Theatre, ritual and transformation

Well known for her work in dramatherapy, Sue Jennings is also a trained anthropologist. She and her three children spent two years on a fieldwork expedition to the Senoi Temiar people of Malaysia: *Theatre, Ritual and Transformation* is the fruit of that experience. It explores the reality of play and drama and brings together the insights of drama, therapy and theatre with those of social anthropology to provide an invaluable theoretical framework for understanding theatre and ritual and their links with healing.

The Temiars regularly perform seances which are enacted through dreams, dance, music and drama. They see the seance as playing a valuable preventive part in people's lives, as well as being a medium of healing and cure. Sue Jennings looks in detail at the role of the seance for the Temiars and at their ideas about women, the body and the soul as expressed through the patterns of their daily lives in which she and her children joined. She describes how Temiar children play in a dramatic form from a few months old and re-create the daily life of the village as well the seances of the adults. This activity clearly demonstrates the developmental model of 'embodiment projection and role' which forms a theoretical basis for play and dramatherapy work.

Theatre, Ritual and Transformation is a fascinating account of a symbolic ritual in its cultural context. It will be of great interest to anthropologists as a detailed field study and also to dramatherapists concerned to understand the ritualisation of life experience and the implications for therapeutic practice.

Sue Jennings is Senior Research Fellow at the London Hospital Medical College, University of London and Honorary Research Fellow of the Shakespeare Institute, University of Birmingham.

Temiar midwife and her *cɔɔʔ*

Theatre, ritual and transformation

The Senoi Temiars

Sue Jennings

London and New York

First published 1995
by Routledge
11 New Fetter Lane, London EC4P 4EE

Simultaneously published in the USA and Canada
by Routledge
29 West 35th Street, New York, NY 10001

Phototypeset in 10pt Times by
Mews Photosetting, Beckenham, Kent
Printed and bound in Great Britain by
Biddles Ltd, Guildford and King's Lynn

British Library Cataloguing in Publication Data
A catalogue record for this book is available from the British Library

Library of Congress Cataloguing in Publication Data
A catalogue record for this book has been requested

ISBN 0-415-05229-7 (hbk)
ISBN 0-415-11990-1 (pbk)

For Johnny and Adoi with love

Contents

Illustrations

Acknowledgements

I have two very special families to thank. My own children, ʔaluŋ Andy, ʔatɛr Ros and ʔaluj Hal supported me throughout our time together in so many ways; but in particular Andy learned Temiar fluently, Ros learned childbirth methods and Hal was healed dramatically by a shaman. I shall always be grateful to the Senoi Temiars, including *Busuuʔ*, *Dalam* and *ʔabiləm*, for their generosity with time and resources and their patience in my stumbling efforts.

I must mention *Tataaʔ* Benjamin for his time and energy and for his generosity like a true Temiar with his own work freely shared.

I must thank my three midwives who have contributed immeasurably to the conception and gestation. *Minonɔɔʔ*, my Temiar midwife, taught me birth procedures and adopted me as her daughter; Dr Andrew Turton waited patiently but used Temiar shaking techniques once labour had started; and Dr Murray Cox sustained the final thesis delivery.

I acknowledge with thanks the financial support from the Evans Trust, Cambridge for my Research Fellowship; additional funding and equipment from the Social Science Research Council; the School of Oriental and African Studies; the University of Belfast; the Jabatan Hal Elwal Orang Asli and the Ministry of National Unity which authorised my field research.

Dato' Nik bin Daud, Dr Salleh Sam and Dr Zanee Merican helped negotiate official paths and medical problems; Veerasamy and Tong Swee were very good friends. Dr Kirsten Summerfelt and the late Professor Anthony Forge helped me before I went to the field and Dr Paul Spencer gave me every encouragement when I got back. The Anthropological Research Student Advisory Group (ARSTAG) and particularly Dr Adrian Collett gave time and patience to preliminary drafts.

Margaret Davies has just kept on typing cheerfully and I am most grateful. Dramatherapy colleagues, students and clients have encouraged and stimulated this process. I must finally mention some special people: Jill Anderson, the late Harry Andrews, David Bryan, Hugh and Jean Dickinson, Audrey Hillyar, Robert Landy, Steve Mitchell, Yiorgos Polos, Suzanne Reading, Sam Rughani and Tony Solomonides for support, sustenance and belief.

Introduction

THE FIELDWORK PROCESS: TRANSITIONS, RELATIONSHIPS AND TRANSFORMATIONS

The title of this book, *Theatre, Ritual and Transformation: The Senoi Temiars*, has been through a series of transformations since I first embarked on the research. What began as a defined research proposal on Temiar dance and body movement before I went to Malaysia changed in emphasis once I was there; these transformations are part of the fieldwork process. It is important to try to clarify this process in order to define some of the many influences and expectations before, during and after fieldwork that all influence outcome.

The process of fieldwork is the dynamic that develops between the anthropologist and the people with whom the research is being done within the context of an alien environment; by alien I mean other than the anthropologist's own. The process goes through a series of developmental transitions. These transitions vary in time and duration for the individual anthropologist but are broadly defined as the journey from outsider to insider, from superficial communication to deeper interactions, and from initial 'explanations' to a more profound 'understanding'.[1] This process is influenced by what the anthropologist takes to the field in terms of roles, expectations and identity, together with life experience. The anthropologist's expectations are of the research, the fieldwork and the researcher's own self. However, these in turn affect the particular choice of topic, the people and the country where the anthropologist decides to work. There are many unknowns in this complex network, and many of the questions do not occur to us until after the fieldwork is completed. The fieldwork process therefore is not just concerned with the dynamics of the fieldwork itself, but must be seen in the context of what went on before

Map 1 The Malay Peninsular

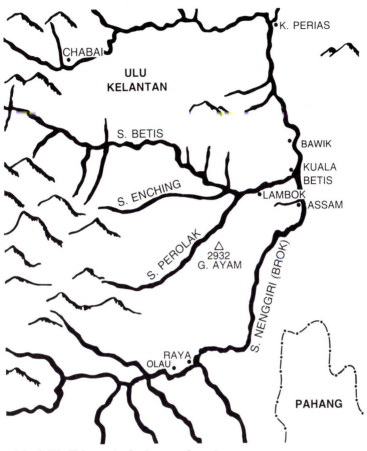

Map 2 Ulu Kelantan (author's research area)

and afterwards, i.e. *the anthropologist and fieldwork in context.*

The purpose of this introduction is therefore to consider the fieldwork process in relation to my own research with the Temiar people. Beginning before I chose to be an anthropologist in the first place, it will describe the various transitions I was involved in throughout the fieldwork. This includes the transitions from psycho-therapy to social anthropology, from drama to ritual, from Britain to Malaysia, and the actual arrival in the Temiar village where my children and I were to spend over a year. It will also look at 'impression management' within the context of the fieldwork process and the emergence of both fieldwork and family identity.

From theatre to therapy

There is no doubt that a training and career in the professional theatre has always influenced my work and thinking. Trained as a dancer from the age of 3 and then a period at drama school, dance and drama had priority over all other forms of education during the formative/ informative years. Having been a dancer and actress in the pro-fessional theatre, the seeds of therapy were sown during periods of 'resting' when I worked as a nursing assistant in a large psychiatric hospital. Part of the treatment programme in this hospital, or rather the recreation programme for the patients, was regular participation in drama groups. Although this was not seen as central to their physical treatment (mainly drugs and electro-convulsive therapy), several doctors nevertheless took it seriously enough for me to be present at case conferences and when discussing patients' progress. It was certainly a progressive approach in the early 1950s.

From this time onwards questions arose about the effects that participation in dance and drama has on people; for example:

- How is it that someone can go on stage with the onset of 'flu and, once 'in role' as someone else, the 'flu symptoms abate?
- Why can psychiatric patients change in mood, awareness and perception after participating in the acting through of a myth?
- Why can a group of so-called 'acting out'[2] West Indian children become absorbed and are able to concentrate after movement to a particular rhythm?

Twenty-five years ago there was no concept of dramatherapy in western medicine. The most active work in drama outside the theatre itself was being developed in drama and theatre in education.

Teaching, followed by remedial teaching with my theatre career, enabled me to work developmentally with drama from the basis of play; although working as a teacher in an education setting, the drama became more 'therapeutic' than 'educational' as I began to work with more disturbed children in schools.

Dramatic intuition was not enough to deal with the kind of emotional depth that clients expressed when involved in dramatic re-enactment – whether using their own personal scripts or the words of someone else. Since there was no formalised dramatherapy training, and a year of psychology had left me only wiser about rats and mazes, personal psychoanalysis seemed appropriate. This I undertook from the late 1960s to the early 1970s. It was a productive, though limited, personal journey which I made in parallel with the task of establishing a centre for the development of dramatherapy and introductory training programmes. However, it also increased my frustration with the narrowness of psychotherapeutic understanding of symbolic behaviour both in Freudian and Jungian philosophies. Two years in a group analytic training gave me some understanding of group dynamics and group process, but sadly little more about dramatherapy – except that group therapy uses the circle, the oldest theatre structure. The practice of dramatherapy and the performance of theatre allowed for more integration between the drama and the therapy in both the emergence of a theoretical base and in drama-therapy practice itself (Jennings 1990).

I was still suffering from what Anthony Storr calls 'Divine discontent' (*The Dynamics of Creation* 1976) as there were so many questions still unanswered, especially about ritual and symbolism, and the *nature of the dramatic act*. Although the practice of dramatherapy was developing in clinical and community settings (as were other arts therapies at that time – in particular art therapy and music therapy), many clinicians remained unconvinced that drama, movement, mime and ritual were anything more than recreational activities. In many psychotherapeutic schools of thought, influenced as they were by the writings of Freud and Marx, ritual had become a perjorative term. It was with some dismay that I realised that at a clinical level, psychiatrists would refer to a ritualistic behaviour as 'meaningless repetitive patterns', and use it in the context of constant head bangings, or else to describe the obsessive acts that the compulsive hand-washer repeats endlessly. Many psychotherapists and psychoanalysts dismiss ritual, especially religious ritual, as opiates for the masses, or as legitimised ways of dealing with neurotic behaviour.

Others are well aware of the power of drama and ritual although perceiving it in different ways. One head of an approved school (now called a young person's prison) hoped that I would use drama to impose a new value system. A headmistress of another school said on no account would she have drama in her establishment; it was very dangerous:

> [I]t would be like opening Pandora's box, you would never know what would come out. They would all behave like savages in the jungle.

It was with these phrases in my head that I cast around for a further area of study through which I could begin to understand the dynamic of drama and of dramatherapy. Psychotherapeutic approaches had taken me some of the way, but issues such as 'the family in context' and 'the group in context' kept concerning me in my work. After many discussions, it seemed that social anthropology could provide a framework within which to answer some of these questions, or perhaps to assist me in asking the right questions. It felt like a big step into the unknown as I embarked on a postgraduate diploma at the University of London.

The transition from therapy to anthropology

As a mature student studying anthropology, I had a very clear idea of what I was seeking. I was looking to social anthropology to enable me to understand ritual drama and symbolism in relation to the rest of social and cultural behaviour. A tall order, I later realised, as so many other people had been asking the same questions for a very long time. However, the whole exercise was most fruitful although I found that my interest and specialism in dance received far more encouragement than my experience and knowledge of therapy. 'Oh, that's psychological' was an easy way to dismiss some of the more searching questions concerning sickness and health in societies. Perhaps the very recent emergence of medical anthropology illustrates the struggle to define boundaries between the disciplines. However, at the time I found anthropologists very sensitive and sometimes even hostile to psychotherapy, particularly in respect of symbolic interpretation. Looking back, it was very productive for me, as the transition had to be made into the anthropological frame of reference.

The two years of full-time study and continuing dramatherapy practice in my spare time proved to be an extremely formative period at every level. I decided to submit my final dissertation based on some actual fieldwork rather than do a library study. Having heard about a hobby-horse trance dance-drama, the *Kuda Kepang*, performed in Indonesia and by Javanese migrants in Malaysia, I decided to go in search of it. I was able to stay in Malaysia for three months and then later return for another month to collect sufficient data for the dissertation. What was important was that I had been able to study *a symbolic ritual in its cultural context*.

Fieldwork and the Temiars

After completing my anthropological diploma I made a decision to pursue longer-term research in Malaysia. Decisions had to be made both on a personal level, as I was a single parent with three children, as well as on a professional level in relation to leaving a dramatherapy practice and an innovative training centre. Once I had made the decision, the obstacles seemed enormous. Members of my extended family and the children's father kept pointing out the hazards of living in a tropical climate and the damage that would be done to the children's education. Academics generally did not feel that the idea of family fieldwork was a good one and even suggested that I put the children in boarding school and go off for six months to do 'a nice little M.Phil.'.

However, other anthropologists had taken their children to the field and I received a lot of support from my former supervisor, the late Anthony Forge, and from Kirsten Summerfelt, who had borne a child during fieldwork in Africa. Funding was a major problem as I was too old compared with most applicants for central funding. The breakthrough came when the Evans Trust awarded me a research fellowship, the only one that year, for a year's fieldwork and asked me to reapply for further funding when I returned. Additional funding was then possible in small amounts from different institutions for specific items such as internal travel, film and tapes.

Although I had not visited the Temiars on my previous visits to Malaysia, I had made two trips into the interior of the tropical rain forest to visit groups of Negritos. The Temiars I had heard of by repute from the writings of Kilton Stewart, meetings with the Department of Aboriginal Affairs (Jabatan Hal Elwal Orang Asli (JOA)), discussions with Dr Bolton in Malaysia, who had founded the aboriginal hospital in Kuala Lumpur, and later, Dr Geoffrey Benjamin at the University of Singapore.

My interest was kindled by the descriptions of the Temiars as being non-aggressive child-centred people who had an ethic of generosity. My original research proposal was to study the Temiar dance in relation to their culture and this fitted with the 'dance lady' persona I seemed to have acquired at SOAS. I found that anthropologists were then less interested in therapy and in fact many debates between psychotherapists and anthropologists were very acrimonious. The area of medical anthropology had not become established then as it has now. So I left the UK in 1974 with three children aged 7, 12 and 14 (Hal, Ros and Andy), and my Jamaican foster-son David, also 14, whom local Social Services funded for a four-month visit. When we left the UK our visas had not even come through, although the research had been approved in principle.

We stopped off in Singapore to visit Geoffrey Benjamin and seek some fieldwork advice, and then entered Malaysia on tourist visas while sorting out the official side once there. I was obviously very anxious, since I managed to get myself knocked down by a scooter in Kuala Lumpur. As my supervisor wryly remarked, that was something that usually happened to people after they had been to the field and not before. Hal also had a serious accident, which resulted in internal stitching in his mouth. It seemed such a relief when, mid-monsoon, we finally arrived in our first Temiar village at Kuala Betis. Although the first week was marred by three of us getting severe dysentery, we had nevertheless at last met the Temiars. It was now necessary to find an agreed way for the research to be carried out. After we began to recover from dysentery, the Temiars started to invite us to their *gɘnabag* with singing, dancing and some energetic trancing. Every day for four nights was enough to begin with.

My main concern was to get a base sorted out and then a plan. I was still extremely anxious that I should not 'miss' anything – my notebooks must be full and curiosity and observation could not let up.

We were then invited to visit a small village two miles up-river to discuss the possibility of having a house built there to serve as the centre of our operations. As the rains had eased off after the monsoon we visited the village of Asam in Kelantan State.

This was our first long walk together outside Betis village which, although normally less than one hour away, took a lot longer because of the mud caused by the monsoon rains. Before leaving I went down to the boat house. The following is the entry from my fieldwork notes.

> I went down to the boat house to fetch some water and the midwife was there. She talks to me in a husky voice. She is most upset. She says her voice is trapped on my tape recorder, which is why she cannot talk and that I should pay the 'bomoh' (Malay term for medicine man) for her treatment. She is quite cross and has a sticking plaster with a poultice on it on her cheeks. I feel embarrassed and wonder if I am trying to do everything too quickly; this awful feeling that no time must be wasted and that notebooks and tapes must be filled as quickly as possible.

We arrived at Asam, which is at the mouth of a very small tributary; it consists of four houses. The oldest living Temiar, Mentri Suleiman, lives there with his married granddaughter, and a daughter and two of his sons have households there as well as another granddaughter. We were invited to eat baked cassava and were given very sweet tea and offered 'home-made' cigarettes in all the houses. We felt at home in Asam and asked if a house could be built for us. There was the half-finished frame of a house standing there which the village people agreed to finish for us for the princely sum of $100 (about the equivalent of £25). This would be a Temiar bamboo stilt house with kitchen, large living area and sleeping compartments for all of us.

We arrived back in Betis and started to plan accordingly. Ros rushed out to join the girls who were going to cut new bamboo for some musical stompers; she grabbed my large *parang* (Malay) and ran, then slipped and fell on to it. She badly sliced her thumb and blood poured out of it – the Temiars nearby fled. Suddenly there was no one there and I was left in the middle of nowhere to deal with a possible haemorrhage! I swallowed hard and decided, it's make-or-break day; staunch the wound with pressure and bind it up with cross-strapping to join the edges. The blood stopped and it slowly healed.

The following is an entry from my fieldwork diary:

> At last our house is ready. We are getting very impatient to move into our own place and be a part of that community. I still remember the cobra in the roof.[3] I am ready to start and I need to be with the Temiars and not apart from them. We move up river into our house with our stuff piled up on a log boat, while the children walk there with more things in back baskets. The

fireplace is still not ready because the village men explain that
they need some special wood for it and they do not have any at the
moment. We have visitors all day long who want to come and talk.
They want to know why we are there, how long we are staying,
and will we go to other villages? They want to know as much as
I do, and it certainly is getting me to speak Temiar. Ros quickly
makes friends with girls of her own age, Hal has three special
friends, and Andy is very popular with the single girls!

The fireplace is at last built of special planks that two Temiar
men bring from another village. They pack earth in the middle of
it and then bake the earth, and finally bring in some tree trunks to
light the fire. Everyone is coming to admire it and we keep boiling
water to brew 'billy-can' tea. *Luŋ*'s wife comes to talk to me and
brings me cassava. She is glad we are here. Hassim wants to be
our friend, but we are a little wary as he does seem to gossip a lot.
They sit around saying what a nice fire it is. It seems like a whole
day of celebration for our fire.

We began to settle into our own routine. I stopped rushing around
thinking I was going to miss everything that might be important. The
children completed two hours of lessons each morning before other
activities took over. Mentri Suleiman's daughter came to the house
after we had been there for a couple of days to tell me the rules of
the river in terms of where we must wash, defecate and so on. A few
days later she brought me some Temiar tobacco and leaves and
showed me how to dry the leaves and roll my own cigarettes. Shortly
afterwards she decided that she was my mother and my family was
adopted. We then had a whole network of relationships up and down
the main rivers.

Impression management

I was well aware when I went to the field that my identity comprised
several quite contrasting roles and also that I took on new roles while
I was there. I kept part of myself quite consciously in the background,
at least to start with, and other aspects of myself came to the fore in
my interactions with the Temiars. I was very aware of role change
when I met outside officials, or visited the large towns.

The three roles of which I was most conscious were my dual
professional role of dramatherapist and anthropologist, and my
family relationships with my own children.

In the early days I self-consciously kept my therapeutic side firmly in the background, being very aware of the stereotype that therapists are people who give explanations of clients' symbolic behaviour and in the main deal with 'deviant' individuals out of their cultural and social context. By trying to shut out this side of myself it became apparent that I was denying a whole range of experience that could usefully 'inform' the anthropologist. The therapist in me was very used to waiting for, but not understanding, long periods of time. I often had to stay with the seemingly chaotic experience of clients, or contain it until they were ready to re-own it. It was after I came back from the field that Cox's book, *Structuring the Therapeutic Process: A Compromise with Chaos* (1978), illuminated both my therapeutic and anthropological work. My established practice of detailed record-keeping as well as my personal diary were also very useful in the anthropological task. A fieldwork diary acts as a kind of internal supervisor (see Casement 1985 for an interesting exposition of this concept), to record and monitor personal feelings and reflections as well as to contain feelings of frustration, homesickness and euphoria. It became a question of allowing the therapist and anthropologist to interact with each other, to be a resource and inform each other. I also realised more clearly that both these roles have anomalous equalities (Jennings 1977).

It was not easy in the early stages to feel that I was both sole parent for the children in a very remote part of the world as well as taking responsibility for any formal education they should receive. My own conviction was that the experience itself would prove to be an invaluable education, although not easily assessed by conventional measurement. It was still tempting to listen to the internal critic who said I was not a good enough mother (and at times anthropologist either!). It obviously changed the nature of our family relationship since there was no escape from the family dynamics, i.e. you cannot march out of the house when there is only a forest full of snakes and other hostile phenomena awaiting you. I am writing up the theme of the family's experience elsewhere[4] but it is obviously going to be constantly present in this book.

Establishing an appropriate and facilitating relationship with the host group – the basis for an anthropologist's research – always takes delicate manoeuvring. The Temiars wanted to be clear why I was there, how long I was staying and whether I would take them *seriously*. The longer we stayed the more seriously they understood my intent, and a gradual working partnership based on mutual trust developed. This was greatly assisted by being adopted into a kinship network.

At times the Temiars expected me to be a law-enforcing agent and, for example, *make* their children attend the local Malay school, since Temiar parents are unwilling to impose their will on their children. However, this gradually changed to an expectation of me as a parent being able to share with other parents the struggle with children. I was also a resource for them in terms of additional food supplies, cash and material goods. I was very much aware that my very presence in the community had its own influence.

My roles shifted when outside officials visited the village on routine checks. Sometimes it would be personnel from the Malay army giving pep talks on security. We were living in an area which was still designated as 'black' because of previous guerilla activity. At other times it was Malay officials taking census details, or members of the JOA wanting to discuss new cultivation projects with senior Temiars. On one occasion a helicopter arrived unannounced with members of a Colombo Plan irrigation project, who were most taken aback to discover a western family living there.

As the Temiars became more relaxed in our presence, we as a family also settled into a flexible routine. Asam village became our base, from which we made regular trips to the villages of Lambok, Bawik, Blau, Raya and Betis. In addition to our making these visits, other groups of Temiars came to see us and would often stay in our house as part of our kinship network. I felt the biggest turning point came when my Temiar mother asked Ros and me if we would help her with a childbirth. At this point I felt I had a designated role in relation to the Temiars and my focus had already shifted away from dance towards indigenous healing. The Temiars began to allow us to enter their complex world.

The family as a resource for fieldwork

Contrary to some observations made before I went to the field, I found the presence of my family a constant source of information and help. The Temiars accepted me far more readily because I was a parent rather than a lone researcher. From time to time they would send discreet messages with the children asking whether I was lonely and needed a husband! The children themselves were able to gain access to information from their peer groups that would not have been available to me. Ros, as well as being an assistant midwife, made friends with a large group of pre-pubertal and adolescent girls and became the most accomplished musician in our family. Andy was sought after by older girls – one in particular – and was able to go out with the men on expeditions where I, as a woman, was not permitted to go. Hal, as my youngest, was a special favourite with the Temiars. It was hard for me to allow him to wander off with his peer group and sleep wherever they decided. David, my foster-son, was very close to the Temiars; they said he was like them because of his dark skin; they thought he was very special.

Sometimes if there were several things to record, we would split up as a team and compare notes on our return. Since, for example, most seances are conducted in minimum light, employing several observers became very useful. We also gradually learned the dances, and I became quite proficient in trance. Andy grew very adept as a photographer as well as making many of the tapes.

Probably the most valuable thing was to be able to process many of our observations and talk them through. The family were very good at helping me keep my feet on the ground. We spent a total of almost eighteen months engaged in this research and we returned to the UK as very changed people. It had been a major personal as well as professional experience and one in which all of us continue to discover insights.

The shift from dance research to healing drama

After the early weeks spent attending seances and learning and observing Temiar dance, it was quite apparent that my interest in ritual, and the embeddedness of dance within ritual, was slowly to become the focus of my research, and this ritual was first and foremost a healing process. Very early in my fieldwork diary there are records of the productive interviews I conducted with indigenous healers. This was further illuminated by my experience of being a midwife, which is considered, like the shaman, as a healing role by the Temiars. Virtually nothing had been written about Temiar childbirth, and as the first woman to research the Temiars, this gave me a good opportunity to gain access to hitherto unrecorded data. I was also particularly interested in the play of children and its relationship with child-rearing and socialisation.

Since shaman and midwives have the two healing roles, it was important to look at their practices in both formal and informal contexts. Dance forms a part of most trance seances, and is sometimes done for its own sake. Dances may be choreographed through dreams and then taught to the community. However, it was the relationship between dreaming and the creative process in a wider sense that seemed the more appropriate focus for research. I was also becoming increasingly interested in the link between two sorts of 'forgetting' that the Temiars talked about – dreaming and trancing and the seemingly paradoxical connection between 'forgetting' and the acquisition of new knowledge – for dreaming reveals the spirit guide by whom the aspiring shaman is taught, and is available to him in seances. The seances are both preventive as well as healing, and are performed on behalf of individuals as well as the community as a whole.

A long time for a thesis

On my return from the field I went through all the experiences that most anthropologists undergo when they emerge from intensive fieldwork. I was not prepared for the long-term effects of culture shock and it took me at least a year to feel that we had surfaced from the experience. I had a professional life to pick up again and obviously being a western single parent to three dependent children made its own demands on me. As I said at the beginning of this introduction, this material passed through a series of transformations before reaching its present form and content. Earlier titles have included *Temiar Dance and Order*, and *Dance and Healing*. I had a lengthy conflict with myself as to whether it should be a 'strictly anthropological' thesis with a major focus on dance, or whether I should allow myself to speak also as a dramatherapist and incorporate the healing data as well as the information on Temiar children within that framework.

It took several years to eventually reach a point where I realised not only that what I had to say was of relevance to dramatherapists specifically (and to psychotherapists generally) but that I was ignoring the whole area of the drama itself both in relation to my own expertise in the theatre and the drama phenomenon that I had actually witnessed. Of particular interest were the changes in role that were made manifest particularly in the dream and trance processes of the Temiars, an enacted continuum in belief and experience for the Temiars between private dream performances and public seance performances.

I had earlier avoided theatrical performance to help understand ritual, and followed more traditional anthropological thought in separating them out as different genres. During this period of gestation I was inspired by new writings from G. Lewis (1980), Tambiah (1985) and Turner (1986) in relation to ritual and drama, as well as from medical anthropologists such as Skultans (1979), Kleinman (1980), Helman (1984) and B.S. Turner (1992). Of course, during my stay away and since I have been back, the whole area and literature of feminist anthropology in general, and writing on menstruation and fertility in particular, have burgeoned. This has been particularly helpful (e.g. MacCormack and Strathern (1980), McCormack (1982), Knight (1983) and Bell *et al.* (1993)).

This book is not a final statement. It is an attempt to bring together the major parts of my Temiar data within a framework which is anthropological but which also incorporates insights from drama, theatre, play and dramatherapy. The Temiar themes that recur in my data relate to play, dance, trance and music within a well-being/illness context as well as a developmental i.e. personal development framework. Marina Roseman, an ethnomusicologist, has since worked with the Temiars on song in healing. Several researchers have been to the Temiars to explore the disputed subject of Temiar dreaming. Benjamin has since written extensively on Temiar language within the context of other Orang Asli languages in Malaysia and within the overall context of Malaysian culture (1976a, 1976b, 1979b, 1981, 1983, 1987, 1991, 1993a, 1993b, 1994). I have had to balance the Temiar data with the greater understanding of theatre and drama and thus dramatherapy. This develops the exploration of the relationship between play, drama, theatre and ritual, through the Temiar epic metaphors of blood, tiger and thunder. The transformation of experiences by these metaphors is achieved through the fundamental nature of the dramatic act (Jennings 1994).

From a thesis to a book: healing theatre and dramatic rituals

The cutting and elaboration of various themes in order to turn the original thesis into a book has again taken time. I have been struggling with many ideas that developed after the doctoral thesis, in particular a 'theatre model of dramatherapy' or as I sometimes call it, 'healing theatre'. The whole subject of dramatherapy has moved on in many ways and there is now established postgraduate training and a formal recognition by the Department of Health. Dramatherapy still swings between the two subtexts of psychotherapy on the one hand and theatre and drama on the other, and it would seem that they can only be understood when one acknowledges the aesthetic process as a therapeutic process. The Temiars taught me so much about the relationship of aesthetics to ecstatic and ascetic experiences of their trance dance-drama: that healing comes about when communication with 'other' – whether spirit-guide or self – is a culmination of our dramatic imagination and performance structures within 'dramatic reality'. Dramatic reality has that quality of 'forgetting' that we experience in dreams, trance or day-to-day absorption, which allows our 'other selves' to become manifest.

In order to be able to take the risks of 'forgetting', we need to develop more healing rituals which are part of our passage through life. People need signposts as they go through major changes in status and relationships, as well as life crises or illness. Rituals assist us to know who we are and where we are, as well as giving boundaries to the journeys of the dramatic imagination.

Throughout this process of dramatherapy, healing theatre and dramatic rituals, I have of course been taken on my own journey. This has culminated in my moving from therapy to theatre, which of course is where it all started. As a professional actress, I am aware how it brings together not only the several aspects of myself, but also those that are 'other'.

AUTHOR'S NOTE

This cumulative research has confirmed for me certain limits of my own competence, especially in relation to the Temiar language and its linguistic analysis. Geoffrey Benjamin has given me immeasurable assistance to fill the gaps and my own lacks.

However, I endorse wholeheartedly his view of the importance of a basic orthography, if not linguistic training, for anthropological fieldworkers. His two-part 'On Pronouncing and Writing Orang Asli Languages: A Guide for the Perplexed' (1985) is an excellent introduction.

Sue Jennings
Stratford-upon-Avon

Pronunciation guide
Notes by Geoffrey Benjamin

Temiar words are printed here in a near-phonemic orthography, corresponding to current usage in Mon-Khmer linguistics. The following description should help the reader to get close to the original pronunciation.

VOWELS

These are pronounced approximately as in the following Malay or English words (but always 'pure', not diphthongised):

i as in Malay *tapis* or English *pit.*
e as in Malay *leher* or like the *a* in (Northern British) English *hate.*
ɛ as the *e* in English *get.*
ə as the *e* in Malay *betul* or (British) English *butter.*
a as in Malay *belah* or (Northern British) English *hat.*
u as the first *u* in Malay *pucuk* or the *oo* in English *loot.*
o as the *o* in Malay *gol* (football) or in (Welsh) English *hole.*
ɔ as the *o* in (British) English *fort.*
ʉ as in (Scottish) English *hus* (i.e. 'house').

Doubled vowels are pronounced longer than single vowels: *lɔɔy* 'wade' vs. *lɔy* 'arrive'. Vowels with a tilde on top, such as *ã* or *ɛ̃*, are pronounced nasally: *kɛ̃ʔ* 'fish' vs. *tɛʔ* 'earth'. Temiar diphthongs are written as vowel-consonant sequences ending in *-w* or *-y*:

kɛwkɔɔw (to call)
lɛylə̃əy (to spread (mat)).

CONSONANTS

These are mostly pronounced as in Malay or Italian. Initial stops, like *p-* or *t-*, are not aspirated. Final consonants are usually pronounced without explosion.

The following need special attention:

> *k* is always a velar stop, as in English. (It is never a glottal stop, as sometimes in Malay.)
>
> *c* is a palatal stop similar to the Malay *c* in *macam* and approximately like the *ch* in English *church*. (Note: unlike Malay *c*, Temiar *c* can occur word-finally.)
>
> *ɲ* is the palatal nasal continuant, like the *ny* of Malay *banyak* or the *ni* in *onion*. (Note: unlike Malay *ny*, Temiar *ɲ* can occur word-finally.)
>
> *ŋ* is the velar nasal continuant, like the *ng* of Malay *nganga* or English *singer* (but not as in *finger*).
>
> *ʔ* is the glottal stop, a consonantal phoneme, like the *k* in the Peninsular Malay pronunciations of *duduk* or *rakyat*, the ' in the Cockney pronunciation *li'l* for *little*, or the unwritten throat-opening sound at the beginning of German *ein*.

WORDS

All Temiar words begin and end with a consonant, never a vowel. (Words that may sound to Malay or English ears as if they begin with a vowel actually begin with the glottal stop, *ʔ*.) Word-stress is always on the final syllable. The hyphen indicates the linking together of several different elements into a single phonological word, with the main stress on the final syllable:

> *ʔɛn-baliik* (on top)
> *nam-ba-bərɛʔcaaʔ* (he will be feeding (someone)).

Chapter 1

Setting the scene

We can learn from experience – from enactment and performance of
the culturally transmitted experience of others – peoples of the Heath
as well as the Book.

(Turner 1982:19)

Life is theatrelike – Theatre is lifelike.

(Wilshire 1982:ix)

Life is not a rehearsal.

(Julie Walters in *She'll be Wearing Pink Pyjamas*)

INTRODUCTION

The Senoi Temiars of Malaysia regularly perform rituals for the
maintenance of health as well as the curing of physical, social and
supernatural manifestations of ill-health. Their preventive and curative seances are stimulated by, and enacted through, dreams, dance,
music, drama and trance media, imbued with complementary themes
of the erotic and ascetic, and an underlying aesthetic sense of creative
performance. I wish to explore the context of these performances in
relation to the Temiar belief system and to consider the complementary roles of shaman and midwives who are engaged in the
healing process. In order to understand the Temiar perceptions, it is
necessary to describe their beliefs and concepts concerning the
human body and the space surrounding the body, both actual and
symbolic; as well as the ritually enforced boundaries of what may
enter or be kept outside of bodies and space. We shall discover that
these phenomena, encapsulated in the ritual dramas enacted at
seances, present the Temiar world in symbolic performance. Dominant themes that recur throughout the Temiar beliefs and cosmology,
tiger, thunder and blood, are epic metaphors which, through their

polysemic properties are constant reminders of Temiar identity. This identity is reinforced both individually and collectively. Ritual and ritual dramas transform undifferentiated experiences into an understandable world within which the Temiars are able to maintain their sense of *self and other*, particularly in relation to well-being and ill-health.

In addition to relevant anthropological material, I draw upon theories from play, drama and theatre, dramatherapy and psychotherapy. Indeed it is through this study that I have achieved a greater understanding of the fundamental nature of the dramatic act and its significance in human development and creativity as well as in therapeutic intervention. I have had to expand my anthropological frame of reference in order to understand the complexity of the Temiar data and its processes. Additionally, I shall draw out the significance of the role of women in Temiar society, not as a subject in itself out of context, but in order to achieve a balance within the whole.

There is virtually no information on the play of Temiar children, which I feel is necessary to more fully understand the Temiar world view. Before describing the Temiars in any detail, it is necessary to develop the themes of play, drama and theatre in relation to ritual.

Play

> The appearance of symbolism ... is the crucial point in all interpretations of ludic function. Why is it that play becomes symbolic, instead of continuing to be mere sensory motor exercise or intellectual experiment, and why should the enjoyment of movement, or activity for the fun of activity, which constitutes a kind of practical make-believe, be completed at a given moment by imaginative make-believe?
>
> (Piaget 1962:162)

> Play is not 'ordinary' or 'real' life. It is rather a stepping out of 'real' life into a temporary sphere of activity with a disposition all of its own. Every child knows perfectly well that he is 'only pretending' or that it was 'only for fun'.
>
> (Huizinga 1949:8)

Play is a developmental activity through which human beings explore and discover their identity in relation to others through multiple media including their own bodies, projective media and a variety of role-play. Play encourages symbolic thought and action and stimulates the emergence of metaphoric expression. In play we learn to create as well as to set limits; we learn about freedom as well as its boundaries. The human body is the primary means of learning, and experiences in play gradually develop in relation to surrounding space. However, play occurs in a symbolic space, a special space set apart that is imbued with significance for the duration of the play activity: 'It is "played out" within certain limits of time and place. It contains its own course and meaning' (ibid.:9).

It is through playing that a child begins to separate out 'dramatic reality' and 'everyday reality' which is essential for maturation.

> The infant is born with creative potential and the capacity to symbolize: indeed, it is the very capacity of human beings to pretend or make-believe which enables them to survive. We cannot envisage a life within which we could not imagine how things are – how they were, or how they might be. The creative imagination is the most important attribute that we can foster in children, and it is the basis of creative playfulness.
>
> (Jennings 1993:20)

The roots of play and expressive behaviour emerge in infants after a few days. Before an infant can walk it can move and make sounds rhythmically, make marks (albeit with food or faeces) and respond mimetically to the facial expression of another. All the experience of sound, movement, mark-making and mimicry are embodied and experienced sensorially in small infants. These are activities which may develop later into music, dance, art and drama. However, in infancy the experiences are undifferentiated, reinforced and heightened by physical handling: touching, stroking and bouncing activity between infant and caring adults. Cultural expectations are transmitted through these experiences, especially those concerning gender and cleanliness. The body is a *primary* means of learning.

About the time of walking the infant is able to project outside of its own body into more concrete media; differentiation between *self and other* is projected into a 'transitional object' or beloved toy (Winnicott 1974). The 'transitional object' takes on a representative role and enables the infant to tolerate absence of the carer for increasing periods of time. He or she is therefore able to symbolise: here/not here and me/not me. Psychologists emphasise that the transitional object is a carer substitute and I contend that other possibilities about its function are neglected. It is my own view that it marks a major stage of dramatic development; for example, the object is usually given a name, is talked to, and answers; it is used to conceal and reveal; for example, when a blanket is put over its head and removed again; it takes on a role, as well as enabling the infant to become that role. It therefore creates a symbolic presence of significant absence as well as enabling projective and role development through objectification and personification (Jennings 1986). Infants today generalise into more extended play through multiple media, and various roles and personalities are tried out. I would describe the play during the first ten months as mimetic; the child *embodies* the voices, gestures and behaviours of significant others, and, as Mead (1934:225) points out, learns more about itself by becoming the other. By ten months the child is the 'actor' and needs an audience (Courtney 1980:45).

I refer to the three stages outlined above as *embodiment, projection* and *role* (Jennings 1990:93), which do not develop in a unilinear way but have a cumulative effect and are carried forward into more complex play activity. I maintain that this progression is essential for dramatic play to develop in children. How it develops and whether it will move into what we choose to call artistic activity is culturally determined. Contemporary psychologists have suggested that the two brain hemispheres control complementary areas of activity: there seems to be a dominance in our society of left brain activity (logic, reasoning, words) over right brain activity (intuition, creativity, metaphor). Education at all levels places greater value on science and technology than on the arts. I therefore suggest that we are left brain dominated. The possibilities that are inherent in early play are not developed equally. It is noticeable that left brain problem solving and computerised play are stimulated earlier and earlier.

I maintain that dramatic playing is essential for healthy survival as the growing child separates out everyday reality from dramatic reality. Failure to achieve this can result in everyday life becoming like a Greek drama.

How does this relate to the Temiars? One could claim that Winnicott's theory will only hold up for western infants, especially since cross-cultural studies of transitional objects and projective play have not, to my knowledge, been carried out. However, the Temiars manage their early childhood development rather differently. There is a strong sense of embodiment of experience in the first year, especially since infants are regularly massaged, stroked and caressed. They are also held tightly but with tension, their ears are covered

during thunder storms, and older people chant 'fear, fear'. Weaning
does not take place at a particular time; infants are breast-fed up to
3 or 4 years of age, not only by their mothers but by other breasts that
may be available. They are also carried constantly until they can

Plate 1 Playing at seance (i)

Plate 2 Playing at families

walk. Once they are walking, they become the baby in children's family play and are carried around on the backs of 5- and 6-year-olds (Plate 2, page 6). Thus the projective stage (without the mediation of a 'transitional' object) emerges in play while breast-feeding is still continuing. Infants gradually take on more roles in family play and differentiate several 'others'. This, I suggest, enables the child to make a more radical transition by the age of 8 when he or she starts to sleep with the peer group rather than close to the parents. Temiar children of 8 and 9 years group together and choose which house they want to sleep in on any particular night. The filial bond is being replaced by the sibling bond as the child's autonomy continues to grow (this was a very difficult thing for me to adjust to when at the age of 7 Hal went to other houses to sleep with his peer group).

Children are also encouraged to talk about their dreams, and dreams are seen as a valuable and creative activity. The concept of play carries over into Temiar adult life with the activities of music, dance, enactment and trance in what are termed play-seances. Children will already have been enacting seances in their own play in or under the house or in a corner of the village (Plate 1, page 5).

I do not wish to elaborate here on the many theories of play and development (Jennings 1993:20), but I do want to draw attention to the importance of play in the ontological development of human beings; although satisfactory play experiences are crucial for the development of gross and fine motor skills, identity, relationships, imagination and conceptual thought, I want to stress the importance of play in relation to what we call the arts and dramatic play and drama in particular. Play itself is the activity that is at the root of artistic expression, and for the Temiars it starts with the dream. I now want to move on to discuss drama and theatre, both as metaphors for everyday life, and as creative performances embedded in human societies.

Drama and theatre

Drama and theatre have been used as metaphors to talk about life for hundreds of years. The quotation from Shakespeare's *As You Like It*, 'All the world's a stage, and all the men and women merely players', is perhaps the most well-used example. Dramatism and dramaturgy are terms used to describe the study of social dramas in which we are all engaged. Harré suggests that the alternative to scientism is a combination of dramatism and praxiology:

[T]hat we live out our lives in accordance with scenarios centred round the local conventions for the representation of character and the restrictions imposed upon the physical means by which we realise practical projects deriving from the nature of the physical and biological world.

(1981:79)

Goffman has contributed to our understanding of social drama through his detailed studies of interaction and impression management. As he says when discussing performances in public life:

The larger the number of matters and the larger the number of acting parts which fall within the domain of the role or the relationship, the more likelihood, it would seem, for points of secrecy to exist.

(1969:71)

Goffman develops his theory of front-stage and back-stage performance of people's social roles. Until comparatively recently, research and writing on social drama had been polarised from drama and theatre itself, with the claim that drama is merely a metaphor for describing human behaviour.

Furthermore, we can see within western education that drama and theatre themselves are separated; drama is seen as creative action based on improvisation, and theatre as a finished product or performance (see in particular Slade 1954; Heathcote 1971). Theatre itself has become marginalised from the experience of the majority of people and is often viewed as an elitist activity catering for a minority. Theatres have closed down for lack of subsidy or turned into television studios or bingo halls. Any school curriculum demonstrates its value by the central position that is occupied by science and technology and the low priority given to the arts in general and drama in particular (a recent applicant for funding was told not to mention the word drama but to talk about social learning through social skills!).

Anthropologists have also fallen into the trap of polarising drama and theatre. Victor Turner was criticised for using the word drama when talking about social action, by both Firth and Gluckman. Drama was considered too loaded a word (Turner 1982:91). Many anthropologists make a clear distinction between ritual and theatrical performance; others have suggested that theatre grew out of ritual. However, one cannot separate theatre from ritual by saying that the former is performance. Performance enters all domains of human existence in both secular and religious fields; the 'dramas of everyday life' as well as the 'dramas set apart', i.e. theatre and ritual. I shall explore ritual in more detail later in this chapter.

The word theatre derives from the Greek *theatron* which literally means a place for seeing. However, it is also linked to the word *theoria* meaning spectacle. It becomes more pertinent to my argument when we consider that spectacle also meant 'to speculate and to theorise'; therefore in the ancient Greek meaning, it was necessary to have something visible, something seen in order to theorise and understand. This was achieved through the spectacle of the drama (from the Greek *dron*, meaning action). However, Plato vilified the person and nature of the actor and said that the art of acting could be morally damaging. If a person can represent a bad character on stage then it follows that he cannot be a good person. Plato maintains that tragedy will excite in the audience emotions that should be curbed:

> Then is it really right, to admire when we see him on the stage, a man we ourselves be ashamed to resemble?
>
> Is it reasonable to feel enjoyment and admiration rather than disgust?
>
> (*The Republic*)

For Plato, the creation of images is the lowest level of mental functioning and art is an avoidance of reality. He said that any actor who could act any part well should be honoured highly and escorted speedily out of the city!

Wilshire claims that in ancient Greek civilisation, reality and appearance are essentially linked. He says: 'An occurrence was denoted by a word from which our "phenomenon" derives directly, and it means literally "that which shows itself". Further "phenomenon" is related to the Greek word for light (phos)' (1982:33).

He suggests that the perceptual sense of things is rendered by theatre, while analysis and synthesis of the embedded concepts come from philosophy. But he warns against developing a mentalistic view of consciousness: 'We will assume that the recognition is between consciousness rather *than between bodies* that are occasionally conscious' (ibid.:166, my emphasis), and 'Most significant is the way a person's body-image is connected with his direct experience of others' bodies as they are immediately lived by them' (ibid.:188).

Wilshire goes on to develop his theory that the essence of theatre is that the audience is *mimetically* involved with the performance: that experiences are *embodied* in the body-self. We suggested earlier that the infant's early experience is an embodiment of the surrounding world. The theme of the embodiment of experience and somatic understanding is one that I return to throughout the book.

Since the turn of the century, dramatists, actors and directors have been re-examining theatre and drama processes in relation to internal and somatic experience as well as observed phenomena. Constantin Stanislavski was more responsible than anyone else for freeing the stylised and postured theatre of his time. Stanislavski took over the Moscow Arts Theatre and developed a new approach to the training of actors as well as to the style of theatre production. He was the first person to develop the 'as if' concept. He worked primarily with his actors on their emotional memory in order to bring authentic feeling to their character parts. If an actor had difficulty with certain parts, then the 'as if' principle would enable them to get in touch with appropriate feelings. Stanislavski (1950/1981) emphasised lengthy, intensive training for actors, the importance of the unconscious and the reality of the actors' own lives. The work of Artaud (1958) too, although revolutionary in its own right, nevertheless has roots in the work of Stanislavski, as have most theatre innovations of the past eighty years.

In the 1970s Grotowski became more and more concerned with the creativity of ordinary people – his para-theatrical work. His concern was to remove the separation between actors and audience, and find new ways of rediscovering an experience of drama and ritual. Grotowski (1969) calls it 'a Theatre of Sources – bringing us back to the sources of life, to direct primeval experience, to organic primary experience'.

Roose-Evans describes this concept as:

> an attempt to create a genuine encounter between individuals who meet at first as complete strangers and then, gradually, as they lose their fear and distrust of each other, move towards a more fundamental encounter in which they themselves are the active and creative participants in their own drama of rituals and ceremonials.

> (1984:154)

There are numerous theatre directors who under the influence of Stanislavski have developed new forms and made new impacts during this century. They are concerned in their research not with formulations, but with a continuous journey. Sometimes this journey is actually undertaken, such as Peter Brook's journey to Africa to see the Ik tribe, and Grotowski's journey to the Far East. There is a kind of restlessness which seeks to go on discovering and resists formulation and static theory. Peter Brook talks about the need to revitalise the theatre, to make it *immediate* (as contrasted with other forms – dead theatre, rough theatre and holy theatre). He says that we should consider the French word for performance – *représentation* – in order to reconcile the contradiction of repetition necessary in rehearsal. It is an occasion when something is 're-presented' and therefore not an imitation of a description of a past event. It abolishes that difference between yesterday and today.

> It takes yesterday's action and makes it live again in every one of its aspects – including its immediacy. In other words a representation is what it claims to be – a making present. We can see how this is the renewal of life that repetition denies and it applies as much in rehearsal as it does in performance.
>
> (Brook 1972:155)

The 'renewal of life' described by Brook is a very apt description of Temiar seance performance, as we shall see in Chapters 4 and 8 of this book.

Recent innovators in the theatre have struggled to rediscover the active interaction between actor and audience, the 'genuine encounter'. However, this encounter is not necessarily a fusion of the psyche of performer and observer; it may be by alienation, by a distancing such as described by Brecht in his work in Germany and America. Brecht never wanted the audience to forget they were in the theatre, that they were seeing a performance of events by actors and he would use various unexpected devices to remind them, such as the actors coming out of role. He believed the audience would thus be prompted to think about what they had seen and learn from it – he was attempting to change the nature of society: 'For Brecht the purpose of the theatre is to teach us how to survive' (Roose-Evans 1984:68).

Simon Callow warns of what happens when drama and theatre become institutionalised, belonging to the directocracy rather than the actors: 'The waste of the actors' intelligence and passion (how can you be passionate about something in which you have no involvement?). All that's left for you is to concentrate on *your role*; unhealthy and counterproductive' (1985:131).

Grotowski echoes social psychologist G.H. Mead when he says:

I am interested in the actor because he is a human being. This involves two principal points: firstly by meeting with another person, the contact, the mutual feeling of comprehension and the impression created by the fact that we try to open ourselves to another being, that we try to understand him; in short the surmounting of our solitude. Secondly, the attempt to understand oneself through the behaviour of another man, finding oneself in him.

(1969:98)

I could say that I am interested in the human being because he or she is an actor – a process that starts at birth, and is essential for our survival (Jennings 1994). However, Peter Brook, Simon Callow and others all suggest that there is a lack of passion in the theatre today. I want to suggest that there is even a *fear* of passion; that the marginality of theatre and theatre experience is based on fears as fundamental as those expressed by Plato thousands of years ago. Plato's arguments were based on the power of the intellect and human beings' capacity to reason. I suggest that the priority given to technology at the expense of the arts is creating a society that is unable to have adequate means of expressing feelings and affect. I have had numerous responses from politicians, educationalists and clinicians who suggest that not only is drama unnecessary but it is also dangerous (see Introduction). Drama is frequently perceived as being Dionysian (Jennings 1985, 1986), and appealing to unbridled raw emotion as separate from the intellect. There seems to be fear of a loss of control, of darkness, of antisocial forces, or of unconscious feelings coming into the open. The Dionysian view of drama is taken to exemplify the 'primitive' forces of nature, the collective frenzy that is set free within such an orgiastic drama.

Pentheus

Shrieking as long as life was left in him, the women howling in triumph. One of them carried off an arm, another a foot, the boot still laced on it. The ribs were stripped, clawed clean; the women's hands, thick red with blood, were tossing, catching, like a plaything Pentheus' flesh.

(*The Bacchae* (Euripides))

The characters within the Bacchae set up the polarity between individual thought and collective emotion, particularly in the character of the Herdsman who comes to report what he has seen on the hillside when, together with other herdsmen and shepherds he witnessed the women breast-feeding wild animals, and then the frenzied collective orgy of the women.

My arguments on this theme are not new in relation to the theatre, though they are innovatory in relation to therapy (Jennings 1985b). Nietzsche expounds his theory of the discharge of Dionysian chorus in an Apollonian world of images:

> The Dionysian excitement is capable of communicating this artistic gift to a multitude, so that they can seem themselves surrounded by a host of spirits while knowing themselves to be essentially one of them. This process of the tragic chorus is the *dramatic* proto-phenomenon: to see oneself transformed before one's own eyes and to begin to act as if one had actually entered into another body, another character. This process stands at the beginning of the origin of drama. Here we have something different from the rhapsodist who does not become fused with his images but like the painter, sees them outside himself as objects of contemplation. Here we have a surrender of individuality and a way of entering into another character. And this phenomenon is encountered epidemically: a whole throng experiences the magic of this transformation.
>
> (1967:64)

and

> Such magic transformation is the pre-supposition of all dramatic art. In this magic transformation the Dionysian reveller sees himself as a satyr, *and as a satyr, in turn he sees the god*, which means that in his metamorphosis he beholds another vision outside himself, as the Apollonian complement of his own state. With this new vision the drama is complete.
>
> (ibid.)

I argue that this polarity between the Apollonian and Dionysian lies at the very base of our attitudes towards theatre, drama and expression of affect. Whereas drama is perceived as being a dangerous stimulus of unbridled emotion, it is in actuality – as is theatre – a structured form of both containing emotion and reaching understanding. In the Greek theatre, certainly in the fifth century, there was a constant attempt to reach an equilibrium between Apollo and Dionysus. The message of the play, *The Bacchae*, is that there is ultimate destruction in either extreme, and that if we *ignore* the passions of the collective we do so at our peril. The problem with a polarity of this kind is that the two positions become mutually exclusive whereas they need to be seen in a dialectical relationship with each other.

Ritual

In attempting to define ritual, we encounter similar problems to those in understanding drama and theatre. I mentioned in the Introduction the pejorative associations that clinicians maintain when describing what they term ritual behaviour. Anthropologists have made their own distinction between ritual and theatrical performance and suggest that theatre has evolved from ritual. They point out that theatre is where people choose to come and where there is an emphasis on aesthetics, whereas rituals are obligatory and aesthetics are not under consideration. Beattie, when comparing early medieval and Greek theatre forms with contemporary spirit possession, defines ritual as 'The performance of expressive acts, usually involving symbolism with the underlying conviction that such performance will, or may, be causally effective' (1977:35). However, he also separates religion from art because ritual is purposive and 'art is also expressive and symbolic but it is done, at least sometimes, not for some ulterior purpose but for its own sake' (ibid.).

I think this is an oversimplification: as Lewis (1982) and Wolheim (1980) argue, the separation of the art object from the process of art and the removal from ritual of its aesthetic intentions is an erroneous one. However, Beattie also states:

> These and other accounts brought home to me that the putting on of a dramatic performance, the acting out of the prescribed ritual possession, was by no means inconsistent with a belief in spirits and in their power over the living. Nor was it inconsistent with the conviction that these spirits might be influenced by means of the ritual prescribed. The play, the drama, was the thing.
>
> (ibid.)

Turner (1982) and Beattie (1977) both suggest that ritual grew out of theatre. They imply an evolutionary process from ritual forms to theatrical models. I think there are dangers in an evolutionary perspective, as it implies a continuous evolution of creative activity. It suggests a continuation of the re-creation of our own history; that somehow our complex societies of today can be understood by the expressive manifestations of the 'primitive'. Duvignaud points out very vehemently that there is no foundation for a so-called primitive origin of artistic experiences. He says, 'It sets out to separate artistic experience from real experience, by associating the former with a privileged kind of existence, pure and detached from all actuality' (1972:25). He quotes André Malraux in the *Voices of Silence*: 'We have *learnt* to see the primitive world which we have always been looking at' (ibid.:28).

Duvignaud says that all art is the perception we have of society at this moment, and that it is culturally conditioned by the way we perceive it: 'Nature as the artist describes it cannot be nature "as it really is" because it has been twice transformed – once by society and again by the artist' (ibid.:29).

Although there is an attempt to separate ritual from drama and drama from ritual, we find that it is almost impossible to refer to one without also referring to the other. La Fontaine (1985) uses the term ritual drama to describe initiation rituals. Turner also finds that he has to use the term ritual drama and dramatic ritual to describe a range of ritual and theatre forms. I would suggest that all ritual has dramatic and performative elements involving changes of role in a space set apart, and all theatre has some elements of ritual such as culturally determined symbols. Ritual, drama and theatre are variations on a theme of symbolic action, stemming from the social and cultural norms of a society. Turner suggests that there is a relationship between ritual and theatre, and social and stage drama.

> Some of these misunderstandings and apparent contradictions can be resolved if we examine the relationship between the two modes of acting in 'real life' and 'on stage' as components of a dynamic system of interdependence between social dramas and cultural forms.
>
> (1982:107)

Tambiah emphasises the communicative aspects of ritual when he says:

> Ritual is a culturally constructed system of symbolic communica-tion. It is constituted of patterned and ordered sequences of words and acts, often expressed in multiple media, whose content and arrangement are characterised in varying degree by formality (conventionality), stereotypy (rigidity), condensation (fusions), and redundancy (repetition).
>
> (1985:128)

He also maintains that all rituals are performative and as such are subject to two different sorts of rules: regulative and constitutive, the former orienting a pre-existing activity and the latter created and understood within the activity itself. Parkin (1992) suggests that steps and movements are the main points in ritual:

> Words may be important elements of ritual performance, sometimes critically so. But while words may stand alone in myth unaccompanied by gesture, they are dependent on the directional movements that make up ritual. It is in this sense that ritual, full of spatial movement and gestural performance, could make the evolutionary transition to drama and theatre, based at first primarily on mime rather than on dialogue.
>
> (1992:17)

However, there is an ambiguity concerning the performance of healing rituals involving spirit possession; although constitutive, their outcome is necessarily uncertain. Tambiah argues that despite the uncertainty, it does not undermine their performance validity.

Lewis (1980) argues that it may be more helpful to think of ritual in terms of stimulation rather than communication. He says that we are affected by ritual; it sets us thinking, and the importance in both ritual and plays is that they are designed to produce an effect on those who are actually present at the performance. He stresses what he terms the 'alerting quality' of ritual, the restricted code; the economy of expression narrows the participant's choice in relation to expectation. Lewis compares ritual to plays and to art generally, and suggests that ritual and art share the same paradox. The artist puts into a work of art in terms of feelings and thoughts more than the observer takes from it, and similarly, the observer takes more from it than the artist ever intended. He says:

> In ritual as in art, he who devises or creates or performs is also spectator of what he does; and he who beholds it is also active in the sense that he interprets the performance. The value of the ritual lies partly in this ambiguity of the active and passive for creator, performer and beholder.
>
> (G. Lewis 1980:38)

He suggests that the quality of 'alerting' enables us to be aware of phenomena that we would otherwise not have noticed: that because our perception is alerted it is less cluttered and we are enabled to see more clearly.

Thus it may be a device of rituals to isolate some familiar object of action, as though within a frame by means of those special features which alert the attention of the spectator, and invite him to discover relations or aspects of that object or action which he would not otherwise or ordinarily see.

(ibid.:30)

Wilshire (1984) says that the theatre may in fact not only allow us to grasp something when the actual thing is not present, but we may also grasp it better. He says:

Life itself is too large and strung out to be taken in as whole by the mind. It is just because we are assaulted by actual particulars in their eluctable, spatial, temporal, and conventional relation-ships to other actual particulars, that only a few can be present to us at once, and those most pressing given demands of survival or imperatives of ego.

(1984:32)

He suggests therefore that the capacity of the theatre to encapsulate the world in the 'world' enables us to understand the whole by the theatre's function of 'organising, compressing, reducing, expanding or speeding up'. However, he emphasises that the theatre 'varies the key theme of mimetic involvement between persons until the theme is taken in *as* such, in its full dimensions by the mind (ibid.:33).

I maintain that any understanding of ritual must also be linked with our understanding of drama and theatre processes. All are performances of some kind, with expectations, including aesthetics, which are socially and culturally determined, and related to the value system of the society in which they emerge. Ritual is society's larger-than-life symbolic representation of the world through multiple media. It can both stimulate and accommodate change.

Play, drama and ritual in relation to the Temiars

My concern now is to clarify some understanding of the properties inherent in drama and ritual that can usefully assist us to understand the Temiars. I earlier described the three developmental stages of embodiment, projection and role that precede the emergence of dramatic play. Although play is a means of mastery, of learning and making sense of the world, the world that children play at is none the less conditioned by the values and controls from the culture itself. In later chapters we shall see that playing is an activity encouraged by the Temiars, both with young children and with adults. Singing, dancing enactment and trance may be termed play performance contrasted with the intentionality of the more serious seances. However, all play is controlled by older people if it is thought to be getting too noisy or out of hand. Perhaps serious is not quite the appropriate word to describe the other seance because it implies that the play-seances are therefore less important. In this context, serious means that there is more prescriptive control from experienced specialists in order to get in touch with the powerful elements in the spirit world, particularly when the seances are held for healing. However there are also non-serious elements in the more prescriptive seances. It is probably only outsiders who invest them with reverence and awe.

Although children's play is extended into adult life, there is the additional focus for the growing child of the essential playfulness and creativity of dreams. Dreams are instructive, revelatory and informative, and considered to be the source of inspiration and new ideas. The dream is an internalised individuated play; all dreams have dramatic form and can be compared to an internal theatre of the individual. The Temiars' dreams are peopled by important characters, namely their potential spirit-guides with whom they will play in the forest or fields, or by whom they may be taught something important to share with the community. Dreaming is therefore developmentally linked with early child play on the one hand and the adult activities of dance, music, drama and trance on the other. All infants and children attend seance performances and are cradled by their mothers or older sisters who play the bamboo stompers.

Pre-pubertal children join in the dancing and singing and sometimes have their own play-seance – and exaggerate the shaking of adults' trance movement – after the main trancing is over.

Healing and *rite-de-passage*

Increasingly, social anthropologists are contributing to our body of knowledge and understanding of healing processes. We are beginning to understand cultural definitions of illness and disease and the inherent symbolism in the way patients talk about their illnesses. We also view health care systems as determining patients' world view of their experience of illness and health and its causation. All ill-health is experienced somatically (Helman 1994).

People are influenced in their perception of illness by their beliefs about their own bodies, both internally and externally and by what goes into and comes out of their bodies. People talk about their bodies, not usually in medical anatomical descriptions but in terms of how they experience their bodies through metaphors relating to cultural perceptions.

Kleinman has suggested that we can identify three overlapping sectors of health care. He describes these as the popular sector, the folk sector and the professional sector. He suggests that the popular health care system, one which is least-researched, is the point of entry into other health care systems. Values and assumptions about illness and health are carried over from the popular sector into other health care systems which tend none the less to be institutionally separate from each other. He says:

> The customary view is that professional people organise their health care for lay people. But typically lay people activate their health care by deciding when and whom to consult, whether or not to comply, when to switch between treatment alternatives, whether care is effective, and whether they are satisfied with the quality. In this sense, the popular sector functions as the chief source and most immediate determinant of health care.
>
> (1980:51)

There is a wide range of people who are consulted in the popular health care system, including bank managers and hairdressers, and people who have had a similar illness are seen as having some knowledge. The Temiar midwife asked me to help deliver a baby. I demurred and said I had not delivered a baby before, so she said without hesitation, 'But you've had three children yourself, of course you know what to do'.

The popular health care system also has strong views about what causes ill-health in terms of food or clothing. Different cultures see different food as health-promoting or as having medicinal qualities when there is illness. The old saying 'Starve a fever, feed a cold' is an apt example of this.

The professional health care sector is based on the modern scientific model. Professional health care is legitimised legally and is strict about who is allowed to practice. Throughout history there has been a debate in terms of who can be allowed to practice, from midwives to chiropractors. Helman (1984) describes the power that medical practitioners have in relation to their patients – to prescribe strong and sometimes dangerous medication, to deprive certain people of their freedom, to pronounce whether or not they are ill. This has profound effects on both the economic and social experience of the patient.

However, Kleinman (1980) and Helman (1984) both suggest that there is currently a move back to include 'folk' (as opposed to popular) approaches to health care. The problem with much professional medicine is that it is distanced from the community of people to whom it relates. As hospitals get more and more 'high-tech', their understanding of the cultural nature of illness and disease becomes more remote. However, for the most part, other health care practices are not tolerated by the professional sector (as the 1986 BMA Report shows). The organic nature of illness is often seen as the real problem and other factors are regarded as secondary. The relationship between doctor and patient is one where the patient is *told* what is wrong and what he or she must do.

The folk sector of health care, according to Kleinman, occupies the space between the popular and professional. Folk healing practitioners are not legitimised in the same way as 'professional' health carers. They can work within the sacred or secular domain and include the well-researched shaman and shamanic practices as well as other perhaps less exotic healers such as herbalists, bone-setters and the village midwife. The folk sector is much larger in non-western societies, although we should be aware of the increasing growth of the folk sector in the UK. Healing ministries in the Anglican Church, for example, are undergoing a revival at all levels, not just among the charismatic movements. I have suggested that dramatherapy and other art psychotherapies belong to the folk sector and are struggling with a mid-life crisis between folk and professional sectors (Jennings 1985, 1986) as they seek clinical recognition for their practice.

Most folk healers come from the culture of the patients with whom they work, and there is thus an understanding of cultural assumptions and the cultural context of the illness. The healer will know the family history and understand the problem 'in context' rather than as a remote case history. The question often asked of folk healers is on what information they base their clinical decisions. I shall explore this further when looking more specifically at Temiar healing practices in relation to their healers. However, it is important to note that the Temiars to a greater or lesser extent relate to all three health care systems, the popular, the professional and the folk, and have their own ideology about all three.

I have suggested in an earlier paper (Jennings 1983a) that any form of treatment or therapy can be seen as a *rite-de-passage* where the concepts of Van Gennep of separation, transition and reincorporation can be identified. The 'passage' from illness to health can be seen as the progression through a series of roles from which it is intended that the sick person may re-emerge as a well person. The liminal time is the time of treatment when hoped-for transitions and transformations take place. Healing rituals in the folk sector are more easily identified when the transition involves say a shamanic seance. However, all healing processes can be seen, even minimally, as passages, although in western professional medicine the cultural and therefore symbolic significance of this is not usually identified.

Professional medicine emphasises its 'scientific' nature; therefore practitioners do not readily recognise that it too has ritual qualities. White gowns and masks and demarcation of space in wards are given clinical veracity and their symbolic significance is usually ignored. A recent study by Orr (1981) demonstrates the clinical reality invested in the wearing of masks in surgery. Orr compared the rate of infection between two operating theatres, one where the theatre staff wore traditional masks and one where they did not. There was absolutely no difference between any resultant infection.

Western healing practice today is usually a very private situation within the doctor's surgery and bound by various secret rules. There are notices in the waiting room that only one person at a time may see the doctor, which makes family consultation impossible (although some surgeries are more flexible). The 'separation' therefore occurs from the moment of the doctor/patient interaction. The relatives are not usually seen as having a part to play in the remediation. The most public form of healing takes place in a theatre – an operating theatre – but the audience is restricted to the supporting actors and probationers who are allowed to observe. The patient's family is not allowed to witness the drama. Members of the supporting cast are usually masked and gowned, thereby suppressing their own individual identity, and are transformed into a collective representation within which the chief actor, the surgeon, is maintained and reaffirmed in his (occasionally her) status. The victim/ hero has second billing in this drama and little attention is paid to his or her contribution to a successful outcome. However, if this drama turns into tragedy, the victim has contributed by being too ill, past hope . . . 'it is curtains for him'.

I would suggest that within the western medical model, the cultural determinants and the accompanying beliefs have been marginalised outside of the treatment setting. For example, hospital chaplains whom I have interviewed frequently complain of their lowly status – that when the doctor enters the room, they are required to leave.

> They usually call for me when it is too late; as if I am only involved with the process of dying; not that I could contribute to the possibility of living.
>
> (Personal communication from a hospital chaplain)

I suggest that the separation of our three institutions of the hospital, the Church and the theatre into distinct domains has removed from healing the total life experience that is possible through symbolic interaction accompanied by belief. Rituals of healing that involve dramatic engagement in a special place set apart may not 'work' in terms of reference laid down by western scientific medicine. Doctors are quick to suggest that it is spontaneous recovery, that people would have got better anyway. However, as La Fontaine (1985) points out, one cannot measure these outcomes by western scientific methods. At the end of the day it is whether the patient experiences him or herself as 'better', whatever the definition of better might be.

The Temiars maintain a range of food and space prohibitions in order to avoid either physically or supernaturally caused illness. For certain illnesses such as conjunctivitis, or accidents such as fractures, they will make use of western medicine if it is available alongside their own treatments. However, soul sickness of the head and heart are only susceptible to shamanic intervention, and other forms of treatment are actively forbidden. The Temiars impose confinement and diet restrictions as part of the healing of illness as well as after childbirth. For serious illness of individuals or the community, the healing seances are performed under the direction of an experienced shaman. However, midwives have a complementary healing role and treat women's disorders, sexual problems and ministrate before, during and after childbirth. We shall see that individuals, groups and specialists are all involved in the maintenance of well-being. Individuals not only have a responsibility towards their own health maintenance but also towards the health of the others.

The role of women

As the first female anthropologist to live with the Temiars I had the opportunity to gain access to much information that would not be available to male researchers. However, I have no wish to study women out of the context of Temiar society. Nevertheless, I will present detailed information on their menstruation and childbirth rituals: ritual dramas that men are not allowed to witness because of both their power and danger. Midwives play a significant and hitherto undocumented role in these rituals and my study was enhanced by the fact that both my daughter and I were asked to assist the village midwife in her work.

CONCLUSION

To fully understand the nature of Temiar healing performances, it is necessary to comprehend the nature of play, drama, ritual and theatre and the essential embodiment of these activities in the emergence and maintenance of Temiar identity. To polarise these mimetic forms is to impose a false division on human cultural experience. For example, to suggest that ritual and theatre are separate forms is to miss the essential nature of the phenomena. Although ritual may be prescriptive, and to a greater extent repetitive, as Tambiah says, 'every field anthropologist knows that no one performance of a rite, however rigidly prescribed, is exactly the same as another performance' (1985:125).

I maintain that the terms ritual, drama and theatre are all means of trying to describe the various forms of larger than life representations involving dominant cultural symbols, artistic media and changes in role, in a designated space set apart. The roots of these creative forms are in early play experience involving embodiment–projection-role, emphasising the fundamental nature of the embodied dramatic act. They establish the important separation between 'dramatic reality' and 'everyday reality', i.e. the imagined world and the real world.

The seances performed by the Temiars are the means whereby the private material of dreams may be transformed into public acceptance and experience. The transformative quality of the seance performance enables the private and individual experience to become public and social.

It is important that both experiences are embodied and enacted. The human body is the means of expressing somatically both the internal and external *self and other* through the trance enactment of a seance performance, i.e. the Temiar belief in two souls – the head-soul and the heart-soul – enables the meeting of the 'good other' in dreams and it incorporates into the human body in trance. The 'evil other' is kept outside the human body and space unless a great shaman can harness its power on his and the community's behalf.

These complex beliefs and practices are elaborated as the main substance of this book. It explores the context and environment of Senoi Temiar health maintenance and healing rituals within their belief system and cosmology.

In my conclusion I suggest that the polysemic, epic metaphors of tiger, thunder and blood, embodied and projected through play, dance, music, drama and trance, enable the transformation and re-creation of the Temiar world as the 'world' of poetic and mimetic performance.

Chapter 2

Introducing the Temiars

The Senoi Temiars form one ethnic subgroup of the Senoi, the other major subgroup being the Senoi Semai who live further south in the state of Pahang. The Temiars number about 12,000 people in a total aboriginal population of some 78,000. They inhabit the tropical rain forest in Malaysia's most northerly states of Perak, Kelantan and Pahang. And yet the Senoi Temiars do not see themselves as forest people. They see themselves as people who live in cleared spaces which happen to be surrounded by forest. Although they acknowledge that they are part of the wider aboriginal population, including the forest-dwelling Negritos, they also know they have different beliefs, languages and practices which have geographical boundaries. The Temiars are also aware that there is some variation in language, shamanic practice, avoidances and cultivation and house-building techniques within Temiar locations.

The name Temiar is an anglicised form of *Təmɛɛr*, and Benjamin (see 1993a and b) argues that it derives from the Austronesian etymon *tembir* (edge). The word *Sɛnʔɔɔy* means people and the Temiars also refer to themselves as *Sɛnʔɔɔy Sərɔk* (hill people). For the purpose of this book I use the term Temiar throughout. The Temiars sometimes use the Malay term *Orang Asli* (original people) to refer to all aborigines in the Peninsular.

There is a wide variation in Temiar physical appearance: skin pigment is from light olive to dark brown, height from 5ft to 5ft 8in, and hair is woolly, wavy or curly. Many rural Malays have similar colouring and hair and the Temiars refer to them as *ʔasal* (original, pure), not as *Sərɔk*. Yet my Jamaican foster-son who was taller and blacker than the Temiars with tight curly hair was told that he was natural *Sərɔk*. This was in contrast to the rest of my family who had to change into *Sərɔk*, and then become Temiars.

Benjamin (1985), who has carried out the most thorough linguistic analysis of not only Temiar but all aboriginal languages in Malaysia, says,

> It belongs to the Central division of Aslian languages, which (together with the Northern and Southern Aslian languages) constitutes the Peninsular branch of Mon-Khmer; the major South East Asian member of the Austroasiatic phylum. . . .
> There is good evidence that Temiar, like other Aslian languages, has absorbed vocabulary and grammatical formutives from some Austronesian but Pre-Malay source that has since disappeared from the Peninsular.

(1985:1)

There is also some Temiarised absorption of the Malay language.

The Temiars live in villages built at the river mouths of the tributaries of the main rivers. The population is concentrated on the mountainous divide between the two most northern Malaysian states of Kelantan and Perak, where the temperatures range from about 85–95 degrees Fahrenheit, with a noticeable drop of 20–25 degrees at night, which makes it unexpectedly chilly for a tropical country. This area receives the full impact of the North-east monsoon (November to February), and the tail end of the South-west monsoon (April to July), so there is little to differentiate the seasons, apart from the fruiting of various trees and some changes in the flora. It rains on average for about 200 days a year.

The vegetation is typically lush with the constant rainfall and heat. The forest is home to a large number of snakes and other reptiles, numerous monkeys, wild pig, tiger and elephant. Barking and mouse deer, wild cattle and tapirs, porcupines and pangolins, together with a vast array of exotic birds and insects, all contribute to this immensely varied fauna. The terrain is steep with 200-foot trees with trailing lianas blocking out daylight. The landscape is broken up by limestone outcrops at irregular intervals, and cross-cut by the large rivers and smaller streams. The rain forest weaves a vast and complex tapestry.

The Temiars build their villages in clearings on the river banks, high enough from the river to be away from flooding during the monsoon. Unlike their nomadic neighbours the Negritos, who build temporary shelters and hunt and gather in the forest interior, the Temiars are settled cultivators who also hunt and gather, and move their villages infrequently for ritual or economic reasons. It is said that in the olden days they would move if someone died – now they only move if many people die. They also move to be nearer more fertile land for crop-growing.

Temiar villages consist either of a single long house with six or eight discrete families in apartments round a central communal area, or a collection of individual dwellings (see Plate 10 (p. 90) and Figure 5.2 (p. 82). The villages are likely to comprise twenty-five to fifty inhabitants, occasionally more. All houses are built off the ground, usually between one and six feet, on sturdy poles; the walls are woven bamboo and the roof is made from *atap* (Malay) thatch (see Figure 5.2 (p. 82) and Plate 8 (p. 80)). A single house will include a cooking area with a large wood fire, one or two sleeping compartments and an eating/meeting area. The villages are well cleared of undergrowth with jungle regeneration constantly being kept at bay.

The Temiars rely on the river for many basic needs, the most obvious being water for washing and cooking. Drinking water is taken from upstream, defecation takes place downstream, and washing and bathing are conducted from the central part of the river bank. The river is also the safest communication link between different areas and although occasionally there are dangerous rapids, the fear of travelling in the forest far outweighs any possible river hazards. The river is the source of fish which are a regular part of the Temiar diet. Nevertheless, when it swells during the monsoon time and debris comes hurtling down from the highlands, the river becomes impassable and even the getting of drinking water is a precarious balancing act.

The river does not only fulfil basic needs for the Temiars, it is also part of their orientation in space. If they are away from the river and particularly if they do not know in which direction the river lies, they feel anxious and disorientated; their capacity to read detailed maps through the river system is quite remarkable. Furthermore, there are restrictions concerning which substances may enter the river and which may not, i.e. human faeces must enter the river and menstrual blood may not. These restrictions will be more fully developed in Chapters 3 and 5.

As I have mentioned, the Temiar house (*deek*) is built off the ground, and although this is obviously for practical reasons such as avoidance of insects, wild animals and flood water, it is more important in relation to the wider understanding of Temiar spatial concepts. This was well illustrated when my Temiar mother gave a

serious admonition to one of her grandchildren who had just learned
to walk, and suddenly went down on to her hands and knees in order
to travel faster. The grandmother picked her up, scolded her and said,
'You must not crawl on the ground like a snake; snakes are dirty and
crawl on the ground on their bellies because they have no legs.' Thus
the Temiars are 'off-the-ground' and their house building reflects
this. 'Off-the-ground' and 'ground' divides the domestic and human
space from that of certain animals and other ground phenomena.
House (*deek*) and forest (*bɛɛk*), a fearful place for any Temiar to
enter, separates the Temiar human world from the non-human world.
The Temiars constantly seek to distinguish themselves from the non-
human world. In all their stories and in the way they organise their
day-to-day lives, the Temiars differentiate between the human world
of the village and he non-human world of the forest. Each is seen to
have its particular order, and certain things in the natural world are
predictable such as the monsoon rains, the fruiting of the seasonal
fruit trees, the full moon and the new moon. The Temiars divide the
lunar month into times when they can go into the forest and times
when they must build houses or do other within-village activities.
However, unexpected upheaval in the natural order such as major
thunderstorms, which are very frightening in their intensity and
destruction, are seen as punishment for certain misdemeanours, i.e.
disruptions in the social order.

The smallest Temiar unit comprises parents and unmarried children; a household usually consists of parents and pre-pubertal
children who occupy a single dwelling house or compartments with
a separate fire in a long house. Several familial units are linked in one
village through ownership of fruit trees, believed to be planted by a
family ancestor. The Temiars say you cannot own land, which has
confused them when the Jabatan Hal Elwal Orang Asli (JOA) has
gazetted various areas for them; you can only own what is grown or
found, be it cultivated or wild, and even that must be shared.
Similarly, houses are not owned as such, they are lived in while the
present families need them. If the family move away to another
village and on their return find a family have moved in, they would
build themselves another house. Houses are erected easily and
quickly and are constantly being changed as new families come to
stay or others move away. The village may change from a long house
to separate houses, and back again.

The question as to who had authority within the village is
frequently posed by outsiders in ways alien to Temiar thinking. How

do decisions come about, and how are wrongs redressed? The Malay government has imposed from without a headman for each village unit, an identified person with whom officials can negotiate. There is also a headman for a larger area, the river valley, who has seniority in a much larger territory (see Benjamin 1968b). The Temiars themselves acknowledge this external authority and usually refer to the headman by the Malay word *Penghulu*. However, in reality the *Penghulu* has little authority as an individual. The Temiar belief is that you cannot *make* anyone do anything, therefore how can an individual impose his will on another? This is a theme to which we shall refer frequently (see also Howell and Willis 1989).

The Temiars nevertheless have respect for age, and most decisions within the village are made by the older people coming together to discuss matters. People are sometimes asked to modify their behaviour but in practice there are few sanctions. Occasionally the Temiars informed me of fines that had been imposed by older men to settle grievances, for example, when a man complained that another man had taken his wife. But there is no authority that can insist on redress. An aggrieved or offending family will sometimes just choose to move away and join another village.

Noone says:

> The extension of kinship bonds, and the differential treatment and reciprocal obligations which relationship implies leaves small scope for individual offences. Where so much is temporary and its ownership shared, the conditions which make theft possible are precluded. Crime and legal procedures are confined practically to quarrels arising out of abuse of the marriage contract. These affairs necessarily do not affect blood-kin, but affines, or relatives by marriage.
>
> (1936:23)

However, supernatural sanction is a constant concern of all Temiars. Possible retribution by the intervention of the malevolent thunder deity (*Karey*) is a part of Temiar waking consciousness. Children are conditioned through a fear response to thunder and there is a range of behaviours which *Karey* is likely to punish, ranging from incest (*gɛɛs*) to laughing at butterflies or other prohibited creatures (*misik*). Intervention from thunder, and also tiger (*mamuug*), and affliction from serious illness are all possible retributions for neglecting various conforming behaviours. Retribution can be against individuals, families or the community, depending on the misdemeanour. Thus every Temiar has responsibilities both towards him- or herself, their dependent offspring, and the community as a whole.

The Temiars are swidden farmers (Benjamin 1985:1), 'slash and burn' cultivators who practice shifting crops which is supplemented by hunting and gathering. They clear areas of forest and plant cassava as the main staple crop, and also hill rice, maize and millet. The 'slash and burn' of the undergrowth is usually undertaken by the men of the village with the women's assistance. The planting and harvesting of the cassava is done by the women. Cassava is a fast-growing tuber which needs to be harvested daily. It forms the basic Temiar diet and is often eaten on its own, baked or stewed. Otherwise it is supplemented by other green vegetables and meat or fish. Women go to the cassava fields daily to bring enough for their own household and for anyone unable to go, for example, through illness. Similarly, they harvested enough for my household since I was often doing other things until I had a Temiar family 'living in' to help me.

The larger villages usually plant hill rice since they have enough labour for planting and harvesting. Hill rice has a much lower yield than the wet rice grown on the coastal plains, and is less abundant. Consequently it is eaten infrequently and tends to be stored and kept for ritual feasting. Maize, yams, millet and sweet potato are all cultivated in small quantities. Women also have their own small domestic vegetable patch where they grow gourds, pumpkins, beans and of course tobacco. Tobacco is grown near the village and shared amongst everyone. It is dried only briefly and is smoked green, wrapped in leaves. There is always great anxiety when tobacco stocks run low and when there is no access to shop-bought cigarettes. Temiars, of any age, cannot conceive of life without tobacco.

The Temiar diet is supplemented by hunting, fishing and gathering. The gathering is done by the women in communal expeditions into secondary forest. Sometimes a family will take a log boat upstream to tend the fields. Mothers and daughters gather various types of fungi, wild berries and green leafy vegetables. By contrast only men are allowed to go into the deep forest. There was no way I could persuade my Temiar friends to take me on a hunting expedition. Sexual division of labour was most strong concerning these expeditions and I would be told very seriously that it would be dangerous. 'Your people in London, in your village, would be very angry with us', they would say. When questioned they would say that Tiger might get me. Danger in the forest is usually conceptualised by Tiger.

Small groups of men go together on expeditions with blowpipes, poison darts and shotguns. They usually stay away for three or four days, and follow spoors; sometimes they build a hide and act on a recent sighting or prophetic dream. They bring back large game such as wild boar, deer or monkey, and various species of bird such as wild chickens or hornbills.

As Noone points out:

> It is necessary to understand the significance of meat in the system of Temiar beliefs and ritual. There is always believed to be danger connected with the consumption of meat. The pregnant woman, and her husband during the period preceding and following the birth of a child, may not even sit close to a meal of which meat is an ingredient, let alone eat it. Before adolescence no children may touch it, and it is the most frequent diet tabu imposed by the medicine man on his ailing patient.
>
> (1936:43)

As Fiddes points out:

> When nutritionists or policy makers discuss the energy, fat, or protein contents of foods, for example, and expect a willing public dutifully to adapt to their habits, they are deceiving themselves in failing to accommodate the numerous other roles that foods play in people's lives.
>
> (1991:41)

There are *grades* of prohibition in relation to the consumption of flesh. Some animal flesh is considered so dangerous that it has to be prepared in one house; those people for whom it is permitted consume it in the same house. However, fruit and vegetables are prepared and eaten within separate dwellings, although they are shared between different households. Most meat waste must be kept in the house and off-the-ground, whereas the vegetable waste is thrown on to the ground or into undergrowth. Certain animals hunted and killed by the Temiars must be 'transformed' before they are brought into the village, for example, their fur may be burnt off. If the hunted animal is very large, such as a full-size wild boar, a small village will invite folk from the next village and it can turn into a spontaneous communal feast. Apart from deep forest hunting, an individual may go off on his own for the day and bring back smaller game. Night-time frogging expeditions are also organised by the men.

Men and women usually fish using different methods. Women line fish from the river bank near the village, whereas men will fish with drag nets from the log boats. Both will use basket traps, woven by men or women. The women also go on expeditions to the tributaries to find river prawns. Occasionally two or more villages will get together to have a fish cull using poison.

There are several ways that a Temiar can earn money, either through regular work with the JOA, such as malaria prevention assistant, medical orderly at one of the forest medical posts, or as a government midwife. These jobs are paid regularly, and in the latter two special training is set up at the Orang Asli hospital in Kuala Lumpur. Additionally there can be casual work on government projects where they are able to earn piece money. Occasionally skilled trekkers are needed for expeditions. Chinese logging companies also find the forest skills of the Temiars useful. Apart from the district midwife, these are all cash paid jobs undertaken by men.

Cash is used to purchase goods that are not otherwise available to the Temiars except through barter of forest produce. Large rafts with rattan and fruit, for example, go downstream to a trading post. Temiars shop in the small logging town two days' journey away, for kerosene, sarongs and shorts, suitcases, metal pots and pans, enamel mugs and plates, batteries, and tinned food such as sardines, eggs, margarine and rice. Whenever possible, they also purchase large quantities of monosodium glutamate, which is sold in packets, and other flavourings. Ready-made cigarettes are also in demand, although home-grown tobacco is preferred, particularly for ritual occasions. However, there is little that is durable apart from kitchen goods, bush knives and clothes, and even the latter are relatively impermanent.

Noone describes the impermanence of Temiar material culture very succinctly when he says:

> To describe the material culture of the Temiar is to tell the uses to which bamboo may be put. Bamboo is indispensable to them for houses, household utensils, vessels, tools, weapons, fences, baskets, water-pipes, rafts, musical instruments and ornaments.
>
> (1936:26)

Midwifery and shamanic healing are the only ritual tasks which are paid for within the community with cash or goods. A shaman may be called to a house for a simple cure or to see a patient who is too ill to be moved, or he may be asked to perform a healing seance. In all circumstances the patient or the patient's relatives will make a payment. The amount will depend on the length of time the treatment takes and the seriousness of the illness. Similarly midwives receive payment from the husband for the baby's delivery, usually in money and clothes. However, there is also a permanent ritual gift-giving set up between a child and its midwife.

Since a village is formed around a core sibling group, marrying out of the village is more likely than marrying within the village. Marriage within the same valley, or on the same river, is preferred. Temiar mothers would say to me that they did not like their daughters to go 'over the mountains' to another place, where customs would be different and they would be too far away. Marriage, the Temiars insist, takes place for love. Young people from different villages meet at seances and 'sing-ins' and have the opportunity to flirt in the dark.[1] Children talk with their parents before they establish a union that already exists in private; there is little ceremony to mark the occasion. Parents of the couple may exchange small gifts such as sarongs or bush knives. Residence is usually changeable at the beginning of marriage, alternating between the villages of both sets of parents. Often the couple live in a compartment built on to the parents' house before eventually building their own separate unit.

Temiars have a respectful relationship with their spouse's opposite sex elder sibling, i.e. the wife's elder brother and the husband's elder sister, and these affinal relations, like the parent-in-law, expect help in the house or fields. Between the spouse's younger, opposite sex siblings there is a co-operative friendship. However, the person has a very free joking relationship with the spouse's same sex siblings, and this often contains a strong sexual content. In our village, Limah's husband had died some years before and she married his younger brother, had more children, and the children of the previous union refer to him as father. Temiar kinship is described in detail in Carey (1961) and Benjamin (1967b, 1993a).

I call the three major stages of the Temiar life cycle which occur between the emphatically marked birth and death rituals *play*, *fertility* and *wisdom*. I have chosen these terms because they encapsulate the predominant characteristics of these life cycle stages, and reflect the Temiar beliefs, values and practices.

Each of these stages is marked by changes in the naming system. Once the dependent infant can walk unaided, he or she is given a name that is different from any other name (see Benjamin 1968a), but this name is used only by parents and within the house. In everyday situations, children are known by nicknames such as 'runny nose', 'running about', 'free' (*pəriih*), borrowed names such as Jimin, Assim, Johnny, or birth-order names, the following being the first five names usually used: *ʔaluŋ, ʔaŋah, ʔalaŋ, Pandaʔ, ʔaɲjaŋ*. The youngest born is called *ʔalʉj* (the same as the youngest born hero in the creation myth). There is no change of name for a couple at marriage, although their parents now call each other *bisat* (co-parent). However, as if anticipating the change in status to parenthood, once the woman is pregnant, she and her husband are often called by the Temiar word for pregnant, *ʔacɔɔʔ*.

At the birth of the first child, or during the time that children may be conceived even if a couple are sterile, the changes in name establish what I term the age of fertility. When the first child is born, the name of both parents becomes either *litɔw* (parents of a boy) or *balɛh* (parents of a girl), depending on the gender of the child. To this is often added the later nickname of the child. For example, I was known as *litɔw ʔandiih* so as not to confuse me with all the other people called *litɔw*. However there are also names for parents with no children and parents of stillborn births. As the last-born child develops increased autonomy, there is a gradual transition of the parents from this fertile time to one of respectful age. Individuals are considered to have knowledge because they have lived long enough. Men are referred to as *tataaʔ* (old man) and women *jajaaʔ* (old woman). 'Knowing' for the Temiars is not the knowledge of information or facts. The Temiars use the words *na-lɛk* (he or she knows) to imply maturity, to know at a deeper level, which they associate with having lived long enough. At death, all names die with you and you are known as old man or old woman of a particular village.

Let us now look at the main characteristics of these three stages which separate Temiar groups, are underpinned by food restriction, spatial avoidance and limitations on trance; and express the polarities of dependency and autonomy, and the later emergence of specialist roles.

THE PLAY STAGE

During the first year of life, the infant is breast-fed on demand, massaged frequently and only leaves the house if he or she is carried by a parent, grandparent or older sibling. Breast-feeding continues for several years but once the infant can walk independently, he or she spends increasing amounts of time outside, often as the baby in children's family games. In the early months infants are washed within the house or on the outside platform where they are also held out for defecation. Once they can walk they spend more time at the river, learning to swim and play and seeing to other bodily functions.

Unless the whole family goes on an expedition to another village or to harvest fields further away from the village, the young infant plays within the confines of the village and river area. Most of the children's games reflect adult activities. For example, they build miniature houses with small fireplaces. The girls play at cooking and the boys go off to hunt to the forest edge. Sometimes they enact a seance and pretend to go into a staggering trance, or learn some of the songs from an older teenager. It was from these *playing-at-seances*, as contrasted with *play-seances*, that I gathered initial information about *gənabag* (communal singing performance) and *lɛslãã* (transformation, a Temiar metaphor for trance). All infants and children (unless ill) attend the seances and join in the singing and dancing. The Temiars believe that children cannot go into trance because this involves freedom of the head-soul and they say that a child's head-soul is not yet strong enough to be free.

As the filial dependency decreases, there is a corresponding increase in individual autonomy and playfulness. At around 7 years, children often sleep together in different houses with their peer groups rather than close to their parents. There is a gradual decrease on food restrictions as fathers experiment with hitherto prohibited food, and if the child suffers no ill-effects he or she is allowed to try it for themselves.

While parents are loving and indulgent to their children, there is a growing awareness of the threat and possible retribution from supernatural sources. From birth, the infant has its ears covered during loud thunderstorms and parents chant 'tuuk, tuuk' (fear) and shiver, and the infant will often whimper and look distressed. As children become more independent in regard to their space and games, inevitably their playing gets louder and sometimes less controlled and parents will call out *misik hãã* (*misik-you*) meaning, if you don't play more quietly then thunder will notice and come closer. This was particularly so when children played noisy games in the river, and jumping-up-and-down games generally.[2]

Schooling provided by the government is available within a few miles. Some children attend more regularly than others, and because

Plate 3 Playing with a young sibling

Plate 4 A 4-year-old washing a 3-week-old baby

my own children were relatively compliant at doing their two hours of lessons most mornings, some of the Temiar mothers thought I could be an enforcing agent and persuade their children to go to school! This was not something they felt they could do themselves, given the value placed on children's personal autonomy. However, it was rather more comfortable for me to join with them in a general moan about children than to impose an external threat or blackmail them.

Children choose at whim whether or not they want to help parents or other grown-ups, but it is very rare for them to refuse to look after a younger sibling (Plate 3). Boys and girls will often request to wash and nurse a small baby (Plate 4), and I have seen pre-pubertal girls try to make a breast in order to suckle a crying infant if its mother is temporarily away. Although there is freedom and lack of responsibility for children, they start to choose to learn about adult activities. There is gender separation as young boys accompany their fathers and older brothers on lesser hunting expeditions, and girls assist their mothers within the village or harvesting the cassava. Boys and girls also dress up as adults as they play-act different activities. The boys tie their sarongs as loincloths and make bows and arrows. The girls re-tie their sarongs over as yet undeveloped breasts and play at being midwife to each other, warming bunches of cassava leaves and holding them against their stomachs. Two boys went round the village with a cut off piece of bamboo playing at taking photographs, which is how they saw me!

At the onset of puberty, marked for girls by the ritual of first menstruation, there is an increased awareness of the opposite sex, and of the opportunities that the seances provide for meeting potential partners. Girls will observe the food restrictions and avoid contact with men during menstruation (since menstrual blood is regarded as dangerous to men by the Temiars), but in general young people enjoy the greatest freedom and playfulness. Their personal autonomy is established and respected, they are encouraged to talk about their dreams and their food taboos are more relaxed. Although they begin to take on adult roles when they help parents or other relatives, there is nevertheless plenty of time for horse-play as they enact more sophisticated versions of the children's games and indulge in comparatively uncontrolled trance-dancing at the play-seances, i.e. not 'playing-at-seances'. Adults can get very impatient if the trance activity of the young people becomes too noisy and goes beyond acceptable limits. At one of the play-seances I attended, girls in particular were bouncing around, falling to the floor, being picked up by their friends only to start bouncing again. One girl stayed in a state of dissociation for over twenty minutes and as the shaman attempted to bring her to consciousness, his more pragmatic wife fetched a cup of water and threw it in the girl's face!

THE FERTILE STAGE

This freedom continues after marriage and during the early months of pregnancy (providing there is no threat of miscarriage). In later pregnancy the woman's diet is restricted both in relation to foreign foods, fruit that has a sticky sap which might impede the birth canal, and the more dangerous meats. Trance in later pregnancy is thought to affect the as yet unformed head-soul of the unborn infant. These restrictions are observed gradually as the pregnancy becomes more noticeable, reaching a peak in the last few weeks when the preparations for the birth are made – especially if it is the first birth.

Childbirth is described later, but I want to stress the ritualised 'point of entry' into the Temiar human world and the major changes in life-style it entails for the parents; it also emphasises a major source of danger and power: post-partum blood. During the post-partum period there is a severe restriction on food and space for both the mother and the midwife and some restriction for the father. Once the bleeding has stopped and the midwife is not in constant attendance, the filial dependent relationship becomes firmly established. Parents and their babies and small children are isolated as a social group by their new name and also the restrictions on foods and activities. The father may have fewer food restrictions than the mother, but he will be the one to try new or hitherto avoided foods. Parents are aware that careless actions and ignoring of 'ground rules' could make their infant ill. My Temiar porter, *Busuu?*, was insistent that he should gather all the wood for our fire. Other people, he said, might not be so careful and therefore gather wood that was near a certain tree which could cause illness in his small children.

Most parents of young children do not go into trance although they attend the seance performances. By allowing the freedom of their own head-soul they could affect the still unformed head-soul of their infant. The young child's head-soul is seen as 'unfixed' and may wander off or react to sudden movement or noise. However, if the father of a small child is an aspiring or apprentice shaman, he will partake in trance activities.

Breast-feeding on demand, as has now been scientifically demon-strated[3] inhibits conception, so Temiar families are fairly evenly spaced with two or three years between births. Temiar women during their fertile years move in and out of lesser and greater food restrictions. During this time there may be the early development of specialist skills which will become established in later years. After giving birth to one or more children, a woman may decide to assist a midwife at the deliveries of other women. I have already mentioned that men may be aspiring shaman; they may also have dreamt of new songs or dances and taught them to others in the village. Women spend time weaving coloured mats and pouches and fishing traps; men become practised at blowpipe hunting, house building, spoor trekking and fish-net weaving. However, there is still a sense that before a rather arbitrary 'middle age' most people do not 'know' because they have not lived long enough.

A young married Temiar schoolteacher was described to me by older Temiar as 'playing at teaching'; he was not considered old enough to teach anybody anything.

THE WISE STAGE

When a Temiar couple are considered unlikely to produce more children (and their youngest child has been called ʔalʉj) or when childless couples[4] are thought unlikely to have children, there is a gradual change from naming with reference to parenting and children to naming in relation to age, wisdom and knowledge (tataaʔ, jajaaʔ). There is a concomitant relaxation of most food avoidances. Older men have greater food freedom than older women. It is at this time that men and women become firmly individualised with greater freedom in their activities, and established in their specialist skills. Men may choose to become shaman and women midwives: these are seen as demanding occupations not to be undertaken lightly. The shaman is persistently attending to the head-souls and illnesses of others, and the midwife managing the dangerous post-partum blood. A shaman does not necessarily have restrictions on his diet, whereas a midwife will have the most extreme restrictions during the delivery and post-partum time, and will always maintain some avoidance, comparable to mothers of young children.

Shaman may develop particular specialities such as death seances, house-building chants and, rarely, 'great' shamanism, i.e.

the tiger shaman. Other men may be known for their skills, for example, in story-telling and men and women alike are turned to for advice on health, hunting and so on.

Midwives and older women conduct hair rituals (see pages 134–5) for appeasing thunder and most adult women take part in the blood ritual if thunderstorms are very severe. The stage that I have termed the age of wisdom is the time from the end of the fertile period until death, when the Temiars consider themselves knowledgeable and specialist, and when certain individuals, namely shaman and mid-wives, take responsibility for the head-soul and blood management of others.

Temiar seances are famous throughout the peninsular to both anthropologists and travellers alike.[5] A popular film has been made of the seances and some writers have described it out of context as a type of erotica, idealised in a way that travesties the Temiars. As part of this introduction I need to establish that the seances are held both for specific purposes, such as healing, or to end the mourning period and also as a regular part of their life-style. Seances can be playful, fun-loving times, when many of the proceedings are not taken too seriously. They are considered to have a preventive as well as a curative function and can be informal as well as formal.

If you ask Temiar individuals why they trance (*lɛslãˉãˉs*) they say things like, 'We must trance', 'We have to trance', 'I can't go for a long time without trancing', 'I long to trance' (*yim-hɔ̃ɔ̃d*: I long or yearn for).

The seance itself is seen as a time when the good influences in the form of small shy spirits of plants, fruits and flowers lodge on the roof of the house or the leaf decorations where the performance is taking place. The shaman enters into a relationship with these good influences and makes use of their beneficence on behalf of the village as a whole as well as the sick. Shaman have first met their own spirit guides in dreams, and both dream and trance activities are considered very important by the Temiars.

I have described how the Temiars differentiate themselves from the non-human world which is considered malevolent and to be avoided, as well as the non-human world which is benevolent, with which the Temiars seek to enter into a positive relationship. All positive and negative entities have designated space, both actual and symbolic. Earlier I described how the Temiars conceptualise their immediate space as off-the-ground and ground, and house and forest. The river is a further means by which the Temiars orientate themselves in space and they use river terms to talk about themselves in space.

The Temiars believe that the world is divided into an upper world (*baliik*) and a lower world (*tɛʔ*), i.e. the idea of heaven and earth. Various versions describe layers between heaven and earth (see Endicott 1979:36 for Negrito variations; and Benjamin 1967a:26 for Temiar accounts).

I found that many of these ideas were imprecise and some of the Temiars I questioned thought they were Malay ideas anyway. However, there is, they say, *certainly* a layered space beyond the sky, including a space that humans cannot see which is inhabited by *Karey* (thunder deity) and his familiars. Various prohibitions act to discourage thunder from coming closer and intervening in Temiar lives. Beneath the earth is a layer inhabited by demons and monsters; the former may intervene through acts of foolishness and the latter may cause the flood water to rise if disturbed. There are also various evil creatures that inhabit river banks and river mouths. They are likely to attack people, particularly at dusk, and to invade their body, especially their heart/blood-soul.

These good spirits can only be seen in dreams; nevertheless they inhabit the world of humans and their positive influences can be felt when they come in close proximity to people. Entities that have a negative influence on the human world live above the sky, beneath the earth or in the forest. By contrast, entities that have a positive influence on the human world live 'in-between' as do people themselves.

Although the Temiars see their Negrito neighbours as like themselves in belonging to the aboriginal races, they also describe themselves in complete contrast to them. The Negritos are nomadic hunter-gatherers who build temporary shelters on the ground, and the Temiars see them as forest people. The Temiars say that the Negritos have knowledge that they do not possess and from my questioning it mainly concerned healing and shamanism. One of my informants admitted a little sheepishly that he wanted to obtain a potion to improve his sex life. He also said that Negrito medicine and spells are stronger but more dangerous.

The Temiars acknowledge that the Senoi Semais are the Asli who most resemble them, although they have some different customs and language variation. Benjamin says:

For the Temiars the cultural system is a traditional function of

territory, and this feature of their world view is an aspect of the
overall categorisation of the universe that recurs in all fields of
Temiar life.

(1966:11)

The Temiars in Kuala Betis, the area where I conducted some of
my field work (Map 2, page xv), refer to the fact that they live in an
area which had previously been inhabited by rural Malays. There is
some anxiety that the Malays might come and oust them out of their
villages but they also say that some of their practices are similar to
the Malays. Their houses are similar to Malay style and they are
familiar with some of the aspects of Malay shamanic practice. One
Temiar shaman in fact held a dual seance which we attended in which
he used both Malay and Temiar forms in parallel. Much further
upstream the house building changes, and there is less familiarity and
awareness of Malay practices. I did not travel right up the head-
waters (because of official security restraints on freedom of travel),
where I was given to understand that there are yet more differences.
Thus there is an important contrast between those Temiars living
nearer to outside influence and those living further away, i.e. down
river and up river.

In this chapter I have given a brief description of the Temiars and
their relationship with the non-human world and other human beings.
I have suggested life-cycle stages of play, fertility and wisdom. I have
also drawn attention to the spatial concepts of 'off-the-ground'/
'ground', 'house and forest' and 'river' as ways in which the Temiar
order their spatial world. Changes in life-stages are acknowledged by
transformations in food and bodily restrictions, naming practice and
dependence or freedom of head-souls. I have referred to sources of
danger – thunder, tiger and menstrual/post-partum blood – as well as
the positive creative activities of dreaming and trancing; women have
an important role in the management of blood and thunder, whereas
male shaman are responsible for most healing, especially of souls.

Chapter 3

Boundaries and transformations

Ethnography ... is an interpretive discipline which aims at the understanding and translation of culture, that is, the rendering of the unintelligible intelligible.

(Carruthers 1992:151)

Launcelot Gobbo: 'Budge' says the fiend. 'Budge not' says my conscience.

(*The Merchant of Venice*, Act 2.ii)

Throughout Temiar thoughts and practices we shall see that there are cross-cutting categories of expected behaviour that establish the boundaries of the human body, the domestic house, social groups and the wider community. Neglect of these constraints can be dangerous, resulting in major illness or death, or, at the least, a small accident. Importantly, individuals can be responsible for retribution both against themselves or against others or towards the whole community.

The Temiar child is born into a world of bodily, spatial and social constraints. These constraints are maintained from the moment of birth with the prohibitions surrounding the birth itself and the way in which the infant is handled in the first year of life. The birth is fraught with dangers because of the possibility of the unwelcome attention of malevolent creatures who might smell the post-partum blood. Newly delivered mothers are seen as being both vulnerable and in need of protection, as well as being dangerous to other people, especially men.

The infant is also vulnerable. This is particularly so because the barely-formed head-soul (*rəwaay*) is free-floating and needs to be strengthened. Actions by both parents, but especially the mother at this time, are seen to affect the strength or weakness of the infant's head-soul. In particular the parents must pay strict attention to the food avoidances which are necessary to maintain the health of the child. These avoidances come under the wider heading of *sabat* and the following categories of people are separated from others by *sabat* food avoidances:

children
women
fertile women
menstruating women
expectant women
expectant women and their spouses
newly-delivered women and their midwives
newly-delivered parents and their midwives
mothers and infants
parents of infants and infants
midwives
unwell people

Although there are *sabat* avoidances for all children and for the husbands of expectant and newly-delivered women, the emergent theme is the predominant connection between fertile women and restricted foods, i.e. menstruating, pregnant, newly-delivered women and mothers of small children all have more strict avoidances.

There is some variation between geographical areas and not all Temiars necessarily agree on the finer detail of prohibitions. However, in broad terms, the foods fall into the following categories:

all flesh
large fish
all other fish
fruit and vegetables
foreign foods (e.g. Chinese noodles)
new and untried foods
salt and spices
tea and coffee

The most stringent restrictions are for newly-delivered mothers and their midwives who are only allowed bland cassava root and warm water. When the post-partum time is over, after the cessation of bleeding, this extreme taboo is broken with a special meal shared between the mother, father and midwife which includes either small fish or non-taboo flesh, green leafy vegetables and cassava. There are no permitted additives. These restrictions continue with a little flexibility – gradual easing up of tea and coffee avoidance and fruits – until the infant is walking. At about 1 year old, the infant is allowed a little bland cassava or plain rice. Meanwhile the father is allowed greater freedom but would not risk consumption of middle or great *gɛnhaaʔ* flesh.

All new food is labelled *sabat* until some older person has tried it first; for example, this happened with my yeast extract. After one of the men had tried it, it was considered permissible for those people who were not infants, or newly-delivered or menstruating women.

Sabat illnesses vary in their severity, the most common symptoms being sickness, vomiting and loss of weight, through to more serious illness (*tɛnruuʔ*) which is manifested in uncontrolled shaking, convulsions and a wasting away of the body. The Temiars demonstrated to me the noisy asthmatic breathing that accompanies severe *tɛnruuʔ* (noisy or laboured breathing at any time causes great anxiety for the Temiars). At its most severe, *tɛnruuʔ* can be the result of a small transformed tiger that enters the *hup*: certain animals and plants are believed to turn into small tigers.

Other *sabat* foods for pregnant women (for example, sticky fruit) are thought to complicate the birth by impeding the birth canal or enlarging the head of the infant. Midwives also believe that their eating habits can affect their newly-delivered infants, and they usually maintain permanent food avoidances. Although food is restricted for women at the time they are considered most dangerous in relation to men (when menstruating and at the post-partum time), the Temiar view centres on the belief that parental acts can affect infants, whether born or *in utero*. *Sabat* foods are therefore concerned with the maintenance of boundaries of the human body as well as the separation of certain categories of people. This imposes a constant vigilance on parents of young children in particular, since their actions can affect their children, and it isolates parents and their small children from other people.

In contrast with *sabat* avoidances of food entering the body, *təracɔɔg* concerns food waste leaving the body; food that has been through the body should not come into contact with the ground. The usual place for defecation is the river, since the fish will eat the faeces before it touches the ground. Infants, once they are standing firmly, will balance on a small ladder at the back of the house, or else their mothers will hold them out to defecate. The debris is immediately consumed by the village dogs which are taught to scavenge. (This can have alarming results for someone 'taken short' in the middle of the night who will squat at the edge of the forest rather than go down to the river. I had the teeth marks for weeks.) I observed a mother call a dog to the back of the house so that it could consume the waste as it emerged from the infant's body. People who are forbidden from going to the river (menstruating women, newly-delivered women, infants and some patients) use the edge of the forest for defecation. We can see how *sabat* and *tɜracɔɔg* regulate what food may enter the body and where faeces may be discharged when it leaves the body. There are other *tɜracɔɔg* restrictions which I shall discuss later in this chapter.

Complementing and cross-cutting the *sabat/tɜracɔɔg* restrictions are those which govern the handling and consumption of certain forest animals. First they are killed away from the village, either at the fringe or in deep forest, and then disfigured in some way before being brought into the house or village – often the skin is burnt off or, with the porcupine, the prickles removed. This group of animals is called *gɛnhaaʔ* and is graded in three degrees of prohibition: great, middle and minor (*rayaaʔ, gagid, ʔamɛs*) respectively. Animals which come into the middle and great categories must be taken into the first possible house when the hunters enter the village and be prepared and eaten in that house. Those people for whom it is not *sabat* congregate in the one house to consume it. All food waste from *gɛnhaaʔ* animals must be burnt on the fire, including the cooking tubes of bamboo, and must not be allowed to come into contact with the ground. Minor *gɛnhaaʔ* animals are still cooked in the first house but shared between the houses for consumption (see Benjamin 1967a for a detailed description of these beliefs and practices).

Under the heading of *gɛnhaaʔ*, at rice harvest a visitor must accept some of the new rice grains either as food or take them away uncooked. This helps preserve the head-soul of the rice and refusing this offering could result in crop failure, visits from tiger and even death – an example of the actions of an individual affecting the community.

Families lay claim to the harvest from their own family orchards while the fruit is still on the trees. Once it has fallen on to the ground anyone can claim it. We would be sitting in our house with the Temiar children listening very intently, and suddenly they would shoot off into the undergrowth; moments later, one of them, the most fleet-footed, would return with a large durian fruit. Temiars can hear a large fruit drop at least a hundred yards away.

Fruit waste from these seasonal trees must *not* be thrown on to the fire. The waste falls underneath the house or is pitched away from the house door into the undergrowth. The Temiars believe that there are head-souls on fruit which would be driven away if the waste is burnt. Head-souls are a positive influence and therefore the aim is to keep them around the house and village. An act that would drive them away (*joruu?*) is seen to be stupid or foolhardy rather than dangerous; i.e. it is seen as a withdrawing of good influence (rather than the invitation of negative influence that can result in severe illness), with resultant vulnerability to outside attack. I became a little confused with the Temiar explanation as to whether we were talking about the head-souls of dead Temiars or the head-souls of the fruit, since all living things have head-souls. (One of Benjamin's informants (1967:148) suggested that the fruits themselves are *human* head-souls.) However, I found it difficult to pin the Temiars down on this. There is a parallel between the domestic house and the human body. *Sabat* and *tɔracɔɔg* regulate what goes into and what comes out of the human body; and *gɛnhaa?* and *joruu?* regulate what goes into or is kept out of the domestic house. *Sabat*, *tɔracɔɔg*, *gɛnhaa?* and *joruu?* control entry and exit of substances and fluids. The neglect of this control can result in uncontrollable bodily symptoms – shaking, convulsions, vomiting and discharge from ears, eyes and nose.

We have seen from the *tɔracɔɔg* beliefs that human waste from digested food must not return to the ground unless it is from a child or from menstruating or newly-delivered women, i.e. a woman that is bleeding. Neither of these categories of people may go to the river where defecation normally takes place. I have already mentioned that animals must be slaughtered away from the domestic domain either in the forest or at the forest edge, and then carried into the first house the hunters reach, depending on which path they take from the forest. Care must be taken that blood from these animals does not drip on to the village paths. It is also very important that women and young children do not go too near the blood of particular animals, including domestic chickens, because the blood is supposed to give off a dangerous smell. The smell of it alone is likely to cause *pocuk*, in which the person shakes uncontrollably and experiences nausea. Care must be taken that children do not go near places where the blood could have been spilt inadvertently.

There is a similarity between the effect the blood of the slaughtered animals may have on women and children, and the effect of menstrual blood on men. Benjamin (1967a:82) suggests that it separates out the domains of nature and culture and also men, and women and children. My interest is in the transformative potential of dangerous substances: menstrual blood and certain plants and creatures can turn into small tigers. The dominant fear in these illnesses is the loss of control – either shaking or vomiting. The correct place for both the blood of slaughtered animals and for menstrual blood is the forest or forest edge, away from possible dangerous contact with people of the opposite sex. Thus gender separation and appropriate boundaried space are the means of protecting people from loss of bodily control or invasion of the body in the *hup*.

There is a large number of avoidance practices that come under the general heading of *misik*. First, *misik* is applied to the range of natural species that must not be laughed at or pointed at, their call imitated, or attention drawn to them in an obvious way. This range includes very colourful and 'different' species, such as butterflies, dragon-flies, various birds, insects and leeches. It was very difficult not to draw attention to an infestation of leeches when they had burrowed through the laces of walking boots and hung bloated in clusters from my feet after a long walk in the forest. However, the removal of the leeches and first aid had to be carried out with no gesticulations, complaint or verbal reference.

Because of its associations with blood, leech avoidance is also referred to as *misik lɔɔt* (blood); Benjamin (1967:117) also refers to the fact that leeches are not allowed to be brought into, or taken out of, the house; if one *is* brought into the house, it must be burned on the fire.

Misik also applies to certain other obvious acts carried on outside which should be done in the house. The Temiars have always joked about the subject, but also kept reminding me it is *misik* to have sex in the daytime, and sex out of doors at any time. This is also given as the reason for restraining people from jumping up and down in the river and for children playing jumping up and down games generally. Thunder might think you are having sex in the daytime. This is in contrast with the laughter and indulgence towards young children when they take part in sexual play. Janum, a 3-year-old boy, ran around the space between the houses with a cassava root, pretending to stick it up the girls' bums and saying '*nɔɔy, nɔɔy, nɔɔy*' (sexual intercourse). Adults and adolescents thought this was very funny and indulged in sexual repartee.

All children's playing, however, is curbed if it gets *too* noisy or seems *too* uncontrolled. Mothers in particular are vigilant that children's play does not involve too much physical speed or that voices do not shriek and scream. The fear response to thunder is effective in dampening down high spirits. I was reprimanded for twirling my umbrella, and was told to make sure that I washed the coloured sleeping mats indoors. As with food, new and untried practices and behaviour are incorporated into this way of thinking. For example, I was told it was *misik* to read a book outside; the fact that it was a first-aid book with diagrams of people's insides may have added to the inappropriateness of this activity. There was no mention of me writing notes in my field-book if I was outside.

There are also *misik* prohibitions that apply on re-entry to the house if people have been away and these must be adhered to for the first few days. Ros, my daughter, after returning from a brief visit to another village, was seriously admonished because she took some cooking pots and pans to the river to wash them. It was also forbidden to use mirrors, squeeze spots or search each other's hair for fleas. This is in contrast to the more generalised sanction against these activities being done outside; after return to an unoccupied house they must not be done at all.

Thunder's disapproval can be expressed in a fairly mild way with distant rumbling and adults looking anxiously towards the sky. However, it could result in a major thunderstorm and decisions are then made concerning the performance of the rituals to dissuade thunder from continuing. The worst result is for thunder to send down thick ropes that can trip or strangle a person or pull them into the fire. These ropes enter the house directly or come up through the floor. At its most extreme, thunder can pull down houses and cause the flood water to rise, creating death and destruction. As a way of explaining his anxiety after he had accompanied me to a new village where there was a dead monkey hanging from a tree outside the village, *Busuu?*, my assistant, told me the following story:

> An old man and his grandson went to Pahang with a blowpipe and blowpiped a monkey. The old man was a big shaman, a shaman of thunder and the ground. He returned and went to someone's house and said he wanted to eat the monkey. The people all came to the house to see the monkey and said, no, he couldn't eat the monkey. He kept saying he wanted it and they kept saying no.
>
> Then the shaman did *jampii?* on the monkey (incantations such

as are used in blessings and healing) and the monkey came alive. The old man said to his grandson, 'Let's go'.

The people put make-up on the monkey, down its nose and on its cheeks. Then the people began to play bamboo stompers and beat drums and the monkey began to dance. All the people began to laugh and say 'Good, good'.

A short time later thunder came and rain came down. Cords came down as thick as my arm. The house fell down and everyone was dead.

(See Endicott 1979:65 for a similar Batek story.)

Misik restrictions impose supernatural limits on human behaviour outside the house. It restricts behaviour that is new or foreign, extremes of children's play or laughter generally, domestic objects being used outside, night-time activities being done in the daytime, and particularly it curbs people's noticeable involvement with phenomena that are distinctive from the natural world. Although the Temiars usually talk about incurring thunder's disapprobation through breaking *misik* restrictions, which affects the whole community, it is also possible for an individual to be afflicted by severe bouts of diarrhoea. *Sabat* and *misik* affect individuals with resulting illness – discharge from the upper or lower body. *Misik* involves the whole community, whereas other rules govern the behaviour of subgroups. Temiars are very anxious at 'in-between' times, such as sunrise and sunset, particularly if there are distinctive phenomena such as rainbows, hot rain, orange sunsets. Children are called indoors at these times and it is forbidden to comment or point at these manifestations.

We have already seen within *misik* the interest that thunder takes in people's sexual behaviour. However, it must not be thought that the Temiars are coy about sexual allusion or sexual activity. I described earlier the sometime sexual connotations of children's play. Men openly joke with each other about missing targets when hunting because their knees are trembling too much from the previous night's indulgence! Pre-marriage relationships are described as playful (*jεhwah*) and include sexual activity. Because of the flimsy construction of Temiar houses it is not possible to be totally discreet, and this often creates a 'ripple effect' in those houses where several families live. However, this is in complete contrast to matters of childbirth and menstruation which are considered by the Temiars, especially Temiar men, to be highly embarrassing and distasteful.

Incest rules, *gɛɛs*, are frequently discussed by the Temiars and, as with *misik*, are something they will constantly check out. Children, once they have stopped sleeping in or near the parental compartment around the age of 6, will sleep much further away, often in another house with other children of that age. Benjamin (1967b:124) says that sibling incest is considered far more serious than filial incest.

Hal, at the age of 7, said to me very clearly when we returned to England, 'There is one reason I am glad to be going home; I shall be able to get into your bed in the middle of the night and no one will say *gɛɛs* to me.'

I found some anxiety about all incest – even avoidance of certain people following each other into the river without a time lapse in between. To marry someone with known blood links would be to incur the strongest intervention of *Karey*, the thunder deity. Thunder takes direct intervention if the *gɛɛs* avoidances are not observed, as he does with neglect of *misik* prohibitions. Thunder's intervention for incest is of the most extreme form and the Temiars told me stories of houses and villages being destroyed by *Karey*'s intervention which resulted in flooding. Certainly *Karey* sends down the ropes and trips the incestuous persons into the fire. Furthermore, incestuous persons are likely to suffer from painful swellings of the thighs and genitals, making further indulgences impossible. The *gɛɛs* rules preserve the integrity of the family by maintaining the separation of any blood links between people who marry. Any mixing of blood that is related is punished severely. *Karey* controls not only those with whom sexual relationships are permissible, but also, as we saw from the *misik* rules, where and at what time sexual relations may take place.

If thunder intervenes there are remedial actions that may be taken, principally by women.

Whereas *misik* and *gɛɛs* are concerned with the direct intervention of thunder, other actions, such as *joruuʔ*, are seen as driving away the good influence, leaving the community vulnerable to thunder's interventions. *Joluŋ* restrictions refer specifically to indiscriminate acts that could scare away the head-souls that are believed to cluster on the decorations set up for a seance on the roof of the house, and generally in the proximity of the village. It is *joluŋ* to bring additional herbs or flowers into the house in the days after a seance, and also to carry bamboo and logs into the house and to leave any part sticking out of the doorway. Bringing new head-souls into the house where such a constellation is already established could scare the existing ones away. The decorations themselves are taken down after a few days, unless there are several seances in a row, when they will be taken down a few days after the last seance.

Thus *joruu?* – concerned with the maintenance of the head-souls of the seasonal fruits by not burning their waste on the fire – and *joluŋ* – which maintains the presence of the spirit guides – are both concerned with not scaring away the good influence of the small, shy spirits which bring the benificence to the village as a whole.

I want to return to a category of behaviour that I mentioned earlier in relation to food waste – *tɘracɔɔg*. There are many *tɘracɔɔg* prohibitions concerned with activity in the forest such as not kicking ant hills or certain tree stumps, as well as others which broadly come under the heading of the disposal of non-human debris. It is prohibited to throw away old tins without first puncturing a hole in the bottom, to throw old clothes into the river, or to pour water (or spit) down the house posts. It is also *tɘracɔɔg* to pull out a cassava root and leave half in the soil, to bring wood that has soil trapped in it into the village, or to come into contact with a split and twisted tree trunk. I was first alerted to *tɘracɔɔg* when I observed my porter making holes in the bottoms of all milk and bean tins that had been thrown away; he said that he was preventing his child from having ear discharge. The most usual illnesses to result from *tɘracɔɔg* are discharge from the ears and nose, deafness, swollen and runny eyes, respiratory difficulty and severe headaches. The latter sounded like a description of migraine, as the Temiars held a band round their heads and said that was what it felt like.

The Temiars are very strict about water being kept away from the house posts. The quite obvious practical side is that the posts could rot, but I am not clear how it fits into any category, unless one sees the house posts as being in the ground, and therefore for saliva or water from the house to run down into it is an inappropriate confusion of boundaries.

The following example (an entry in my fieldwork notes) was given to me of 'headache' *tɘracɔɔg*:

> Busu has been very busy with the new extension on the house so I suggest he asks one of the others, perhaps one of the young men, to fetch a new tree for the fire. He says no, he must do it himself because of *terachog*. When asked to explain he said that someone else might bring a tree that had touched a *terachog* tree and he illustrated what it looked like by wrapping his arms round each other. He said it could cause his children to be ill

with very bad headaches or runny nose.

When *təracɔɔg* rule-breaking results in discharge from the nose or ears, it would appear that fluids that should reside in the body come out through inappropriate orifices.

One factor in several of these prohibitions is the mixing of categories, such as throwing old clothes in the river, and letting water accumulate in discarded tins. I suggest that some of these beliefs concern keeping things separate that should be separate, and others seem to describe things being split that should not be split, i.e. the cassava root and the tree. However, all concern appropriate behaviour outside the house and also in the forest. *Təracɔɔg* does not have supernatural intervention as a consequence, but an individual or child is ill as the result of a parent's careless actions. Other phenomena also have prohibition against certain 'mixtures': under *gɛnhaaʔ*, story-telling and seance performances are not allowed to take place on the same night; under *sabat*, fish and meat may not be eaten at the same meal, and of course with *gɛɛs* certain people are not allowed to 'mix'.

In the early months I found it difficult to adjust to the Temiars' apparent obfuscation. I already knew before I went to the field that certain things had avoidance names. For example, one can use the Temiar word *Karey* for thunder, but not *ʔɛŋkuuʔ*; and *mamuug* (tiger) is forbidden but the Malay word *harimau* permissible. Similarly, other large animals such as elephant, and elements such as wind and rain also have permissible and non-permissible names. However, it took time for me to adjust to the avoidance of naming most meat while it was being eaten and digested. Only the generalised name *ɲam* (animal) is used. When men hunt in the forest they do not announce where they are going, since tiger might overhear and lie in wait for them, so they say they are going to the river or to visit some friends. On other occasions they would just seem to disappear. With an anthropologist's tendency to ask questions rather than wait for answers, I found this very frustrating! It was as though the Temiar have to carry a strong *internal model* of appropriate limits of behaviour within the forest and outside generally but it must not be talked about.

I have discussed a range of food avoidances and limits on behaviour in both house and forest space. I want now to describe those expectations of Temiar social behaviour which place obligations on people. There is an expectation of sharing food and goods between people. One of the worst insults one Temiar can call another is to call them stingy (*karyɛd*). If someone is asked for something, there is an expectation that it will be given, otherwise misfortune, such as a fall or a bite, will come on the person who asked in the first place. The capacity to give is noticeable in very small children (a quality usually designated developmentally much later in western psychology); for example, when toddlers are asked for flowers or tobacco they willingly give. I observed this in infants from as young as 1 year old.

Səlantab is a form of ritual generosity. Whenever a newcomer visits a Temiar house, tobacco and food are always offered and must be accepted. The most traditional tobacco offering is home-grown tobacco wrapped in leaves (the same that is usually smoked at seances); when one visits a long house where there are several families, a cigarette is given from each household. If food is not immediately available, a child is sent quickly to another house to obtain cassava or rice that is then cooked and proffered. One of my assistants explained painstakingly to me that if we could not accept the food or tobacco, then we had to take a small piece of it and rub it on our calves saying, '*sɔh, sɔh, səlantab*'. She was clear that it was a substitute, but nevertheless obligatory, otherwise we might well have an accident or get bitten by snakes or other creatures. There is also an obligation, when a promise or undertaking is given, to carry it out; for example, the Temiars are very chary of people promising to come back and see them unless that can be guaranteed, since to make a promise and not carry it out brings misfortune to the recipient of the promise. When I and the children were leaving our area for a couple of weeks, I was about to tell my Temiar mother that I would be back soon. She stopped me by saying *parɛnlʉk*, which is the misfortune she would suffer if I did not keep my word.

We have seen in this chapter how individuals and groups are separated by various cross-cutting restrictions on food, waste, space, play, sex and all those activities that come under the heading of creativity, i.e. singing, dancing, trancing and story-telling. Thus we can see that physical, spatial and social relationships between individuals and groups are organised and maintained by these very complex expectations of people's behaviour.

The title of this chapter, 'Boundaries and transformations', underlies the fundamental methods whereby the Temiars maintain their world view in relation to each other, the non-human world and the supernatural world. The house and the forests are separated out as separate domains, and the house and the human body have their own integrity which is maintained by the limits of what may enter and exit. Inappropriate mixing of categories of food, activities and people are also prohibited.

The river which runs through both the forest and the village is also spatially separated with its own sanctions. It is not permissible to throw clothes in the river or to contaminate it with post-partum or menstrual blood, yet it is the appropriate place for the disposal of human food waste. Games that could be misunderstood as sexual activity must not take place in the river, and persons between whom a sexual relationship would be incestuous must not enter the river at the same time.

The blood of animals and the blood of women is a recurring theme, as is its capacity to transform into tiger and be dangerous to the opposite sex. These tigers may gnaw away at a person's *hup* or suck their blood.

Throughout, we have a differentiation between groups of people and spaces, yet at times this differentiation is deliberately blurred. Humans are differentiated from the non-human world, yet must not stand out from it. Human beings are differentiated from each other yet must be in a constant state of giving and taking.

The agencies of control, the most powerful and malevolent tiger and thunder, are external to Temiar society but will intervene if behaviour is uncontrolled. Similarly illnesses involving sickness, diarrhoea, shaking and convulsions, and accidents to the self, e.g. cuts or snake bites, all uncontrollable, are the individual's affliction for transgression. Thus it is the community as a whole that is violated by thunder, and an individual who becomes ill by their own actions or who is violated by a transformed tiger. The paradox of this is that the Temiars, who prize individual autonomy and are constantly emphasising that you cannot make anybody do anything, nevertheless have very powerful sanctions to control human behaviour in all its aspects and encourage responsibility to the community as a whole.

Chapter 4

Temiar body

Control and invasion

There was a time when all the body's members
Rebelled against the belly, thus accused it:
That only like a gulf it did remain
I'th'midst o'th'body, idle and unactive,
Still cupboarding the viand, never bearing
Like labour with the rest, where th'other instruments
Did see and hear, devise, instruct, walk, feel,
And, mutually participate, did minister
Unto the appetite and affection common
Of the whole body.

(*Coriolanus*, Act 1.i)

... one that converses more with the buttock of the night than with the forehead of the morning. ...

(*Coriolanus*, Act 2.i)

The scope of the body as a medium of expression is limited by the controls exerted by the social system.

(Douglas 1970:70)

Intrinsic to the Temiar beliefs which maintain the integrity of their bodies is the control exerted on individuals and groups in relation to the crossing of bodily boundaries. These boundaries concern the inside and outside of the body, the upper and lower half, and substances which enter and are transformed in the body. These categories are encapsulated by the complex set of beliefs and practices concerning human hair and blood, and their relationship with the head-soul and blood/heart-soul. I shall now explore these themes in more detail and relate them to Temiar movement and dance. It is impossible to talk about bodies without referring to spaces within and across which bodies move. We have already seen the complex Temiar controls and beliefs regarding the use of space and its boundaries, both horizontally and vertically.

There is only a brief period of time when Temiar bodies are completely unclothed, and that falls roughly between the age of sitting up and final weaning – around 3 to 4 years old. Small babies are wrapped in old sarongs apart from the times when they are being massaged by their mothers or midwives. Once they are able to sit up and begin to be mobile, clothes are worn infrequently unless a child is carried out of the house, when its head will always be covered in order to protect its still weak head-soul. Once a child can walk by itself it will play outside and there will usually be no covering of any kind. Girls begin to wear clothes before boys, at 4 to 5 years old (see Plate 5). It can be at age 6 or 7 years before a boy is habitually clothed; even then there is less concern about nudity – for example, boys will strip off by the river and run in and out of the water with no embarrassment. Girls will rarely do this once they have started to wear clothes unless they are with an all-female group. However, towards the onset of puberty, bathing tends to be segregated. Younger boys may accompany the teenage girls when playing water games in the river.

The freedom of exposure of the top half of the body is in complete contrast to the concealment of the lower half of the body. As I mentioned above, covering up starts earlier for girls than for boys, but before puberty genital concealment is firmly established. Young

Plate 5 Temiar children playing (girls covering up before boys)

girls will be teased by older children if their sarong is worn carelessly: 'I can see your vagina' (accompanied by giggling and nudging). Although pubertal girls will bathe together with little embarrassment at their own nudity, adult women will conceal their pubic area even when bathing together. They perform a most elaborate routine of co-ordination as they enter the water and keep their pubic area covered with one hand while they pull their sarongs over their heads with the other. On emerging from the water they do the same as they hastily replace their sarongs. However, there did not appear to be the same modesty between men when naked together; they would strip off and enter the water with no effort at concealment. Even during childbirth there is great concern for preserving the modesty of the lower part of the body and it is covered as far as possible. I also noticed during trance sessions that when a girl became unconscious there was concern from her friends lest she lose her sarong, and they usually re-tied it very tightly to prevent this happening. Thus we have a separation between the upper body and lower body in terms of concealment, and once puberty is reached the lower part of the body is concealed by everyone. However, there is a question of degree, and it would appear that females will usually cover up when with each other, whereas males will not.

Although the lower half of the body is covered in order to *conceal* it, heads are covered in order to *protect* them. Head protection starts almost from birth, as the head-soul is seen to be small and weak. Whenever small babies are carried outside, their heads will be covered. However, head covering is less frequent once a child is walking and more independent. Pre-pubertal and pre-married young people rarely cover their heads in the village. If they accompany older relatives outside the village they often wear a cap or turban. At pregnancy and childbirth head covering again increases.

The Temiars differentiate their clothing according to whether they stay within the village or go outside it. The most usual day-to-day dress for the Temiars is sarongs for both sexes or shorts for the men and boys. On leaving the village the head is always covered either with a turban or a cloth. The women journey a short distance to the cassava fields and the men into the forest. Sometimes the men will tie their sarongs like a loincloth. Usually everyone has bare feet when leaving the village but may wear flip-flops within the village. Some men acquire army clothing and wear green drill trousers. However, Mentri Suleiman, the oldest living Temiar when I was in Asam, always wore his sarong tied like a loincloth and would don a new sarong if he was going 'officially' to another village to consult or advise.

For the Temiars there is no notion of modesty towards the body from the waist upwards.[1] On the occasions when they do wear a tee-shirt or blouse it is for decorative purposes. Similarly, some of the women have acquired brassieres and wear them as a 'top' at performances. The Temiars described to me how in the early days both men and women wore small pieces of bark cloth which were tied round the waist, and covered the genital area back and front: 'When the Malays discovered us they laughed at the bark cloth and the quills through our noses so we wore sarongs' (fieldwork notes).

Even so, as with other customs that the Temiars have assimilated from Malays, they have their own distinctive style of tying their sarong which they would often demonstrate to me. Teenage and young women would 'play' at being Malay and would scrape their hair back straight, lighten their skin colour with talcum powder, make their lips very red, and re-tie their sarongs and wear a blouse. On one occasion when I had been photographing family groups and children in the village, two of the women said that they wanted me to take some photographs for *my mother and other people* of them looking like Malays. The women dressed up in the manner I have already described and the men put on shirts and shorts or trousers and all posed in a formal grouping. They said that the photographs of themselves as Temiar were for me, but these photographs were for me to show other people.

Their willingness to adapt to *gɔb* (foreign) in terms of their external bodies did not seem a problem. The Temiars told me that they had been asked by the JOA that Temiar women should cover up their breasts when being visited by officials. It had almost become a reflex action in my village. We would hear a motorboat on the river and the women would untie their sarongs at the waist and tie them above their breasts; when the officials had left they would promptly lower them again.

Traditionally the Temiars used to tattoo their faces, especially their foreheads, by using porcupine quills to puncture the skin and then rubbing ash into the hole. I only came across a handful of older people, men and women, who still had tattoos. Similarly, the Temiars traditionally used porcupine quills to pierce holes through their noses and would wear quills for dancing and at seances. Now they use the quill to pierce their ears, oiling it before gradually inserting it into the toddler girl's ear lobe and slowly pushing it through until the thicker part of the quill is in place. This takes some weeks, and the quill is then held in place and regularly turned until the hole has healed. This hole will be large enough to take a half-smoked cigarette or a large flower. It is used decoratively for the seances. Piercing is no longer practised on men, although I was told that in the old days all men and women could have tattoos and nose piercing.

As well as tattooing, the Temiars paint their faces. There are two sorts of painting,[2] one that is curative which I will discuss more under healing, and one that is decorative, which is reserved for the seances. Men rarely use face paint these days, and women tend to use modern products rather than the traditional vegetable dyes. However, these are still used from time to time, and the Temiars thought it was very important for me to wear them when they dressed me up as a Temiar for my first major seance.

They use lime to paint white dots (Plate 15, Chapter 9) and other colours – charcoal for black lines, and red from the areca palm for red lines and circles as well as for reddening lips – to paint designs. Sometimes these designs would be very quick and haphazard, with random strokes and patches – usually for impromptu singing and dancing events. However, for planned events far more time and care and great patience was taken to draw the designs accurately.

Temiars feel that body hair is very unpleasant. Women are most particular about not having excessively bushy pubic hair. They say that it is 'not nice', it's 'dirty', it's 'not pretty', and they shave their pubic hair to a minimum with a bush knife. It is rare to see beards and moustaches on Temiar men; an individual will occasionally grow one, but in the main facial hair is sparse and will be shaved off regularly. Temiar head hair is usually short and wavy on men, while the women grow theirs to its longest length to their shoulders. Some Temiars, as a consequence of intermarriage with Negritos, have very woolly hair, but others have straight hair like the Malays. A small child, once its hair has grown, has its head shaved but a small patch is left for the head-soul; otherwise, it is said, the head-soul would have nowhere to rest. All waste hair is kept carefully within the house and tucked into small pockets in the house wall. It is used in the rituals to appease thunder, when it is burnt on a log in the doorway.[3] When I became concerned that so much of my hair was disappearing when it was cut off for these rituals, I was told by my Temiar mother to save the waste hair from my comb. However, when I asked the same question of *Busuu?*, my assistant, he said, with ribald laughter, that once a person's head was completely shaved, they must start shaving their pubic hair for the rituals! When the Temiars suffer discomfort from head-lice they offer their hair to someone else to be searched. The other person searches and picks out the lice but gives it back to the host who squashes it between his or her thumb nails.

When asking the Temiars about the insides of their bodies, most responses concerned soul and blood beliefs rather than precise anatomical details; there was the expressed unease about the first aid book I carried because it showed the organs within a body. A few young people were willing to try and draw the insides and name the different parts, though their locations and proportions were more notional than accurate. The organs that are most frequently referred to are the lungs, liver, heart and *hup*. The *hup* is located at the base of the sternum and they would press their fingers just below the rib-cage to indicate this. One informant said that the inside of the body was like a branch of the *rambutan* tree, with all the different organs, like the fruits, joined to the branching stem, and she clasped her hands and fingers together to illustrate this. The Temiars say the *hup* is essential for life; it is where a person's feelings are located, and is compared to the liver (which for the Malays is the seat of feelings) and to the heart (which for the European is the same). The Temiars also said that it is connected with breathing (*hɛmnum*), and respiratory difficulty (*na-sɔlood*), which causes great anxiety and indicates sickness in the *hup*. Thus we can see that the *hup* represents the functions of the heart, liver and lungs in terms of a living, breathing, feeling person. Sickness in the *hup* can cause lack of desire or will to do anything. Furthermore, there is a constant reference to the *hup*'s connection with blood when we remember the possibilities of small tigers invading the *hup* and eating it away, gnawing at it or sucking its blood, especially at such 'in-between' times as sunrise and sunset. There are also dangerous entities near the river that will invade the *hup* if sufficient precaution is not taken. These are graphically described by Benjamin:

> More serious are two types of water demon living in the sand of the river bed that send out creeping tentacles in the early morning and late evening. These tentacles eventually come upon a human waist to attack, whereupon they liquefy and enter the upper body to eat away the blood of the man's *hup*, the seat of the emotions. The largest of these two demons is known as *Bahyaa?*. . . .
>
> The smaller is known as *Paad*, a Temiar root meaning 'to suck dry', as when a person chews a sugarcane or *Karey*, the thunder deity, sucks dry the flesh of men who misbehave. It also occurs as

a curse *nam-pɛdpaad* 'may he suck (you) dry', shouted at
someone who passes wind inside the house. It is also believed that
Paad affects the rump of a person who sleeps too close to his
parents, and it thereby bears some relation to incest regulations.

(1967a:134)

The theme of tentacles, cords and threads is a recurring image of
Temiar thought, and these threads are able to symbolically cross from
non-human to human boundaries. Some threads have a malign
influence such as *paad* and *bahyaaʔ*, and go through a transformation
before entering the *hup*. Others have a benign influence and enter the
hup transformed into a spirit guide essence. The Temiars would use
their fingers to describe how it felt to be eaten away in their *hup* and
a claw-like movement to burrow into the sternum. They also believe
that the heart-soul (*jərəək*) is located in the *hup*. Unlike the head-
soul, which is labile and can leave the body, the heart-soul is enclosed
inside the body and only leaves it at death. Severe sickness in either
soul can cause death.

Benjamin (1967:162) suggests that, given the links between the
heart-soul and blood, it is more helpful to refer to it as the blood-soul
as a translation of the Temiar concepts. Since the *hup* is the location
of the heart-soul and the Temiars refer to outside agencies sucking
the blood of the *hup*, it seems appropriate to describe it in this way.
I refer to it as the heart/blood-soul, thereby retaining both images.

In contrast to the *hup* where the heart/blood-soul (*jərəək*) resides
inside the body, the head-soul rests on the crown of the head on a tuft
of hair. It is capable of leaving the body voluntarily in dreams, trance
and finally at death, but also involuntarily in certain soul sicknesses.
As I have said, the newborn infant has a weak, unformed head-soul
and is dependent on the strength of its parents' head-souls. Various
protective measures such as confinement in the house, head cover-
ings, massage and careful diet, all assist in the strengthening of the
head-soul. In dreams the human head-soul can meet with its spirit
guide (usually the head-soul of a non-human species) and be taught
songs and dances; it can be innovative and creative. Both the head-
soul and the blood-soul are seen as necessary to life and finally leave
the body at death. Both are susceptible to sicknesses brought on by
the neglect of boundaries concerning the human body and the space
in which the bodies are located.

I discussed in Chapter 3 how important it is for the Temiars to
regulate what enters and leaves the body in relation to food and food

waste, and how untoward entry into the body must be avoided by restricting entry through the mouth. The mouth is also essential for respiration, and laboured or difficult breathing is a serious sign of sickness. The Temiars draw attention to the mouth in other ways. Temiar children are breast-fed for several years and it is not unusual for mothers to place home-made cigarettes[4] in their mouths after breast-feeding. Encouragement to smoke starts from a few months old and at 5 years Temiar children usually have their own small tobacco supply or else help themselves from parents or older siblings (Plate 6). It is very rare for Temiars not to smoke and there is heightened anxiety if there is a shortage of tobacco.

Cigarettes are given to visitors on arrival and it would be bad manners to refuse a cigarette. At the more serious seances carefully rolled cigarettes are placed on a tray with the other ritual objects, and these are usually smoked after the seance by the shaman and those who have been in trance. It is usual for those who have been heavily in trance to have a cigarette placed in their mouths as they are 'coming to'. Generally there is a mass 'lighting up' which is in contrast to the darkness or semi-darkness of the major seances. At some seances the smoke from a dish of charcoal, on which aromatic herbs are sprinkled, is passed around to those who have been in trance and either they or a helper will waft the smoke over the trunk and limbs but especially the head and face.

Plate 6 Established smokers

Although vomiting causes anxiety, there is social and ritual use of saliva. Adults and young people also engage in betel nut chewing, the saliva being spat out between the slats of the floor (Plate 7), as with ordinary spitting. Saliva is used by the midwife during childbirth when, as a healing technique, she spit-blows on the woman's stomach during the second stage of labour. I also saw spitting used in non-seance healing by certain shaman.

> There were screams from Hal as he emerged from playing hide-and-seek with Abus in the long grass; raw wheals were coming up on his leg (my fear of course was a snake bite). It appeared to be a bite of a 10" centipede. Mentri Suleiman immediately came to our house and sat in the doorway. He ran his hand over Hal's leg, then started to mutter his *jampi*, most of which I could not hear, but he was talking to *dato? lengri*; in between his muttering he spat on the inflamed area.
>
> (fieldwork notes)

I shall discuss healing and illness, and techniques used by shaman and midwives later. However, I mention here that the mouth is the focus of attention when the shaman practices healing. He clicks his tongue and teeth and then sucks the offending area through a clenched fist to remove the object or substances. He blows back into

Plate 7 Chewing and spitting betel nut

the area through his fist, having first 'milked' his own blood/heart-soul.

Thus the mouth has the multiple function of regulating the ingestion of food and maintaining it within the body, as well as the means of breath and smoke, two human necessities, entering and leaving the body. Spitting is commonplace, but it is utilised specifically in betel nut chewing as well as in shamanic and midwifery healing practices.

We have already discussed bodily orifices – the control of faeces and menstrual and post-partum blood, and also ear discharge as a result of *tɘracɔɔg* negligence. Ears are an important feature: older siblings and adults hold their hands over the ears of babies and infants during a loud thunderstorm and chant 'fear, fear'. Temiars spend a lot of time cleaning their ears with leaves or stems from the nipa palm. Normal nose discharge is ejected away from the house or through the slats of the floor. However, a persistent runny nose gives rise to concern and in children is thought to be connected with *tɘracɔɔg*, as is ear discharge.

> My porter quite happily accepted Western medicine for his daughter's runny nose, but at the same time went round puncturing holes in all the tins where rain might have gathered, i.e. to right the situation.
>
> (fieldwork notes)

The eyes of small children are also covered when there is lightning. I have mentioned above that tears do not appear to have any symbolic significance for the Temiars. However, conjunctivitis is fairly commonplace and if persistent causes concern. Since it is also very contagious it can spread quite rapidly and I found my antibiotic ointment in great demand, although they would also go to the shaman for his cure (the shaman uses spit on the eyes).

Before moving on to describe dance specifically, I want to draw attention to some more general aspects of Temiar voluntary and involuntary movement. In Temiar day-to-day movement there is a marked degree of control exercised from birth onwards. The young infant is contained within the house and is constantly held and massaged. Often when asleep a baby is suspended in a sarong from the ceiling of the parents' sleeping compartment. Young children will use sarongs to make swings underneath the house, and old boxes to hide in and play rides. Children's play is sharply controlled if it appears to get physically too energetic, noisy or out of control. Boisterousness is curbed and young people's games are co-operative rather than competitive. This is evident in games of football or handball across a net – scoring and winning is not predominant. When I visited Malay schools where Temiar children had been integrated, the teachers remarked on the lack of competition in both sports and classroom subjects, and on the lack of importance to them of winning a prize.

It is virtually unknown for Temiar parents to strike either their children or each other. They are physically indulgent towards their children and spend much time fondling and caressing them. On the rare occasions when I observed an infant or teenager lose control in a tantrum by hitting out or throwing things, the response was for everyone to move away and isolate the person until they had calmed down.

Temiar body movement is slow and measured; their walking is from the ball of the foot rather than the heel. As we have already seen, pointing or laughing at and imitating fast-moving insects and animals are forbidden; they risk inviting a *misik* thunder intervention. Similarly, jumping up and down in the river or anywhere else will tempt thunder to come and look. Involuntary shaking and convulsions are to be feared as they are symptoms of major sickness, and are connected with contact with or proximity to menstrual blood or animal blood. Involuntary shaking and convulsions are also symptoms which can be produced by accidental or careless contact with the lower part of certain trees – the equivalent of the tree's lower body which some Temiars consider to be the sap. Voluntary shaking is used only in childbirth to encourage the baby to be born as quickly as possible. It is done frequently during the second stage of labour when the woman has a contraction. However, less controlled shaking and arm flailing is a feature of Temiar trance-dance, but there are limits placed on total abandon by the shaman or other older people in the village. When dances get very energetic, with stamping, turning and bouncing, the whole house can collapse, with everyone falling into a heap. The collapse of the bodies can lead to the collapse of the house which everyone finds highly amusing, and there is a pause while the house is being repaired.

Although Temiar movement within the village is highly controlled, it is even more controlled in the forest. Sounds and footsteps are muted in all forest expeditions and the Temiars seem invisible, blending with the environment. In addition to this capacity for muted body movement, the Temiars have a fine and lively dexterity. They are able to scale trees, often a bare trunk. They handle bush knives and blow pipes with precise accuracy. I was initially alarmed to see small children being allowed to use bush knives for cutting fruit. Their co-ordination is very advanced compared with a western infant. Although relatively small in structure, the Temiars have a strong physical control, demonstrated when they navigate boats and rafts despite currents and rapids; they maintain a balance in a fast-flowing river when hauling in heavy drag-nets. Large tree-trunks are balanced on their shoulders when carried from the forest, without using their hands. Men and women alike carry produce and water in containers on their backs, unlike the Malays who usually carry things on their heads. The Temiars, in contrast to the upright posture of the Malays, stoop forward from the waist.

We can see that the Temiar body movement is characterised by its control, strength and balance, the lack of voluntary, quick or sudden expression, except in dance, trance or as a symptom of sickness. Involuntary movements, such as shaking and convulsions, like uncontrolled emissions from the body, are believed to result from a neglect of bodily and spatial boundaries.

The Temiar word for dance is *sisɛʔ*, although they occasionally use the Malay word *joget*. *Sisɛʔ* is the word used for dance *per se*, when there is not the intention to enter trance. Dance with trance is usually termed *pɛhnɔɔh* and, when coupled with the word *jɛhwah* (play, playful), indicates that there is no intention to seriously call down the spirit guides and *lɛslã ãs* (transformation: often used to describe a trance state). However, the Temiar word for community singing, *gɜnabag*, also includes the activities of dance and playful trance. Thus the boundaries that we maintain in the west by the terms of dance, music and drama do not apply in the way that the Temiars talk about expressive activities.

Little has been written about Temiar dance that is not in the context of their seances; these reports are mainly descriptive of the more exotic aspects of seances. However, they appear exotic to the non-Temiar observer rather than to the Temiars themselves. Williams-Hunt says, 'The Temiar Senoi are by far the most graceful dancers and prepare elaborate flower and leaf ornaments for their cere-monies' (1952:28). Richard Noone reports his brother Pat as saying: 'These people are going through a profound social crisis and for them this dance is a spiritual lifeline. The dance is called the Chinchem' (Slimming 1958:57).

Stewart says that the shaman progress through different dance styles in their advancement to attain recognition. He describes a dream revelation (1947:277–331) whereby an ailing shaman was taught this new dance, together with various new food prohibitions and changes in dress style. In his summary Stewart says:

> We have traced the progress of the shaman through the *G Nsak* phase where his dream character gave him a song while he slept and assumed control over him in the public dance; through the Jingjang phase in which he became expert in using his dream forces to promote the social life of the group and take responsibility for various group projects; through the stage of the shaman's temple where this erstwhile fantasy force of childhood is used in giving support and succour to the sick and dying; to this Chinchem inspiration, the expression of which reacts upon the ideational norms of the group, causing individuals to renounce their most favourite plentiful food and to don foreign clothing as their Malay neighbours do, and to introduce women into the ceremonies of the group in a way which gives them a higher status than either the Malay or the Chinese women have.
>
> (1947:238)

I do not have further data on the detailed origins of the *Ciɲcɛm* dance; however, it is an example of the revelation of an individual shaman which spread through the area. Nor do I have information concerning the progression of shamanic dances as described by Stewart. Nevertheless, there is no doubt that for the Temiars, original choreography of dance comes from dream revelation and new dance patterns are taught to people by aspiring or established shaman at the seance. Acceptance of a new dance or song of healing helps to establish the reputation of a shaman.

Benjamin (1967:293) observes interestingly that in the Temiar area north of the Perolak Valley, the distinction between male and female dancing is very marked, whereas further south, men and women tend to perform in a similar manner. He also noted that 'The highest grade of shamanship is noticeable for dispensing with the dance as an element in its performance' (1967:261). He suggests that this serves to emphasise the 'ecstatic' nature of ordinary shamanism in contrast with the 'ascetic' quality of great shamanism.

I shall argue that Temiar dance cannot be studied in isolation from trance, dramatic performance, body categories and spatial boundaries. Dancing among the Temiars is more than a mere pastime. It is a process that can only be fully appreciated in relation to the fullest range of cultural context and as an integral part of their social life.

As a dancer, I found Temiar dance uninteresting, especially in terms of their choreographic content and repetitive movement. There were no narrative dances that could compare with the Temiar songs which relate their myths and legends. Story-telling is not permitted at the same time as seance performance. There were no dances that could be termed celebratory or *rites-de-passage*. However, as an anthropologist I found Temiar dance exciting and complex, and it provided an essential clue towards understanding their highly intricate social and cosmological system.

Most of the children's play is imitation of adult life, including the dance and trance sessions. Sometimes these will be imitations of actual sessions that had happened the previous evening. Sometimes the children will spontaneously devise their own. I refer to such behaviour as playing-at-seance. These play sessions happen outside or in a corner of the house. Children use small pieces of bamboo to imitate the stompers and they will dance and sing and sometimes imitate the giddiness of the trance behaviour. Occasionally a young adult will join in and show them rhythms and tune. However, if the playing becomes too loud and obtrusive, older people are quick to tell them to calm down. Parents were insistent on obedience to behaviour governed by cosmic rules, even though children did not always take them too seriously. In this way children were being taught to control their spontaneous play.

As well as play, spontaneous playful dancing and singing sessions also occur among adults in the house in the evenings. These can involve anyone who happens to be in the village, even foreigners. There is usually little, if any, preparation and decoration for an adult play-dance. It may start with a small group getting together and singing, others gradually joining in. There is an atmosphere of lightheartedness and fun. Sometimes trancing is involved in a spontaneous form among young people, when it is regarded essentially as play. Sometimes older people will come and watch; again they will also bring the playing to a halt if they think it is getting out of hand. For example, if there was screaming and shouting to a rhythm beat on a metal tray, an older man or woman would tell them curtly to calm down, to do it 'properly', sometimes demonstrating a rhythm.

Temiar dance occasions also provide an opportunity for flirtation among young people, both as an aside during the more serious dances and as a central feature of their play-dances. There may be some pairing and touching between the sexes at the play-dance, but overt bodily contact is avoided. Pubertal girls frequently queue for the attentions of a young shaman who overtly practises his developing skills while covertly responding to their advances. He may place his forehead on theirs, or press the flat of his hand between their breasts, or hold them close from behind and sway with them, whereupon the girls would start trancing vigorously.

Dancing takes place at night, commencing after dark and sometimes continuing until dawn but never into daytime. There are a few Temiars who do not *dance*. The exceptions appear to be older people of both sexes, although older women often join in for a short time. Certain categories of shaman who would not use dance in their seances still dance in ordinary sessions like everyone else. Pregnancy is not a bar to dance, providing that the mother is considered 'well'. However, I have already mentioned that those members of the community who are allowed to *trance* are far more limited.

Although singing sessions may occur in anyone's house, there is usually one house in the village where dancing takes place. If the village consists of a single long house with discrete family units, these are built along the sides of a large central area where dancing takes place. Where a village is made up of separate houses, it is usually the house with the largest central area where dancing takes place. The Temiars make sure that the supports beneath the house are strong enough for what will be an energetic session. The floor is made of slatted bamboo which gives a yielding surface for dancing.

Dance does not occur outside on the ground. The only occasion when a group of women danced, amid giggles, on the ground was when they wanted me to show them an English dance. On another occasion, when some officials tried to encourage a Temiar get-together, they made the mistake of organising it in an open space outside. There was a little desultory singing which eventually petered out and most Temiars went for the free food before returning to their houses.

I observed two instances of spontaneous dancing with a division of the sexes and an element of transvestism in the spirit of play. In one, a group of women were gathered in one house and spontaneous singing developed into dancing. Then one woman tucked her sarong well above her knees and started imitating others, whereupon there was much laughter and horseplay, sexual allusion and so on. On another occasion I happened to be visiting *Luŋ*'s house – he was one of the older men in our village – and became aware that something was going on in his house.

Long was the only adult present and was watching very carefully as a group of teenage boys, with their sarongs tied above their nipples (as women sometimes tie them) were dancing around in a circle and singing as they did so. All Long could tell me was that they were all 'playing' (*jɛhwah*) but there was no attempt to stop it when I arrived; however, I had a feeling of slight embarrassment as if I had intruded on something very private.

(fieldwork notes)

Temiars dance in an anti-clockwise circle. Variations can include turning outward from the circle at an angle of 45 degrees, and then back into the circle. The big circle may break up into smaller circles (this always happens in trance: see Figure 4.1). The dance steps are based on a simple walking pattern. One foot is thrust forward, with the weight

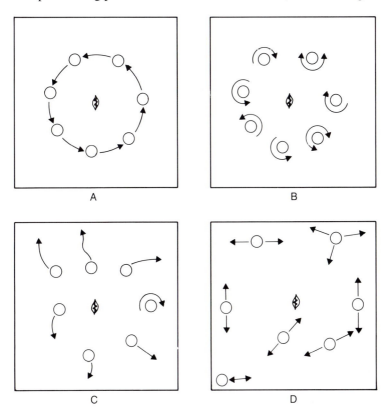

Figure 4.1 Dance to trance pattern of group and individual movement

transferred on to it, the second foot is placed alongside the first, and at the same time the person gives a slight spring forward (Benjamin (1967:297) describes this as 'double hops'). The men bend forward up to an angle of 90 degrees as they spring, each arm alternating and parallel to the floor. Variations can include a small jump, emphasising both feet going into the floor rather than away from it, or both feet sliding forward together. Women may dance this step or use a strut walk (*sapooy*) as they turn their bodies into the circle and out again. Their arms hang by their sides, or they place one arm on their hip, the other arm (or both arms) weaving and swaying. Roseman (1993:161) describes this as a 'strolling-in-place' movement and compares it to the swaying movement that women do in everyday life. She says:

> These motions, in turn are associated with the waving of palm fronds and jungle foliage in the wind. *Lɛylɔnɔɔy* 'bending, swaying' an expressive found in song texts and poetic speech, refers both to the quality of swaying in human movement and in wind swept foliage.
>
> (1993:162–3)

Older women occasionally demonstrated for me a dance which they said dated back to the old days when men and women performed different dances. The body is supported on bent knees with a transfer of weight through the hips from one leg to the other; the arms are extended and the wrists circle as they lean from side to side. The movement is very controlled and sustained and could be seen as an aesthetic development of *sapooy* described above, the difference being that this dance is done for pleasure and display. There is a sense of being a good dancer in its execution and it does not lead into trance, whereas the movement described above is freer and more relaxed in its performance and usually does lead into trance.

The basic walking and strut pattern constitutes the dance activity in the spontaneous play-dances, and often precedes the more serious trance-dances. However, it is noticeable that there is less dance in the initial stage of a trance session although there is often a return to it after the trancing is over. The following description is of a more typical play-seance which involved a lot of dancing and spontaneous trancing as well as some brief healing.

> Mariam called to our house and said, 'Come and play, we are going to dance'.
>   We said that we would join her in a few minutes and quickly changed sarongs and combed our hair. We went to Busu Selbon's

where people were already gathering and there was a lot of chatter and elation. Some very hasty decoration had been put up – a few bunches of leaves from the ceiling. There were several young men standing in the centre, talking to each other, deciding who was going to start the singing (I later realised that all of them were aspiring shaman and had begun to try out their skills). They wore very colourful sarongs and one of them had bead necklaces round one shoulder and under his arm. Two of them had flowers in their hair.

Apek started singing, squatting in the centre of the floor, his fist against his cheek (very like the Malays when they sing religious chants); the chorus of girls were a bit giggly, but soon settled down in sequence, pounding out an even rhythm together; Apek did some preliminary calling, *Ma-lɔɔ??* Ma-lɔɔ?? (where?), coughed and started singing.

Most of the young girls got up and started dancing round in a circle (mainly girls and young women with a few young boys). There were a few older people but they were sitting chatting amongst themselves. One of the girls said that she was going to dance like they did in the olden days and started to sway gracefully and extended her arms in circular gestures [as described earlier]; the other girls didn't know the dance and whispered to me that this girl was very clever at dancing and 'knew' the old styles.

Another of the shaman took over the singing, which he did standing up and as the girls went on dancing Mariam started to flay her arms round and lose her balance; Adoi tied her sarong very tightly round her waist, and she and Halimah held Mariam by both her arms as she leapt around the floor before eventually collapsing. Adoi and Jelimo line up for the shaman to press their chests with his hands, and they too were away, flailing their arms and stumbling. More women help to tie their sarongs; the singer and the musicians keep going as the room seems full of flailing bodies, with people trying to keep up with the entranced, and more girls going in. Mariam lay on the floor and looked very dazed, so Busu Selbon's wife sprinkled water on her face. In between the trance, the dancing continued. The atmosphere was very charged with a lot of energy. The older people seemed as if they were there to keep an eye on things, and one or two of the older women joined in the dancing.

The girls all had a rest, as did the two singers, and everyone lit cigarettes; one of the young shaman started to press his forehead against the other young one, and then he began to stagger and fall all round the room. The young men, including the shaman, start to move round in the circle. One of the older men takes over the singing and it felt as if he was bringing a little order into what had been a seemingly frivolous and very erotic outburst. In the circle one of the young men, Tengah (Mariam's husband), started to trance sponta-neously and fell over; onlookers helped him to stand upright, and he leapt around the room and people backed away frightened.

He tripped over a piece of floor and fell down, having cut his foot. It roused him out of the trance and he sat there looking a bit dazed. The others carried on singing and dancing with occasional trance. Another man took over the singing, and the older man went over to his grandchild and performed the blowing on the head-soul. Everyone danced until they were exhausted and then we all curled up where we were and slept in our sarongs. As always, one singer kept singing until we all slept; he bent over to see if I was awake and I opened one eye. 'I won't stop singing until everyone is asleep' he said, 'It's the Asli custom'.

(fieldwork notes)

Tengah was very frightened when he cut his foot, in particular because it was bleeding. Blood spilt from the body causes extreme anxiety, even when the amount is relatively small. Tengah said that he was going to have a rest from trancing and it was apparent that the degree of loss of control had disturbed him greatly. Mariam, his wife, did not seem unduly disturbed and said that it was only playing, although she often passed out for ten minutes at a time at the seance. Apek, one of my assistants, said that the trance-dance made him feel as if he were flying; he said, 'I am flying like a bird, I am free'. He held out his arms and made swooping movements with them. Apek said he had to trance very often; that he *had* to. While he was living with us he slipped away to as many trance-dances as he could.

Trance and dance are very popular activities with the Temiar and, apart from taboo times, are held regularly often for several nights in a row. The contrasts I have described between the play sessions and the more serious gatherings are grades of the same activity and should not be considered to be totally separate. Temiar dance exhibits a developmental spectrum from the informal and spontaneous play-dance to the formal and planned trance-dance. The extremes at either end are easy to recognise, but the middle is more blurred. Dance can just happen; music and singing start, followed by dancing, and may result in spontaneous trancing. Intentional trance is usually planned, with decorations and ritual objects. There are various degrees of trance and dance at seances, and the most notable is the tiger seance which dispenses with dance completely.

There is some difference between male and female dance but this is thought by the Temiars to have been more marked in the past. Dance is an activity that is always done off-the-ground and in the house. It is permissible for all people to dance, whereas trance is only available to certain categories of people whose head-souls are not currently at risk. We see an absence of both dance and trance at highly dangerous times such as following death, and an absence of trance at the most powerful tiger seance. Dance and trance in relation to the Temiar life cycle is illustrated in Chapter 6.

So how may we begin to understand the broad spectrum of bodily concepts manifested by the Temiars in their everyday life as well as in their performances?

Blacking (1977) stresses the need for greater understanding of bodily affect in the research of social sciences. He says:

> Techniques of the body are not entirely learnt from others so much as discovered through others. The cognitive consensus that makes the social and socio-physical bodies possible is not always fully perceived or cognized. Many things happen to us for which society has no labels. Since I maintain that the body is never infinitely malleable, it follows that there can be tension between people's training and education in the techniques of the body and their bodies' own inner force and proclivities. I would even go so far as to say that this tension between 'inner' and 'outer' reality is a crucial factor in motivating human behaviour and action, and that the measure of its influence is to be found in the meaning of a feeling in any given situation.
>
> (1977:4)

We saw that small babies are massaged from birth and have their bodies, particularly their heads, 'pressed' for several months, which, while strengthening the head-soul or rəwaay, also emphasises its importance. Infants have their ears covered during thunderstorms and their eyes shielded from lightning and are thus constantly alerted sensorially to the evil presence of Karey. Temiar babies are discouraged from crawling and are held on their feet from 2 or 3 months old. Before an infant can walk independently, and therefore be allowed outside on the ground, it has embodied the most important restrictions, the institutionalised feelings, reinforced by a fear of supernatural punishment, that are basic to Temiar life.

As described in Chapter 1, the three developmental stages in the infant before dramatic play emerges are *embodiment, projection* and *role*. For Temiar infants, embodiment of belief and feelings continues throughout life and is reinforced through the soul beliefs which are activated even more strongly in trance and dance performances. Children's play extends the value system that has been experienced in the early months and body control reinforces role relationships. Children learn that creativity, innovation and mastery come through their private dream experiences; thus the autonomy which is highly valued by the Temiars is developed through its links with innovation.

The Temiars transmit to their growing offspring the orderly way in which the physical body should be controlled. There is instruction as to what stays inside the body and what is allowed to come out of the body, provided that it is discharged into the right place. There is also a clear separation between the upper and lower body which is demonstrated by the exposure and concealment of the pubic area and head, as well as dance which emphasises so strongly the mobility in the upper half and the static or simple supportive walking role of the lower body. Dance, clothing, hair and blood beliefs all contribute to the horizontal divide between the upper and lower body. We can see from this exposition that most aspects of the Temiar body are controlled both in movement, exposure and emissions. There are strict observances concerning bodily boundaries and the maintenance of the integrity of the whole body, as well as the relationship between the upper and lower body, symbolised through the head- and the blood/heart-souls.

Both head- and blood/heart-souls are subject to sickness. The head-soul can wander off or be startled, and shamanic intervention is needed to retrieve it. The *hup* does not leave the body but is subject to invasion from outside. It may result in loss of bodily control through shaking, convulsions, accidents, vomiting, diarrhoea (*sabat, gɛnhaaʔ, pocuk, tɛnruuʔ, misik*) or more serious invasion from outside forces into the *hup* itself where they will gnaw the flesh or suck the blood (*pacɔg, bahyaaʔ, paad*). At its most serious there is a transformation of the blood of certain animals, and menstrual blood, into tigers which also enter the *hup*.

This double theme of uncontrolled transformation of blood into tiger which enters the body and controlled transformation of shaman into tiger in the tiger seances, which then leave the body/house/village, is central to Temiar belief and practice.

Chapter 5

Temiar space
Order and disorder

> Hear you me, Jessica
> Lock up my doors; and when you hear the drum
> And the vile squealing of the wry-necked fife
> Clamber not you up to the casement
> Nor thrust your head into the public street
> To gaze on Christian fools with varnished faces,
> But stop my house's ears – I mean my casements.
>> (*The Merchant of Venice*, Act 2.v)

The house is, as Cunningham has said (1964) in his article on the Atoni house: 'one of the best modes available to a preliterate society to encapsulate ideas'.

> (quoted in Turton 1978:113)

The spatial categories with which Temiars conceptualise their world are off-the-ground/ground and house/forest. They regulate the human body with upper/lower and inner/outer schemata. In this chapter I develop further this spatial grid in relation to the Temiar physical world of house/village, forest and river. Although I shall discuss them under separate headings, it is important to bear in mind that they are interrelated and not discrete phenomena. Since the Temiars have the same word *deek* for both house and village, I shall discuss them under the same heading (see also Roseman 1993:4).

When I first arrived in Kuala Betis and lived in a Malay-style plank house that belonged to a teacher, there is no doubt that this ascribed a certain status and relationship to me that changed markedly when I moved into a Temiar house. The Temiars were friendly enough but nevertheless 'formal', and it was some time before I was invited to one of their houses. I was impatient to move into a village and into a Temiar house and after our initial visit wanted the whole enterprise completed as soon as possible. There was a house frame standing in the village of Asam and it was agreed by Mentri Suleiman, the most senior Temiar in the area, in consultation with others, that we should pay Malay $100 for the finished house. As time went by and although some work had been done on the house, it was still not complete, I came to realise that house building can only take place at certain times each month. The Temiars make a distinction between village and house-based tasks and forest-based tasks, and these must not take place at the same time. Each month, based on a lunar calendar, is roughly divided into alternate times of staying in the village and going into the forest. Each period of time is between five and seven days, although the first day is always taboo. I had to wait for the appropriate time before my house could be completed. Eventually it was finished apart from the fireplace, and I was eager to move in. The Temiars agreed reluctantly but they did not seem happy about it. We cooked on a small camping stove which we had brought with us but there was unease that we did not have a fireplace. I shall elaborate on the theme of fireplaces later in this chapter.

Temiar houses are built high on the river bank to be away from possible flooding during the monsoon, but near enough to be able to fetch water easily. The back of the house, i.e. the door to the kitchen area, is constructed on the forest side of the house and care is taken that public paths do not pass too close to the door (see Figure 5.1). The importance of this is illustrated in the following example. An extension had been built on to a house belonging to the parents of a young couple who were imminently expecting their first child, and the construction abutted on to the usual communal path down to the river. The girl's father insisted that the path be re-routed round the other side of the house and the former one not used. Childbirth takes place at the back of the house in the space nearest the forest. The location of childbirth is related to the blood themes which are discussed throughout this book.

Temiar houses in this area are constructed from walls of woven, split bamboo tied on to a wooden frame and roofed with *atap* thatch. Flooring is also made from split bamboo, apart from the kitchen where it is usually constructed from slats in order to allow the debris to drop through to the ground beneath. The fireplace is made of wooden planks surrounding a square filled with earth and ash. Windows are uncommon and when they do occur they are in the kitchen and living area only. Small balconies may be constructed at the front or back, and the front door, which faces the cleared space in the village, leads into the main activity area. Since houses are built off-the-ground, a ladder or steps are necessary at both the front and

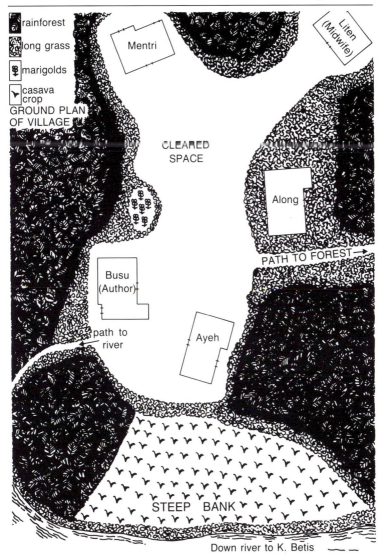

Figure 5.1 Ground plan of village

back doors (Figure 5.2; Plates 8 and 9). The house is either a communal long house, where there are separate units built in a rectangle with a large communal area used for seances, or separate houses built in a cleared village space. The Temiars said that in the

Plate 8 Front of Temiar house

Plate 9 Back of the same house

Attap thatch (see Plate 8, p. 80)

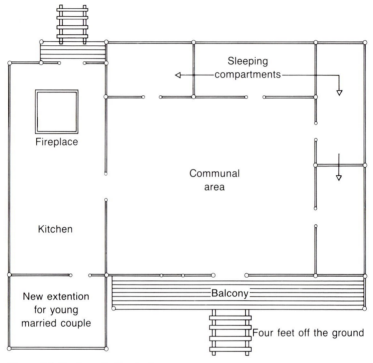

Figure 5.2 Section of a Temiar house

past they always lived in long houses but now they lived in either. In one village I visited they were in the middle of changing from a long house to individual houses. People said that living in the long house was easier because all the food could be taken round without going outside, but that it was difficult for everyone to live so close together. Each of the units in the long house contains a separate family consisting of parents and their unmarried children. Occasionally an older single relative may stay too, but usually they have their own unit. Each household has its own fireplace, even the households of single people.

The house style I have described is essentially Malay in influence. The Temiars thought it was most appropriate for that particular area since it was once inhabited by Malays. Further away from Betis the Temiars built quite different houses. They used horizontal lengths of bamboo strapped to each other with rattan to form the walls, and slats of bamboo for the floor, with an *atap* roof (Plate 11, p. 91). The Temiars complained that many of the Malay houses had corrugated iron roofs (such as the cluster of houses and the school at Kuala Betis) and that they were far too hot. Additions may be built on to a house when children marry or new families move in and so on. The Temiar house can be in a constant state of change in size and occupation. In concept the long house is essentially the same as the individual houses which have a cleared space in the central village area. There is usually a main door in the long house into the communal area and two or three back or side doors which are close to the forest.

It was not until later in my stay that I was able to observe the building of a new house from beginning to end and the rituals that this involves. The first task is the sinking into the ground of the strong support posts; the holes are dug by the house builder. Usually the older men of the village help each other with the assistance of the younger men. However, the initial stage is always undertaken by an older man with the assistance of a shaman. Before the corner posts are inserted into the holes, a pebble is placed in each hole by a shaman or older man (often it is the same person), who mutters *jampii?* and pours water from a bamboo tube into the holes to prevent *təracɔɔg*. The posts are then placed firmly in the holes and the earth around pressed down.

Once the posts are in position, the work progresses quite quickly with the walls and flooring, and finally the *atap* roof is woven and tied firmly in place. The Temiars were most unhappy when one of my children planted some marigolds in the tops of the bamboo posts that supported our balcony and asked us to take them down. Bamboo must not be taken into the house if it has earth trapped in it. It seems that *təracɔɔg* keeps spatially distinct the house and the forest, and the house and the ground. The only earth that is allowed into the house has been cooked and is used for the base of the fire place. Old timbers are never used to build a new house as it is thought that they could bring misfortune.

The main structure is built first – the support posts, cross members and major partitions – followed by the walls and roof. Once the external building is complete, the Temiars pay attention to the inside of the house. As I mentioned earlier, the fireplace is considered very important and the Temiars were not happy about me living in my house until the fireplace was ready. It was built of stout wood surrounds and then filled with ash from another fire and earth, which was baked before the fireplace was ready to use. The Temiars said that the earth had to be cooked. All the village came to visit us and comment on the fireplace. After it had been baked, *Busuu?*, my Temiar assistant, went to fetch large logs and we cooked our first meal (Plate 12, p. 110). After the fireplace is built, various small partitions, shelving and outside doors, all of bamboo, are constructed and put into place. The space is divided into a kitchen, a large communal area, and sleeping areas, which are small and more private, where a couple, small children and older unmarried children sleep (Figure 5.2).

I have referred to the fact that Temiar children are kept within the confines of the house until they can walk, unless they are carried by their mother, father or older sibling. In any case, they are kept within the village area and washed and bathed in the house or on the balcony at the back of the house. Children therefore must be kept off-the-ground, and for the most part, in the house. These rules are gradually relaxed once the child can walk independently. There is not a first-footing ceremony such as the Malays practice, which ritualises the first steps the infant takes on the ground. However, this is the time when Temiar children begin to have more freedom outside and are given their unique name. The child usually plays outside with other children and is often the baby in family play. Toddlers are still kept very much within the cleared area of the village except when they go with mothers and aunts to the river.

The most popular games that young children play in the village are family games. They build small shelters with fires, heat water and bake small pieces of cassava. Small boys go off to hunt with bows and arrows and return to eat in the playhouse. I described earlier how young children learn to play-at-seance and to sing, accompanying themselves with bamboo stompers. Toddlers are the babies in these play-families and 4- and 5-year-olds are strong enough to carry a toddler on their backs in a sarong. Children also play many games in which they give each other rides in cardboard boxes, on branches, and swing each other in sarongs tied to the cross-members under-neath the houses. Young children also accompany their mothers to harvest cassava and to the river. If they feel like it they assist in fetching vegetables and water, although there is no pressure if they choose not to help.

All cooking is done within the house by men and women. However, as we saw earlier, not all foods can be taken into the house without some ritual preparation. The cooking of cultivated and wild vegetables and fruits takes place in all houses and the waste is thrown on to the ground. Similarly the skins from seasonal fruits, which are not cooked (apart from the banana on occasions), are thrown on to the ground. The areas beneath the Temiar houses accumulate much of the vegetable and fruit waste, and periodically the women sweep the ground clean with a broom made of twigs, and brush it into the undergrowth.

Animals which live in the village or house are never slaughtered or eaten.[1] The Temiars keep tame dogs, cats, goats, chickens and geese as pets, and they are treated as members of the family and named accordingly. They use the word cɔɔʔ for tame animals which is the same name that a midwife uses for a child she delivers.

Children use small animals as babies in their games, carrying them in the folds of their sarongs. I observed girls using small chicks as play objects, first dyeing their feathers. Very occasionally the Temiars slaughter chickens for a special meal but I only observed this twice during my stay. Similarly the Temiars were quite happy when I bought eggs from the shop to eat but they would not let me take eggs from the nesting boxes under the house. Furthermore, they would not allow me to milk the goat that I was rearing but engineered its disappearance, and I later discovered that it had joined a herd of goats in another village! All these tame animals have the freedom of the village and special pets come inside the house.

Food is thus related to Temiar spatial concepts. Animal flesh killed in the forest is partly processed before it is brought into the domestic space; it is then kept within the house, usually the same house, and waste is kept off the ground. Fruit and vegetables are not prepared before entering the house and may be transported between houses; waste is thrown on to the ground. Live, tame animals are kept within the house or village and are *not* eaten.

Earlier I talked about a large number of beliefs associated with thunder which come under the heading of *misik*. Some of these are directly connected with activities that may or may not go on in the house. There is a range of activities that, even though they are house activities as such, should not be engaged in for several days when first occupying or reoccupying a house. These include weaving, carving, rattan scraping and using metal pots and pans. It is the *misik* regulations that attract the notice of the malevolent thunder deity who will send thunderstorms if the restrictions are disregarded. All these activities are said to allow a person to be noticed; therefore not to engage in them is not to stand out. The most serious action within this category is the use of mirrors. Many households do own mirrors and use them when they squeeze spots or apply face make-up; but the mirrors must *never* be used outside the house and must be covered up in the house during thunderstorms.[2] Similarly they must not be used when first occupying or reoccupying a house. I mentioned that waste hair must be kept in the house and then used for thunder appeasement if storms are too violent. The umbilicus[3] and nail clippings are also retained within the house in scraps of material and tucked into the bamboo walls.

Waking time in the village/house is social time, and visits to each other's houses are frequent unless people are in seclusion due to illness or menstruation. Doors are only closed when people settle down to sleep and my own idea of privacy, to have some time to myself, was not understood by the Temiars. Dentan says of the Semai:

> The lack of privacy serves an important social function. There are very few ways in which a Semai can be forced to conform to the standards of his community. But each person must know that his neighbours are watching him. If he does such a simple thing as start for the river to defaecate or bathe, someone is going to ask him where he is going and what he intends to do there.
>
> (1968:29)

And:

> Privacy would render gossip less effective as a means of social control.
>
> (ibid:31)

The Temiars in my village would have been dismayed if I excluded them from anything I happened to be doing. If I was writing up my notes or teaching the children, they would still call by and sit and watch, or wait until I was free to chat. Partitions in the houses are so thin that anything can be heard through the walls (cf. Roseman 1993:4, 5). At times when we were staying in another village in someone's house, we would hear conversations and jokes late into the night through the walls of the sleeping spaces and the main rooms. Visitors often sleep in the main area if there does not happen to be a spare sleeping compartment. Usually there are no spare rooms as Temiars build their houses to suit the needs of the people actually living there. On the one occasion when I did shut my door and tie it shut, the Temiars who called just waited outside until I opened it again! This lack of privacy amongst people in the village is in marked contrast to the obfuscation of the Temiars in relation to the non-human world. I mention in the introduction and again later in this chapter how the Temiars use avoidance words or use circumlocution in order that tigers or the souls of natural species should be unaware of their actions.

At this juncture I need to make some reference to seance and other ritual activities that are confined to the house. Group activities, i.e. activities that are shared throughout the community even if not everyone participates on every occasion, such as feasting, dancing, trancing and story-telling, take place within the house, as well as the preparation of ritual objects for the seances. Singing is the only one of these activities that is ever done alone (see Roseman 1986, 1993 for an ethnomusical study of the Temiars); lone Temiars sing to themselves in the early hours of the morning. However, singing, dancing and trance as performance embody the formal and informal seances that the Temiars create for recreation, celebration and healing. These performances take place in the communal area of a long house or in a large space of an individual house. Decorations hung from the beams include particular leaves and aromatic herbs that are fetched from the forest. A special garland is made on a circle of rattan, or sometimes a bunch of leaves, as a resting place for the good spirits. The head-souls of beneficent spirits are encouraged to come down from the hilltops and tree-tops, and often from far away, following the path of the rivers. These spirits are coaxed to come close the house and settle on the roof, the beams or the decorations themselves. The centrepiece could be described as a 'house within a house'. As we shall see later, the tiger seance is based on a similar idea. Great care is taken after the seances to maintain the good influences of these spirits and not scare them away; it is *joluŋ* to bring fresh, sweet-smelling plants into the house after a seance as this could frighten the good spirits away.

During seances, various people go into a trance state and their head-souls leave their bodies. While their bodies are safely contained within the house, their head-souls can go and play with other head-souls, in the garden, the forest, the fields or hillside or follow the path of the river. It is the shaman's skilful management that enables the head-souls to rejoin their human bodies before the end of the seance.

If a head-soul is startled away or taken by another head-soul, then its retrieval is not so easy. The shaman say that it may have gone on a long journey and will be difficult to summon, particularly if the lost head-soul is enjoying itself playing. Head-soul loss is considered an illness (*rɛywaay*) and part of the ensuing treatment may be seclusion in the patient's house while the shaman is trying to effect a cure. Head-soul freedom, however, is a state of dissocation which is longed for by the Temiars. This tension between freedom and control is a constant theme of Temiar life. Seances and the creative media of song, dance, drama and trance are all communal activities which take place in the house and firmly off the ground. If a seance is likely to be very energetic, men in the village strengthen the house posts and the floor before the performance starts. However, Temiar houses often start to sway when dancing gets vigorous and floors are known to collapse and dancers fall through to the ground. It is not uncommon for the whole room to collapse and dancers, decorations, musicians and onlookers end up in a heap on the ground. The Temiars' response is laughter and hilarity when these off-the-ground activities end up on the ground. As an observer I would have expected this collapse of house, bringing about a collapse of boundaries, to result in danger or supernatural intervention. However, paradoxically, the Temiars treat it as an amusing and not an embarrassing or alarming hiatus and take a break while the house is repaired.

We have discussed Temiar beliefs and practices in relation to the house and village, and have seen that they are often brought into a relationship with the forest. The forest appears to represent for the Temiars the complete antithesis of the house and village. Dark, dense and damp, difficult to penetrate, the typical rain forest of South East Asia contrasts sharply to the light, intense heat and open space of the village clearing. The forest is felt by the Temiars to be encroaching on the village space, and time is frequently spent in cutting back any regeneration of growth around their domestic area. The forest is the habitation of many real and imagined dangers, in particular the arch-enemy of the Temiars, the tiger, considered to be so dangerous that the Temiars use a nickname or Malay word for it. The Temiars do not hunt tigers, as it is certainly not suitable for eating, though they may be killed for protection.

The most common animals hunted in the forest are porcupines, certain monkey species, wild boar and various birds. The main motivation for entering the forest is to hunt for food, and shorter journeys are made for gathering firewood and logs. There are marked transformations of self in the preparation men make before entering the forest and in their behaviour once inside it. They usually wear more traditional clothes such as loincloths, and travel as light as possible, with shotgun or blowpipes, a small basket which contains food if they intend to stay overnight, and a bush knife. They do not announce that they are going but quietly slip away, unnoticed and invisible. On one occasion, my Temiar assistant put on his loincloth and carried his blowpipe to be photographed; he took it off again and said he would go hunting later. He said that tiger could already have seen or heard him. However, he also felt an obligation to go, now that he had said that he would. He slipped away later that afternoon, almost melting into the environment.

Although Temiar behaviour is not at all extrovert, apart from lively seances, it is noticeably more muted in the forest. Talking is minimal and hushed; physical movement is very controlled; and there is a paucity of gesture and gesticulation. Many of the creatures which come under the *misik* category and must not be laughed at, imitated or pointed at, are encountered in the forest. Much is communicated through nods, glances of eyes and pouts of the mouth. In contrast to the men, women and children are only allowed into the secondary forest when collecting wild vegetables, fruit and fungi and also when gathering small shellfish from the beds of the smaller rivers, but they are never allowed to go into deep or primary forest, and even their expeditions to the more open fringe areas are tinged with a sense of danger. They always cover their heads and usually go in groups of about six people. They are constantly on the look-out for snakes and seek to avoid animals rather than confront them. Women also come to the forest edge to gather the various bark, pith and leaves for decorations for the seances. Men, on the other hand, will travel great distances through the forest to the higher altitudes to get the special bamboo for making blowpipes. The bamboo needed for house building, and also for making the musical instruments, is found nearer the village.

The Temiars are reluctant to travel long distances if they are likely to encounter beliefs and practices different from their own. *Busuu?*, my assistant, was always far more anxious if we were out of the immediate area. The Temiars say that they prefer other Temiars who live locally, and mothers say they would not like their daughters to live 'over the hill' as they would miss them and long for them (*rəyaak*). They said the same when we finally left the jungle to return to the UK. It was the fact that we were going a long way. The Temiars

Plate 10 Asam village

Plate 11 Old style Temiar house (inhabited by a recluse shaman)

usually measure their journeys by cigarette smokes; for example, when asked how far it is to another village, they answer, 'two cigarettes'. So although in their physical world the Temiars travel relatively short distances, their head-souls (*rəwaay*), particularly those of shaman, are able to travel very long distances, following the paths (*nɔŋ*) of spirit-guides who may reveal important information in their dream encounters of hunting sites, new dances, songs and cures.

The contrast between the village and the forest is most strongly differentiated between domestic houses and forest shelters. One could speculate at a practical level that Temiar houses are built off-the-ground for protection from damp, leeches, scorpions, snakes and other animals (Plates 10 and 11). If this were so, then there would be even stronger reasons for building forest shelters off the ground. However, the reverse is true. If the Temiars need to build a shelter in the forest because they are staying overnight, then it is a temporary, lean-to shelter built on the ground. It can be a few palm branches leant together, or a slightly firmer structure with a small frame. Benjamin (1967b:51) defines the name *diŋ-rɔb* as a hastily-built house![4] When the hunters sit or lie down in these shelters, there is only a symbolic separation of leaves or cloth which keeps them 'off-the-ground'. Although one could suggest that in essence this is off-the-ground, perhaps the clearer distinction is ground/raised above the ground. These palm shelters resemble those used by the tiger-shaman in their special seances (see page 168).

The beliefs of the Temiars in relation to village and forest space are in complete contrast to those of the Batek Negritos. Endicott says:

> The Batek are not afraid of the forest and do not build symbolic defences against it. Their easy intimacy with the forest is clearly expressed in the layouts of their camps. The huts at a campsite are scattered here and there, facing at various directions. No deliberate effort is made to remove the undergrowth from the space between the huts or to set off the area of the camp from the surrounding forest. When the thatch of the huts is still green, a Batek camp blends into its surrounding so well that only the sound of voices and the smoke of fires betray its presence to an observer a few feet away. Thus the Batek, unlike most forest-dwelling agricultural peoples, do not attempt to carve out an island of culture in a sea of nature.

(1979:53)

However, the Temiars see themselves as being more like the Negritos when they are in the forest. As I said earlier, the Temiars do not see themselves as forest people but feel they live in villages that happen to be near a forest.

I have described the changes in behaviour and activities between the village and forest and how the bodies of animals are altered before being brought into the village and the bodies of people are transformed before they journey into the forest.

I want now to describe the different spatial practices in relation to birth and death. I have described how childbirth takes place at the back of the house and firmly off the ground. The placenta is tied in a cloth and given by the midwife to the father who ties it to a tree in the forest well away from habitation. Stillborn babies are given tree burial in even more remote forest areas. However, deaths of ordinary mortals are dealt with in the following way. I limit my discussion here to the description of burial spaces. Graves are always situated across water, usually the other side of a river, as the dead person's ghost is thought to have difficulty in traversing water. The Temiars in Asam and Kuala Betis described how they dress the corpse in its old clothes and then wrap it in its sleeping mats. The body is then wrapped round with split bamboo and hung from two poles in order to be carried to the burial place. People who are not closely related to the person carry the body and dig the grave. The Temiars described how they build a house under the ground to act as a grave. They dig the hole and clear the soil out very thoroughly, put a bamboo floor in it and then place the corpse on the floor with its head facing to the west. They make sure that no soil can possibly come into contact with the corpse. They build a sloping roof at an angle, similar to the backrest used at childbirths, before replacing the soil. They place objects that belonged to the person such as cooking pots into the grave, together with home-made gifts such as jewelry, a bush knife and money. The grave is finished off with a mound of earth on the top. Sometimes a fence is built around the grave to keep away intruding animals, and fires are lit, especially at the head and foot; this also happens at childbirth outside the house where the birth has taken place.

By complete contrast to the interment of ordinary people in the ground and the tree burial of placentas and stillborn babies in the forest above the ground, great shaman are left exposed on the platform of their houses and the rest of the village move away. I was told this by Temiars rather than witnessing it. There are very few great shaman. I was also told that the great shaman's head-soul turns into a tiger at death. The great shaman's corpse is not transported to a place of burial. I can only speculate that it is too dangerous to be in contact and therefore safer for everyone else to move away; similarly it is unsafe to be in touch with the great shaman when he changes into a tiger during the seance.

There is a repetition of the theme of blood and tigers within the ground/off-the-ground differentiation. This is linked with the burial in the ground of menstrual clothes at the edge of the forest, and post-partum blood that is allowed to soak into the ground, or else into branches which are then disposed of at the forest edge. These relationships are summarily presented as follows:

placenta stillborn babies		mortals
:	:	
tree burial		ground burial
:	:	
off-the-ground		in-the-ground

or:

placenta stillborn babies		menstrual and post-partum blood
:	:	
special category		ordinary category
:	:	
maintained off-the-ground		buried in-the-ground

I want now to emphasise the separation between house and forest, and the transformations that animals and people go through when moving from one to the other. The vertical opposition between off-the-ground and ground, and the horizontal opposition between house and forest may be said to be mutually reinforcing. In this schema, I would argue that the forest fringes act as some kind of 'in-between place' that is safe enough for women to visit, bury their menstrual cloths, participate in the ritual of first menstruation and for their placentas to be buried. However, it is still contrasted with the very deep forest which is the domain of men.

The river is also an 'in-between space' and is a very important feature for the Temiars; they use the expression 'from the source to estuary' to denote tradition and history, and also to describe the long journeys undertaken by head-souls when they leave the body, and when spirit-guides visit a seance.

We may recall that Temiar villages are always built on the banks of rivers, usually at the mouths of the small tributaries where they join the main rivers. The Temiars told me it would be impossible to live anywhere except near a river. When I told them about a proposal to build a great lake nearby (a Colombo Plan project to store water from the monsoon), they said they could not live near water that did not move. When I took a group of Temiars to see the sea, they were most perturbed that it did not move in one direction but seemed to move forward and back. However, Endicott (1983:230) suggests that traditionally the Temiar houses were not situated at the river's edge but rather on a ridge where they would be easier to defend. He suggests that their preference for long houses may also have been a means of defence, especially against slave raiding in which all Orang Asli groups were involved prior to the twentieth century.

The river is the preferred means of travel for the Temiars rather than the dangerous treks through the jungle. They use log boats large enough to contain a whole family when they go to see relatives or when they want to hunt in a new location, or visit distant crops or fruit trees. If a log boat is not available, they will build a raft out of bamboo which has a small raised platform in the middle. Both boats and rafts are poled up and down the river, even when the rivers are quite fast-flowing and there are dangerous currents. The river is also the source of the most taboo-free protein – fish. Everyone can eat fish (apart from one of the less common large species) and it is the most popular food for children and recently-delivered parents, and fishing is an activity undertaken by both men and women.

Naturally the river is of central importance to the Temiars for their water supply. There are trees that yield water in the forest if they get thirsty on long walks, but the river supplies all their major water needs. Water is fetched in bamboo containers in a back-basket and leaned against the kitchen wall. Most houses in modern times have acquired a kettle, metal pots and pans, which are used for fetching water. Unless there has been some Malay influence (some areas have had talks on river-borne diseases), the Temiars happily drink water straight from the river. I always thought it was a gymnastic feat that they were able to wade into the river and bend over to drink without wetting their clothes. However, during first menstruation, childbirth and illness, water is always warmed (not boiled) on the fire, before being drunk or used for ritual bathing.

The Temiars spend much of their time in the river. They bathe several times a day apart from at monsoon time when the river is too swollen to be safe. If the day is hot, the preference is to go to the river to keep cool. The children learn to swim very early and play chase and floating games in the river. However, the river is not the preferred place to be at twilight or after dark; the water demons may send out their tentacles which invade people's *hup* and suck their blood. Encounters with other wild animals after darkness are also feared. However, men do organise night-time fishing and frogging expeditions. When returning from these trips they stand over the fire to ward off any evil entities that may have become attached to their clothes or bodies in the night-time dew.

We may recall that the river is forbidden to those people who may endanger others because of contamination through blood or those who need protection until their head-souls are strong enough to leave the house. All these people wash in their houses or else at the forest edge. The restrictions of *tɔracɔɔg* also regulate behaviour concerning the river. For example, it is not permissible to throw old clothes or tins into the river. It would seem once again that the world of human beings is being kept separate from the non-human world. However, I occasionally observed some people throwing small flower heads into the river, where they floated gently downstream. A Temiar man explained that it is to guard the head-soul of a child, and is a protective ritual performed by parents of surviving babies and infants. This is in contrast to the burial of corpses across rivers so that their ghost is discouraged from returning to the village to haunt people.

To summarise, the river is a most important spatial domain for the Temiars, as a means of travel, a supply of safe food and as providing major spatial co-ordinates, enabling the Temiars to orientate their bodies in space. This is manifested in several ways. One of the most spectacular is the ease with which they can map-read from rivers. They can trace very complicated Malay maps with no hesitation, once they see a recognisable river. When I described maps or asked about rivers further away from Kuala Betis, they would use their hands to indicate the shape and relationship of one river to another. In particular they use the fingers of both hands to describe and illustrate the river sources of the mountain divide between the states of Kelantan and Perak that feed the river valleys on either side. Similarly, if any Temiars lost their way in the forest they would find their way to the nearest river and immediately know where they were. The river is also important in establishing referential areas for the Temiars in relation to non-Temiars and other aboriginal groups. The Temiars also acknowledge differences as well as relationships with people living further up-river and down-river.

We have considered relationships between the house, the forest/ forest fringe and now the river. In these I suggest that the river is the physical intermediary between the human world of the house and the non-human world of the forest. Whereas the house/river and house/ forest are also complementary to each other, they also relate triadically as inter-dependent units of space both physically and conceptually in terms of everyday Temiar life.

We have seen in this chapter how the Temiars separate their spatial categories vertically and horizontally and designate appro-priate behaviour within those spaces. When trying to tease out relationships between concepts of other people, it is tempting to ascribe meaning where perhaps the people themselves do not explicitly make the links and connections. However, in relation to bodies and space, it is argued here that the Temiars themselves, in their linguistic terms and their behaviour, do see the categories upper/lower, inner/outer, off-the-ground/ground and house/forest in systematic opposition and relationship. They frequently use the word *hunt-tɛʔ* to describe the Negritos,[5] and also behaviour that is messy, confused, careless or chaotic (such as dropping something or missing a target with a blowpipe or describing something that 'is all Greek to them'). The word *tɛʔ* means ground (for an etymological analysis deriving *hun-* from *hup*, therefore connected with will or feelings, see Benjamin 1967b:31), and they use the word to describe going hunting in the forest. Thus disorder on the ground is indicated by the phrase *hun-tɛʔ*. By contrast, the word *hum-booʔ* is used to describe tradition, culture, the correct way of doing things. *Booʔ* is the Temiar word for mother. Therefore *booʔ* is associated with the house and things off-the-ground, with order (although paradoxically it is also mothers who are dangerous because of their uncontrolled blood). Benjamin (1967a:312) reports that *ʔalɥj*, the original youngest-born, first taught people the correct kinship terms, prior to which they had related to each other in a *hun-tɛʔ* manner. Thus *ʔalɥj* is seen as a bringer of order, whereas the two most feared entities are bringers of disorder: tiger from the forest floor and thunder from above the sky. And thus the Temiars themselves strive to emulate *hum-booʔ* in their daily life, avoiding the *hun-tɛʔ* confusion of behaviour, bodies and space except of course in the more chaotic trance experiences.

Benjamin (1994) has written about the relationship between mother and child together forming a tree. The word for mother, *boo?*, also means tree-trunk, and I have already described the importance of family trees. So *hum-boo?* implies some stability in relation to both mothers and trees, i.e. rootedness, in contrast with the *hun-tɛ?* of the unexpected and potentially dangerous uprootedness of thunderstorm damage.

Chapter 6

Dreams, souls and trance

And thou art wrapp'd and swathed around in dreams,
Dreams that are true, yet enigmatical;
For the belongings of thy present state,
Save through such symbols, come not home to thee.
(Newman, *The Dream of Gerontius*)

An immediate difficulty in any attempt to write about dreams is the
sheer bulk of literature in the many disciplines that address the subject.
For example, dream interpretation forms the basis of both Freudian and
Jungian psychoanalysis, and provides material to be worked with in
most other arts and psychotherapeutic interventions. A further problem
is that dreams and their understanding have taken on a life and meaning
of their own, frequently removed from the personal, social and cultural
context in which the dreaming may take place. Dreams are seen as
sources of prophecy, resolution and a means of gaining access to the
hidden dark regions of unconscious experience. The last few years
have seen a particular surge of interest and debate concerning Temiar
dreaming in Europe and North America. Here I shall attempt to
summarise and contextualise the historic and current material on
Temiar dreaming.[1] It should be noted that theory and literature
concerning Temiar dream practices is usually referred to as Senoi
dreaming, but the people being written about are the Temiars.

Kilton Stewart, an American anthropologist, visited the Senoi
Temiars in the 1930s; he also spent time with Pat Noone who had
already conducted considerable early research (e.g. Noone 1936).
Stewart collected data which were to be included in his doctoral
thesis (for which he registered at the London School of Economics),
entitled 'Magico-Religious Beliefs and Practices in Primitive Societies: A Sociological Interpretation of Their Therapeutic Aspects'
(1947). This included data from three cultures: the Senoi Temiars, the

Negritos of the Philippines and the Yami of Botel Tobago (near Formosa/Taiwan). In his thesis Stewart, who, with others, has since written extensively on this subject, describes the basis of his dream theory as well as a formulated practice of Senoi dream therapy.

Stewart's claim is that the Senoi teach their children how to make use of their dreams through a maturational process. Young children are encouraged to have free-floating dreams and not to fear them; by adolescence they are being taught to control their dreams, to overcome adversaries present in the dream as well as pursuing pleasure to its utmost limits. He says:

> The net result of dream expression and interpretation in childhood – as will be seen – is to produce frustration dreams, then guidance dreams. The fear dreams of early childhood become more complicated, then give way to a higher and higher percentage of frustration dreams, then to dreams in which there is agreement between the destructive characters and the authority characters and the 'I' factor.
>
> (Stewart 1947:120)

Stewart claims that by regular dream instruction from parents, children are able to make use of their dreams and change them. Thus initially destructive forces such as snakes, tigers and lightning behave as destructive in the dreams of small children, but: '*as maturation proceeds, although the dream authorities usually go on acting like social authorities, the destructive dream characters become constructive and co-operative*' (ibid:124). Stewart describes how the Temiars have 'informal morning councils' in order to plan their day, based on important dreams and their directions: 'This informal council on dreams is the focus of Temiar group life' (ibid:103). He then proceeds to give details of a typical morning council, and goes on to talk about the 'family council' in which children are encouraged to recount their dreams to the father and older brothers at the morning meal. This will mean that 'A Child's Dream is Focus of Family Interaction Which Formulates His Daily Progress, Expresses to Authority His Anti-Social Dream Actions, and Shapes Him for Shamanism' (ibid:112). Stewart describes the intervention of older people in the dream life of the child. For example, they may explain some of the child's antisocial acts; describe his/her antagonists as 'masquerading spirits'; and recommend that the child perform social gestures towards people who may have been the recipient of the dreamer's antisocial feelings. Stewart goes on to say:

In these dream interpretations, co-operation and responsibility are often encouraged, interest in the arts and crafts is sponsored, and the child is made to feel important by being regarded as a possible vessel for vital spiritual communications of significance to the whole group. Thus, in the morning council, the tensions and frustrations of daily life released in dreams, are again attached to the group by authority and re-directed from anti-social into co-operative channels.

(ibid:114)

In later papers and published works (1953, 1954, 1975) Stewart elaborates his theory and practice of Senoi dream education and Senoi dream therapy as a means of therapeutic intervention for developing mental and emotional health. He describes an idealised life-style of the Temiars that is happy, peaceful and stress-free, and he attributes this to their dream practices. Numerous psychologists and therapists took notice of these works and elaborated a practice, particularly in America, of Senoi dream therapy, and established Senoi dream clinics (see, for example, Latner and Sabini 1972; Hudson and O'Connor 1981; and Kaplan and Williams 1980).

I found it very disconcerting during my fieldwork that I was unable to verify the practice which Stewart had described. After a discussion with Benjamin I discovered that he, too, had not discovered anything as formalised in his fieldwork as Stewart had described. Reassured, I continued my research and collected whatever dream information I could gather. In his own thesis Benjamin (1967b: 233–8) summarises Stewart's approach but at that time did not overtly challenge it. Not until after I made a brief return visit to the Temiars in 1984 did I discover from several researchers that the whole Senoi dream therapy issue had reached great proportions and was receiving the attention of many writers (see, for example, Dentan 1983a; Faraday and Wren-Lewis 1984; and Stewart 1983).

William Domhoff was the first to directly challenge the issue, asking how it was that no anthropologist who had been to the field and could speak Temiar had actually verified Stewart's research. Domhoff collaborated with Robert Dentan and eventually published *The Mystique of Dreams* (1985). (Dentan also published several papers, including 'Senoi Dream Praxis' (1983a), and 'A Dream of Senoi' (1983c)). Domhoff gives us a detailed account of the development of interest in Senoi dreaming as well as presenting a most stimulating hypothesis in terms of why Senoi dream therapy took hold of America in the first place. Stimulating though it is, that particular discussion does not interest us here. However, reaction against the challenges of Dentan and Domhoff has resulted in the suggestion that the Temiars have in fact drastically changed through outside influences, through the Emergency, and that their dreaming belonged to an original practice and is perhaps still continuing in remote areas (see, for example, Randall 1983). However, as Benjamin has pointed out (personal communication), there are no undiscovered Temiar groups living out of contact with other groups. Domhoff (1985) himself says reports from Noone, who had lived with the Temiars in the 1930s, when compared with later researchers, such as Benjamin, Dentan and Robarchek, demonstrate very little cultural change.

Furthermore, on my brief return visit to the Temiars in 1984, I met Anne Faraday (a psychologist and author of two books on dreams) and John Wren-Lewis who had just been to visit the Temiars. They agreed with me that in no way could Stewart's claims be considered accurate. Their findings are reported in the *Dream Network Bulletin* (August 1984). They conclude:

> Sadly, we must report that not a single Temiar recalled any form of dream control education in childhood or any such practice among adults; in fact they vehemently denied that dream manipulation had ever been a part of their culture. And dreams play such a integral part in their whole religious life that we cannot conceive of a major-dream practice being allowed to fade into oblivion when the religion itself is so very much alive.

> (p. 10)

I now propose to examine Temiar dreaming in relation to soul beliefs and trance.

The Temiars place great store by their dreams and if anyone says that they have dreamt then there will be plenty of people to listen to their dreams. Usually people report dreams that could contain useful information for the group and will see dreams as being predictive of successful places where game can be found for the hunter, or where fruit and vegetables can be foraged. The Temiars usually act on their dreams in this way. Endicott (1979) reports similarly for the Batek Negritos and says that dreams and trance are sources of knowledge. Although Negritos do not value information gained from another human being any less than dream knowledge, there is an assumption that the human knowledge will originally have come from the *hala asal* (original person). As I mentioned in Chapter 4, during sleep, the head-soul *rəwaay* of the sleeper is free to wander and meet with the *gonig* or spirit-guide and the relationship between the dreamer and spirit-guide is a filial one; one way that the dreamer may recognise his or her *gonig* is by the *gonig* addressing the dreamer as parent; the spirit-guide is the child of the dreamer. However, there is another relationship between dreamer and spirit-guide and that is between teacher and pupil; the dreamer refers to the *gonig* as both child and teacher (*guuʔ*). *The gonig* is believed to teach the dreamer something new, and dreaming is therefore seen as a source of innovation and knowledge as well as creative and playful.

Roseman (1986, 1993) goes further than the child/teacher roles of the spirit-guides. She says:

> Overtones of longing, flirtation, enticement and seduction pervade the cross-sexual relationship between humans and spirit-guides. While Temiar mediums are predominantly male, their spirit-guides are predominantly female. A common term for spirit-guides, *gonig* derives from the Malay *gundik* (consort). Bemoaning the fate of transitory dream encounters, mediums often comment: 'I sleep with her at night, but in the morning my bed is empty'.
>
> (1986:16)

A young male or female spirit-guide appears in the person's dreams as a small person (Benjamin 1967b:139, mannikin).[2] For ordinary mortals a *gonig* is the head-soul of flowers, fruits and trees and animals that are classed as above the ground. Everyone is believed to have encounters in dreaming between their head-souls and these child/teacher head-souls of natural species. Repeated encounters with one or more spirit-guides is an indication of the potential for shamanism, for the individual to be *halaaʔ* (knowledgeable, adept).

The Temiars do not necessarily share their dreams and some people who may be potential shaman keep their dreaming private if they do not want to take up the responsibilities it would impose on them. However, having knowledge that is felt could benefit the whole community imposes an obligation to share. Thus dreaming is an activity in which everyone engages and is a source of knowledge to the dreamer. The dreamer may be taught not only ground or forest-based information such as the whereabouts of successful hunting places, but also new knowledge concerning the essentially off-the-ground, house-bound activities of music and dance. New songs, dance patterns and steps are taught to the dreamer, who in turn teaches them to the community at a seance. Dreaming is therefore very much a creative process which occurs through personal encounter with the individual's spirit-guide, child/teacher.

Before considering the relationship between dreams and trance, I need to expand our knowledge of Temiar soul beliefs.

I have already described briefly the Temiar soul concept in Chapters 3 and 4, concerning the existence of a head-soul (*rəwaay*), and a heart/blood-soul (*jərəək*), the head-soul resting on the crown of the head and able to leave the body, and the heart/blood-soul residing in the *hup*, the place of feelings, which only leaves the body at death. As I said, although a literal translation of the *jərəək* is heart-soul, Benjamin refers to it mainly as the blood-soul. (Stewart 1947 refers variously to the *jərəək* as heart-soul, liver-soul and liver-bile-soul.) The Temiars (Benjamin 1967b) also refer occasionally to an eye-soul, *kɛnlɔɔk*, and to the shadow-soul, *wɔɔg*. As with *jərəək*, *kɛnlɔɔk* and *wɔɔg* only leave the body at death. Therefore in humans the *rəwaay* and the *jərəək* are the upper body and lower body-soul respectively.

Dentan explains the Semai concepts of soul in the following way:

> The Semai think of a person as made up of a set of six interlocking things or processes. The two most important components of this complex are *ruai* or 'soul' and *kaloog* or 'spirit'. The *sangiid* or 'thought' is localized in the heart and expressed in the *laham* or 'breath'. The other two elements of a person are his *sakoo* or 'aura', which can be seen as the flush of good health in the face of a robust person, and the *nadi* or 'arterial pulse', which is primarily located where it is most strongly felt, in the left breast. . . .
>
> Daylight, a sensitive and intellectual West Semai man, says that to grasp the relationships between the six components of a person one can think of a person as a car. *Ruai* would be the battery, *kaloog* the driver, 'thought' the running of the engine, 'breath' the gas, 'aura' the paint, and 'arterial pulse' the speedometer.
>
> (1968:82)

In contrast, Endicott (1979) reports that the Batek Negritos believe in a wind-life-soul which 'animates man and other mortal animals' and is manifested in the breath and voice. They also believe in a shadow-soul which can leave the body and be seen in dreams or trance. In illness (as with the Temiars) a person's shadow-soul must not fall on the sick person. Endicott also describes how a fever will result if the shadow-soul of one person falls on the shadow or body of another.

For the Temiars, entities in the non-human world also have head-souls which are labile – trees, mountains, animals and so on. (I must mention here my appreciation of Benjamin for helping me to clarify the following data on various soul terms.) Although fruit trees and plants also have *rəwaay*, the 'head-souls' of some mountains are referred to as *məntərii?* (minister). Conversely, some plants, trees and animals have particularly dangerous lower-body-souls called *kənoruk* which are believed to wander forth as tigers. (We have already noted in Chapter 4 how spilt blood turns into small tigers and the human heart/blood-soul turns into a tiger at death.)

However, the lower-body-souls of certain mountains are referred to as *sarak* and are believed to transform into large tigers who roam the countryside.

The head-souls of all entities, human and otherwise, are free-moving and can leave the body during dreams and trance. Often the *rəwaay* is thought to go and play while the person is in trance or is described as going on a journey (*nɔŋ*). When the Temiars first taught me to trance and I was unconscious for some minutes, the shaman said that he had to send his head-soul on a long journey to fetch mine back. Head-soul loss needs shamanic intervention and lengthy absence of the head-soul away from the body causes death. However, in the case of young children whose head-souls are still being formed, their head-soul can slip off by accident which is why great care is taken by the parents not to endanger it. Head-soul sickness or loss is referred to as *rəwaay*.

Shamanic intervention is necessary with head- and blood/heart-soul illnesses. I want to describe the involvement of the shaman's own souls in the healing process. The shaman's spirit-guide(s) assist in the healing, whether it is at a formal healing seance or less formal treatment which takes place in the person's own house or the house of the shaman. Although the healing strength of the spirit-guides is present in concentration at the seances, a shaman has his own guide's healing power available to him all the time. This is important when seances are prohibited, for example, during mourning.

Although the shaman may prescribe avoidance of certain foods (*sabat*), seclusion in the house, and use prayers and chants, his most frequent resource for healing is his spirit-guide(s). Most shaman derive spirit-guides from species that are off-the-ground; it is major and great shaman who are helped by the power of the more dangerous off-the-ground creatures or entities.

Before pursuing the topic of Temiar trance in more detail, let us look briefly at what we mean by the term trance in this context. As with dreams, there is a vast and varied literature on trance. As with dreaming, there is a tendency to take trance out of its cultural context, particularly when it is dramatically ecstatic, and invest it with ethnocentric assumptions. The phenomenon of dissociation takes many forms, some of which are very visible and physical, others less obvious. I.M. Lewis suggests that trance is a neutral term for describing states of dissociation. He says:

> For our purposes all we need to note for the moment is the universality of mystical experience and the remarkable uniformity of mystical language and symbolism. We also require, however, a neutral term to denote the mental state of the subject of such experiences. Here I shall employ the word 'trance', using it in its general medical sense which the *Penguin Dictionary of Psychology* conveniently defines as: 'a condition of dissociation, characterised by the lack of voluntary movement, and frequently by automatisms in act and thought, illustrated by hypnotic and mediumistic conditions'.
>
> (1971:38)

Trance behaviour usually responds to the expectations of a particular culture. For example in societies where it is expected that children will trance, such as Bali, then children trance. The Temiars believe that people cannot trance until puberty, and that the head-soul is not strong enough to leave the body. Therefore they considered that only my son Andy and myself were able to trance and they were eager to teach us, with some success. However I want to emphasise that dissociation happens in many cultures and contexts and that there is a wide range of degree of dissociation, from mild absorption to total unconsciousness. It may be caused by a variety of stimuli such as hallucinogens and hyperventilation, to name but two. However, it can be produced with no external stimulus within a particularly focused context. I refer in particular to the experience of many actors when they report experiences of being possessed by the roles they are playing. Johnstone (1979) says that many actors report 'split consciousness' or what he terms 'amnesias'. He quotes Fanny Kemble who said, 'The curious part of acting, to me, is the sort of double process which the mind carried on at once, the combined operation of one's faculties, so to speak, in diametrically opposite directions' (1979:151). He goes on to say: 'Most people only recognise 'trance' when the subject looks confused – out of touch with the reality around him. We even think of hypnosis as 'sleep'. In many trance states people are *more* in touch, more observant' (ibid:153).

I want to emphasise that trance is a somatic experience, it is felt in and through the body with changes in temperature, heart and pulse rate. It involves a partial letting go of conscious control in order for the experienced 'other' to emerge. It is in enactment that the trance allows the experienced 'other' to be made manifest. We shall see from further exploration of the Temiar beliefs about dreams, souls and trance that they have a conceptual framework in which embodiment and enactment and soul freedom are the means by which dreams and trance are made visible.

I want to pursue the relationship of the head-soul with the activities of dreaming and trancing. We have seen how head-soul freedom, providing that the *rǝwaay* has not been startled or stolen, is the source of creative encounter in its playfulness and journeys. The *gonig* child/teacher it meets will from time to time teach the person something. The *gonig* of ordinary mortals are head-souls of off-the-ground entities who manifest themselves as small people to the dreamer and reveal something new.

The Temiar word for a dream is *pɔʔ* and dreaming is seen as an essentially active and controlled pastime. To meet with one's spirit-guide is known as *halaaʔ* which as we have already seen is also a word used for shaman. Anyone has the potential for *halaaʔ*; it is the experienced development of it into shamanism that enables someone to become a designated *halaaʔ*, whether minor, middle, major or great.

The Temiar word for trance is *pɔɔh* and, as with dreaming, the head-soul is believed to leave the body and go on journeys and to play with other head-souls. Very often the Temiars gather together for playful dances where there is dancing, singing and often spontaneous trancing. They refer to these sessions as *sisɛʔ jɛhwah* (play-dance) or *pɛhpɔɔh jɛhwah* (play-trance) as contrasted with the more serious trance sessions (Chapter 8) that are usually conducted for healing. The decision to 'play' is often on the spur of the moment, few decorations are made, though sometimes there is a token bunch of leaves. Although it is considered that a person's spirit-guide is around at the time, there is not the intention to call down the guides. Not all dancing and singing leads to trance although it is often a time for uncontrolled trance as I have described in Chapter 4. Sometimes aspiring shaman display their prowess at these play sessions and encourage young women to trance vigorously. There is a high discharge of energy through the dancing and trancing and older people would sometimes curb the noise and lack of control of the young people at these sessions. Most young adults dance and trance but parents of small children (apart from shaman) refrain from trance to protect the head-soul of their child (Figure 6.1 illustrates dance and trance in relation to Temiar life cycle roles).

Trance is not exclusively a shamanistic activity. Like dreaming it is something that everyone can do (providing they are not prohibited through illness); and it would seem that whereas dreams are a personal activity with individual encounter of one's spirit-guide, the seances are a communal time where the availability of one's *gonig* is there to share. It may also be the time that a Temiar will try to teach the group a new song or dance pattern learned in a dream. We shall see in Chapters 8 and 9 how the seances, although still public, take on a different quality, particularly in relation to healing. However, even at play trance-dance, healing may take place. If an aspiring shaman or an adept is in trance, he will blow on the head-souls of children who are watching, or of someone known to be unwell. Nevertheless, trance can happen at all seances, whether play or serious and as an activity it is longed for (*na-rəyaak*) by the Temiars. They complained of the taboo of the

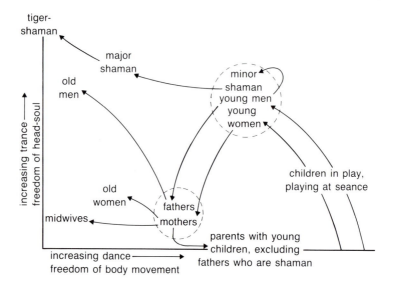

Figure 6.1 Dance and trance in Temiar life cycle roles: freedom of bodies and head-souls

mourning period which did not allow seances or trance. When it is playful and experienced by ordinary people, it is a time for head-souls to go on creative journeys; when it is serious and experienced by shaman, then it is for specific healing of sick individuals, to make the head-soul of the village strong, or to try to avoid possible sickness in the future. Seances are felt to have a preventive as well as a curative function. The other words used in relation to trance, as well as *pɔɔh*, are *leslaas* (transformation) and *wɛlwəl* (forgetting),

On occasions at playful seances, the shaman is in trance and, speaking as his spirit-guide and therefore as his child, he uses the opportunity for reminding people of their responsibilities. This is carried out in a joking fashion with mimicry and caricature. Ali Songkok, a minor shaman (Plate 12) who lived near Kuala Betis, used to clown around, imitating animals and impersonating outsiders as examples of how not to behave. On other occasions the shaman takes this opportunity seriously if he feels that people need to be reminded to work hard, or work together, or to share their produce generously. Since the shaman is talking as his child spirit-guide, he can directly communicate with people whom he would normally avoid. Thus he can call his mother-in-law grandmother (his wife is addressed as mother).

We can see in dreaming and trancing that encounter with and playing of various roles is possible. In trance, the shaman becomes the child, whether playfully or seriously, and is able to address people with whom he would normally have avoidance relationships. When not in trance, the shaman or spirit-guide becomes the teacher and is able to transmit the knowledge that has been revealed to him. Thus dreams and trance enable people to cross boundaries that are forbidden in waking life.

I have already mentioned the erotic content of some of the encounters of younger shaman at the seances, and Roseman, quoted earlier in this chapter, describes the flirtatious and seductive quality of dream encounters. I would argue that dreaming and trancing provide the opportunity within controlled settings for multiple role encounters and the expansion of multiple selves. The several internalised 'others' – the creative, the playful, the erotic, the healing selves – are stimulated and enabled to interact with the many external 'others' both in the human and non-human world. Thus there is a continuum of the dramatic act from private revelation to public manifestation.

Our understanding of dreaming and trancing as creative activities expands even further when we consider the language of Temiar creation myths. There are many variations of these myths which describe how the Temiar world came into being. One of these stories, which is told in several variations, describes the Temiar origins as the

Plate 12 Ali Songkok, a minor shaman, about to trance

result of the creative acts of an original founding mother-shaman-midwife known as Chingkai.[3] Chingkai was one of two mountains left behind when the original flood waters began to subside. (The Temiars point out the two mountains on the upper regions of the Nenggiri river.) Chingkai created the first Temiar brother and sister who in turn were the founders of the Temiar human race. Chingkai and her familiars created the major features of the Temiar topographical and calendrical world, their shamanism, and also thunder, who was created last. What is interesting for us here is that Chingkai and her familiars *dreamed and tranced* the Temiar world into being. Dreaming and trancing were thus the means by which human beings themselves were created. Dreaming and trancing are considered by the Temiars as ordinary but essential activities that are available to everyone and that are essentially joyous, creative and playful. There is a tendency for travellers and ethnographers to treat Temiar trance with awe, whereas the Temiars themselves laugh, joke and are entertained by it.

Having examined the relationship between dreams, souls and trance which are encapsulated in the drama, I want to return to the seance performances where people are allowed public freedom of head-soul and where the beneficent head-souls of others donate their healing powers. In Temiar seances the shaman is a spirit medium for his spirit-guide even though his head-soul and those of other participants are free to go on journeys. Thus the Temiars combine an essential duality of soul freedom on the one hand and spirit medium on the other.

Endicott says that both the Lebir and Aring Batek regard trancing as the most effective means of communicating with the *hala asal*. He says:

> According to Batek theories, trancing is a sort of controlled dreaming, in that the shadow-soul can be deliberately sent to any part of the universe. It is guided by the songs that accompany the trance, different songs being used for different destinations. The shadow-soul is variously described as flying or being carried by the incense smoke, the wind or the *hala' 'asal*. It may also use its tiger-body to make journeys to earth. The shadow-soul of the shaman is able to meet any of the *hala' 'asal*. This way the shaman can negotiate directly with them, because he is a friend of the *hala' 'asal*, he can get whatever help and information he needs. The great advantage of trancing over ordinary dreaming of course is that in the former the shaman can decide what *hala'* to

visit and can determine the topic of discussion, whereas in the latter the dreamer plays a passive role, without any influence over which, if any, *hala'* will visit him, or what information it will impart.

(1979:145)

For the Batek there is the contrast between the passive role of the dreamer and the active role of the shaman in trance. Whereas Benjamin says of the Temiars (1979a:10; 1983a:92) that dreaming is essentially an activity, and most of the time a controlled activity, trancing is also a controlled activity. He emphasises the private/ public nature of dreaming and trancing. What is dreamt is often taken to seances and taught to participants: songs, dance-steps, music. Trancing may or may not follow an instructional session. The connection between the two activities (dreaming and trancing) is the guidance of the spirit-guide.

Trance for the Temiars is essentially an activity that is manifest at seance performances. All seances, whether playful or serious, informal or formal, may contain trance as part of the proceedings. Playful seances may have spontaneous trance whereas the more serious seances have the intentionality of trance. Playful seance may be a spontaneous group activity where many young shaman try out their skills and the formal seance is under the direction of a single experienced shaman, though others often assist. Between these two extremes is a range of seance performance that includes elements of both. What clearly demonstrates the contrast is the calling down of the spirit-guides on to the decorations and the specific shamanic techniques used for dispensing the essence from the guides, which is described on pages 143–4. The degree of dissociation is not always obvious to the observer. Young people dance themselves into trance, often in a very energetic way, whereas older people sway backwards and forwards with a minimum of physical movement. No drugs, alcohol or hallucinogens are used and it would appear that the pounding rhythm, the sprung bamboo floor, the semi-darkness and degree of hyperventilation are all conducive to trance.

We have already seen in Chapter 2 that there are people who do not go into trance for fear of further endangering the vulnerable head-soul of themselves or their children. In healing seances the patient never goes into trance and the shaman, as a means of contacting a concentration of his spirit-guide power, is in controlled trance for the healing ceremony. It is noticeable that the shaman is in a lighter trance state than that of the participants. Entranced participants may eventually fall to the floor and need reviving by the shaman who fetches back the person's head-soul which has travelled too far. Older people do not usually become unconscious and emerge from the trance state themselves without the intervention of the shaman.

Endicott says of the Batek:

> Batek trance is not usually deep; the loss of consciousness is not complete. . . .
>
> Usually a shaman in trance just goes on singing, with eyes shut, describing in song the journey of his shadow-soul. Sometimes the shaman stopped singing when he goes into trance, but continued to sit with eyes closed, swaying in time to the music. It is said, though I have not seen it happen, that shaman sometimes dance and then fall down in a stupor. . . .
>
> No alcohol or drugs are used by the Batek to induce trance though good-smelling leaves are worn and incense burned and their odours may have some small effect on the shaman's state of consciousness. Batek shamans do not normally answer questions when they are in trance. This is consistent with the theory that the shadow-soul is absent from the body at that time. The shaman is not aware of his surroundings while in trance, but he may be able to recount the adventures of his shadow-soul after he revives.
>
> (1979:149)

This is in marked contrast to the Temiar shaman who is very aware of his surroundings to the extent that as the spirit-guide-child he is able to address people present in changed kinship terms and to use the opportunity to impose a form of social control both on individuals and groups. He does answer questions and converse with people while in trance. He is both spirit-medium for his spirit-guide, his own feelings temporarily put to one side, and in a state of dissociation with the absence of his head-soul.

The visiting spirit-guide transmits his or her power to the shaman through liquid. The spirit-guide, which rests on the central decorations, is said to let down threads which transform into a liquid (*kahyɛk*). The shaman usually catches the liquid in the palm of his hand and then uses it in the process of healing. There are two methods in which it can be used and these are described in Chapter 8. There is sometimes actual fluid in the palm of the shaman's hand; at other times it is said to be there and only visible to people in trance. On occasions the shaman will place a bowl of water underneath the decorations and use a palm-frond to flick water on to a whole group of people or on to an individual patient whom he is curing. The shaman touches his own chest to allow the liquid to enter his *hup*; thus the liquid comes from inside the shaman, as well as being externally present through his ministrations.

Essential to the Temiar understanding of trance is the process of transformation. The Temiar word *na-lããs* (change into, transformation, metamorphosis) is used quite specifically: for example, in the tiger-seance, when the shaman is said to change into a tiger, and also for the substances which turn into tigers (menstrual blood, spilt blood, etc.) which can enter the *hup* and gnaw away at an individual. However, at seances the word is used to describe being in the trance state, and may carry with it the notion of more serious trancing compared with the play-seances described earlier.

The Temiar terms *na-lããs* (verb) and *lɛslããs* (noun) usually relate to the more serious shamanistic context of forgetting of feelings (*na-wəl*). This may happen at any casual singing and dance performance when there is some sense of dissociation, or the more focused trance performances. The Temiars also say that onlookers can be startled into trance during any kind of seance. The belief is that the head-soul has been frightened away and the individual usually starts to shake violently. This can be controlled by the ministrations of the shaman within the seance, and sometimes the antics of such people can cause much amusement for the onlookers.

One such episode that I witnessed happened to a man who told me that he used to trance frequently but tonight he was just going to watch. He was sitting observing when suddenly he got up and started to jerk violently as if in a spasm; he stumbled and fell round the room, bouncing in his own circle. The movements gradually became less controlled and he then performed *tɛnhool* (blowing through his clenched hand) on the heads of his wife and child.

In this chapter I have described the essentially private activity of dreaming in relation to the public activity of trancing, both activities involving the interaction of head-souls with head-souls of others. Both enable the person to engage in changes in role of self and other. The concepts to which we keep returning are those of freedom as contrasted with containment, and the idea that freedom must be controlled or it will lead to head-soul loss. The idea of play, creativity and knowledge is essentially at the core of the dream and trance process, as it is in the creation story in the creative acts of the founder-creator-shaman-midwife and her familiars. Dreaming is an individual activity when the person has personal encounters with the child/teacher of the spirit-guide; this is contrasted with the group activity of the seance where the skills and experiences of the spirit-guide are made available to everyone present. While I was developing my ideas on the relationship between dream and trance I speculated on the earlier problems discussed in relation to Kilton Stewart's work. There seems to be a confusion between dreams and trance in much of what he writes.

Stewart's insistence on dream maturation as a way of educating children through the imposition of dream control appears to be more consonant with the way in which young people are encouraged to control their trance behaviour and their play. On several occasions I witnessed adults teaching young people how to control play-seance behaviour as well as playing-at-seances.

I am particularly interested in the concept of self-and-other, or selves and other selves – the internalised and externalised others. We have seen through trance that shaman internalise the other-self of the spirit-guide and how everyone, whether in dreams or trance, is able to detach their head-soul as a means of making journeys and meeting others. Therefore each individual has at least two selves – the blood/heart-soul and the head-soul – which are most prominent in the semiconscious or unconscious life. In everyday life they are most prominent through their absence in sickness. In the activities of dreams and trance the Temiars identify and embody internal and external roles. However, before pursuing this concept further I want to look at a more recent work by Benjamin entitled 'The Anthropology of Grammar: Self and Other in Temiar' (1983a). Benjamin suggests that it is reasonable for the Temiars to have developed a distinct middle voice, in which subject and object become one, because 'the individual's empirical self or felt subjectivity is thus portraying as a dialectical composite of Self and Other' (1983a:92).

He discusses this specifically in relation to Temiar soul-beliefs, and suggests that it is in soul-beliefs that the Temiars come closest to talking about ideas concerned with the conceptualisation of the person; the following extended quotation illuminates the Temiar complexities:

[I]t is then that the mutual entangling of Self in Other becomes patent. Animate beings are said to possess two souls, one associated with the upper part of the body (the head-hair roots of humans and animals, the leaves of trees, and the summits of mountains) and the other with the lower part (the heart, breath and blood, the roots and the subterranean mass). Dreamers and spirit-mediums report that upper-body souls when met with are like young men or women in appearance, but the lower-body selves are like tigers; in other words, upper-body souls are seen as familiar, domestic and Self-like, while lower-body souls are seen as strange, wild and Other-like. Yet it is the person's heart-cum-tiger soul, the *hup* that is claimed to be the source of his will or agency: it is one's *hup* that makes one do things or lacks the desire to do something. Tigers, of course, are clearly Other; but it is also possible to perceive as 'other' the usually autonomous beating of one's heart (also *hup*) or one's breathing (*hɛmnum*, the -*n*- infixed form of *hup*), since these can be directly monitored by the individual without their needing to be controlled. The head-soul, *rəwaay*, on the other hand is clearly 'Self'-like in its association with the incessant but unobserved growth of the hair – the marker of bodily integrity. But it is cast in the role of a patient-like, non-controlling *experiencer* of whatever befalls the individual in dreams, trance and sickness (one form of which is *rəywaay* 'uncontrolled soul-loss').

Thus for the Temiar, the controlling *hup* (the 'I') is seen as an autonomous other inside the person, while the experiencing *rəwaay* (the 'me') is seen as an equally autonomous, but non-controlling, Self. In other words, *hup* beliefs imply that my actions are at the same time something that I undergo while *rəwaay* beliefs imply that the things that I undergo (growth, dreaming etc.) are at the same time my actions (as in one's dreams which are regarded as controlled activities for the Temiar).

(ibid:91–2)

It has been suggested by philosophers and psychologists alike that an individual develops a sense of identity, a sense of self, by also experiencing 'other'. Mead (1934) talks about the importance of 'taking the role of the other' as a significant factor in early development. Mead, quoted in Wilshire, says:

The self arises in conduct when the individual becomes as object in experience to himself. This takes place when the individual assumes the attitude or uses the gesture which another individual would use and responds to it himself, or tends to so respond.... It arises in the life of the infant through what is unfortunately called imitation, and finds its expression in the normal play life of young children. In the process the child gradually becomes a social being in his own experience, and he acts towards himself in a manner analogous to that in which he acts towards others. Especially he talks to himself as he talks to others and in keeping up this conversation in the inner form constitutes the field which is called the mind. *Then those objects and experiences which belong to his own body,* those images which belong to his own past, become part of this self.

(Wilshire 1982:116, my emphasis)

However, most philosophical writers (for example, Hegel) consider a person's experience of themselves to be a mental rather than bodily experience. The importance of Mead's work is that there is an acknowledgement, albeit undeveloped, of the bodily experience of 'self and other'. Wilshire has developed this as a basis for his argument of self as body-self in the following:

It is a conscious or potentially conscious body which must be identified as a self, and it is under the following conditions: when it can experience objects or persons which are in fact other than itself – but with whom it is mimetically involved – and then can reproduce it *as* other in their absence. This includes its ability to deliberately reproduce its undeliberate mimetic involvement and identification *with others' identification and objectification of it,* and in their absence. The body must be able, to some extent, to appropriate *as* its own *its* mimetic reproduction of *them.*

(1982:152)

Wilshire develops these ideas in relation to the necessity for theatre and theatrical activity as a condition of the body's realising this. My own broader concerns in the field of dramatherapy are based on the premise that for many of my patients there is an absence of developed self; and bodily experienced image is often manifested as a frozen self, unable to experience 'other' (Jennings 1987). However, my interest here in relation to the linguistic model of Benjamin (1983a) is how the Temiars both experience and conceptualise 'self and other' in their dreams and trance activities and their soul-beliefs, through the medium of their own body (both collective and individual) and their bodily interactions with symbolic and actual 'other'

The Temiars believe in two major souls – one outside the body but resting on it – the *rəwaay* or head-soul which in the human infant is undeveloped and liable to slip away unless constant precautions are maintained by the parents – and one inside the body – the heart-

/blood soul (*hup*). The restrictions on food, space and soul freedom, emphasised by changes in name, maintain a parent–child dependency which does not modify until the infant can walk independently, i.e. is able to walk on the ground as a separate person. The transition is a gradual one from filial to sibling dependency within which individual autonomy is encouraged and reinforced. In children's play there is a free flow of enacting other roles, particularly in playing-at-seances, with an imitation of trance behaviour. However, the noise and extrovert quality of this play is curbed through threat of supernatural intervention. Inner encounter with the 'other' is encouraged through private dreaming, an activity which is enjoyed and even longed for by the Temiars (see Roseman 1993). The Temiars listen to and learn from the 'other' encountered in dreams through the interactions of the body-based but mobile head-soul. The rewards from these dream encounters benefit the community as a whole through the creative acts of singing, dancing and healing. The head-soul encounter is with another miniaturised person, both like oneself in being human, but also like 'other' in being non-human.

The second major soul is the blood/heart-soul, located inside the body and conceptually of the lower body. It governs feelings and desire, the individual's will; it does not leave the body but is susceptible to invasion from outside principally from lower-body agencies of destructive 'others', the most destructive 'other' being symbolised by the tiger. It is the shaman who is able to become 'other' in trance at the seance when his *hup*, his feelings and desire, are put aside; he enters into a dialectical relationship with the essence of the spirit-guide which enters his *hup* in order for him to become a mediator for actual others, i.e. the assembled people. In his voice he becomes 'other' when he addresses the others. This is personified by him quite literally when he behaves as teacher and instructs others how they should behave. The great shaman is one who can allow the lower-body essence to enter his *hup* from ground creatures, epitomised in the transformation of the great shaman who personifies the most dreaded and evil 'other', i.e. tiger. Therefore the Temiar sense of identity is embedded in both individual dreaming and collective trancing through the creative media of play, dance, drama and singing and the emergence of an interrelated duality of self, experienced through and located in the body, of head and blood/heart-souls (Jennings 1985a).

The development of these themes, particularly in relation to women through their transformational roles towards blood, is the theme of Chapter 7.

Chapter 7

Women and blood

I'll warrant him for drowning, though the ship were no stronger than a nutshell and as leaky as an unstaunched wench.

(*The Tempest*, Act 1.i)

Be bloody, bold and resolute; laugh to scorn
The power of man; for none of women born
Shall harm Macbeth.

(*Macbeth*, Act 4.i)

This chapter is primarily about female blood and the role of Temiar women in the management of this blood. I shall discuss three main areas where blood and women have a central position: menstruation, childbirth, and the rituals acted out to appease thunderstorms. I shall elaborate the theme of childbirth when I discuss pregnancy together with illness and death in Chapter 8.

I have addressed women within the general context of my Temiar data in previous chapters. In particular I have discussed women's roles within the Temiar subsistence economy, preparation and prohibition of certain foods, parenthood and their place in the naming system. Additionally, in Chapters 4 and 5, we have seen that women complement men in relation to Temiar beliefs and practices concerning body and space.

It is only in recent years that anthropological writers and others have begun to address themselves to themes that are central to women such as menstruation[1] and childbirth. Scant attention is paid in Temiar ethnography to these two themes in particular. Benjamin (1967b), although writing in great detail on blood beliefs in the wider sphere, in the main only describes menstruation and childbirth in relation to the effect they have on men. There are certain difficulties for men in researching these themes with the Temiars, as Benjamin says:

Childbirth and menstruation are topics that the Temiar find highly embarrassing to discuss when men are present – including myself among them – although sexual matters as such are talked about very freely indeed, in mixed company and in the presence of children. The only occasion on which I noticed a blush suffusing the dark cinnamon features of Temiar friends was when I turned the conversation to talk of menstruation.

(1967b:166)

As the first female anthropologist working with the Temiars I have been able to redress that balance to a certain extent. Similarly, like Benjamin I was able to receive little information from men, though my older son was able to obtain some insights. My daughter was also invaluable in exploring these themes, with a close peer and adoptive sibling group of pre-pubertal and pubertal girls.

Recent writings on anthropology have challenged many assumptions concerning women and bodily functions. These writings were only available to me on my return from the field and have greatly assisted my understanding of the data.

MacCormack and Strathern (1980), together with contributors, discuss in detail the assumptions concerning the placing of women in binary opposition to men, particularly in relation to menstruation. Menstruation, because of its cyclicity, is seen as belonging to nature and therefore to 'wildness' (Ardener 1975). In the same volume, Bloch and Bloch describe how many philosophers accepted that women were closer to nature because of their experience of sex and motherhood. This was often used as a basis to exclude them from political and intellectual domains. Since 'nature' was seen as something to conquer and regulate, it followed that women too must be subordinated. Thus because women were closer to 'nature' they were capable of unbridled passion which needed 'taming'. Attention was drawn to women's cravings during pregnancy which were associated with cannibalism by Lametri (ibid.).

This is not the place to discuss these issues in detail (see also Reiter 1975; MacCormack 1982). However, I want to consider the Temiar material against an increased understanding of women. As MacCormack (1980) says:

Menstruating women have a cyclicity as nature does, therefore they are wild and untameable. But wildness can also be an implicit meaning of maleness. Because metaphor is based upon the polysemic and open nature of words it has great potential for both contradiction and for 'redescribing reality' and must not be taken as truth in any literal sense.

> (Ricoeur 1978, in MacCormack and Strathern 1980:169)

and:

> Much of the ethnographic literature suggests that rather than viewing women metaphorically in nature, they (and men) might be better seen as mediating between nature and culture, in the reciprocity of marriage exchange, socialising children into adults, transforming raw meat and vegetables into cooked food, cultivating, domesticating, and making cultural products of all sorts.
>
> (ibid:9)

Most of the literature on menstrual beliefs associates two cross-cutting themes of power and pollution. Women are considered dangerous because of the power and pollution associated with their menstrual flow and thus it is something that men wish to avoid or to emulate. Hogbin (1970) describes the practice of male menstruation amongst the Wogeo of New Guinea. He says, 'The technique of male menstruation is as follows. First the man catches a crayfish or crab and removes one of its claws, which he keeps wrapped up with ginger in it'. Then late in the afternoon, having fasted for the day, he goes to an isolated beach and:

> wades out till the water is up to his knees. He stands there with his legs apart and induces an erection. . . . When ready he pushes back the foreskin and hacks the glans, first on the left side and then on the right. Above all, he must not allow the blood to fall on his fingers or his legs.
>
> (1970:88–9)

When the 'sea is no longer pink' he walks ashore, wraps his wounded penis in leaves, dresses and returns to the village men's club where he has to remain in seclusion. (For a detailed discussion on Hogbin's work see Knight 1983, where he describes the phenomenon of women having 'an extraordinary marriage-regulating power'.)

The Wogeo believe that the power of menstruation blood is that the flow cleanses impurities (Hogbin 1970:88). It is a commonly held belief in our own culture that periods represent a monthly clear-out of the body's wastes, and non-menstrual blood flow, for example with leeches, is also seen as having purifying results.

However, Lewis (1980) warns us against making the assumption that ritual penis bleeding is necessarily a symbolic male menstruation. He argues that we can only make that assumption if the actors in the ritual acknowledge the link themselves. He stresses that there must be an intellectual component in recognition of symbol and metaphor. Unlike the Wogeo, the Gnau studied by Lewis made no connection between penis bleeding and menstruation. Furthermore, although the Wogeo do use the same word for menstruation for both men and women, Hogbin tells us that it is not 'symbolic', i.e. both men and women 'really' menstruate. If the observer chooses to say that the men menstruate 'symbolically', then it is a concept imposed by the observer, not by the Wogeo themselves.

> The same argument applies to 'metaphor' when used by anthropologists in relation to the ideas, words or actions of other people. The people must recognise distinctions between two concepts for one to be used *metaphorically* of the other by them.
>
> (G. Lewis 1980:112)

Gillison (1980) describes how discrepancy between stated beliefs and actual practice in relation to menstruation amongst the Gimi robs women of a *negative power* (my emphasis) invested in them by male beliefs. She says that Gimi men genuinely fear menstrual blood, speak of women with contempt and go to great lengths to avoid them. However:

> They are also attracted to women's dangerousness. Sitting around the fire inside a hunting lodge, men discuss the delights of heterosexual sex. Their songs celebrate the eroticism of menstrual blood: 'I follow the River to its source. As I climb along its course, I see blood staining the rocks. As I round the bend I see you standing naked in the water, beautiful red blood streaming down your shiny black legs! When shall we have sex? Now? In a moment?
>
> (1980:152–3)

We need to look no further than Judaeo/Christian beliefs concerning the powerful attributes given to blood. In the story of the woman with the 'issue of blood', Jewish social and cultural values are evident in the attitudes of the disciples to the woman. However, she is persistent:

> And there was a woman who had had a flow of blood for 12 years,

and who had suffered much under many physicians, and had spent all she had, and was no better but rather grew worse. She had heard reports about Jesus, and came up behind him in the crowd and touched his garment. For she said, 'If I touch even his garments, I shall be made well'. And immediately the haemorrhage ceased; and she felt in her body that she was healed of her disease.

(Mark 5, verses 25–30)

Attention is usually paid to the actual healing of the haemorrhage; I think the loss of power is interesting: 'And Jesus, perceiving in himself that power had gone forth from him, immediately turned about in the crowd, and said, "Who touched my garments?" ' (ibid.).

Orthodox Judaism insists that women are ritually cleansed by bathing when the menstrual flow has ceased. I conducted a recent interview in Israel with the now grown-up daughter of a Rabbi. She described to me when she was a young child how women would queue up to see her father to show him their underwear and ask if the period was sufficiently ended to resume sexual relations with their husbands. She vividly remembers at the age of 8 that if for any reason her father was not available, the same women would ask her, and accept her opinion. Christian beliefs regarding menstruation are currently being treated very seriously, through the heated and acrimonious debate concerning the ordination of women. Although rarely stated publicly, priests have euphemistically said to me that a woman would not be available at all times to minister to her flock.

Blood must be understood as a polysemic category in all cultures; and menstrual blood in most cultures has ambivalent beliefs and attitudes attached to it, particularly concerning power and pollution.

I want to suggest that these themes of power and pollution are in fact variations of the same set of beliefs and attitudes. The segregation of women who are menstruating from contact with men, often accompanied by rules concerning the handling of communal food, is a statement of the power of menstrual blood. Whether it is expressed in terms of disgust or danger, they are variants of the same power that is invested in women's cyclic emissions.

Bearing this example in mind, I now want to discuss the Temiars, who I feel have certain particular characteristics. For the Temiars, *all spilt blood* is dangerous. As we saw in Chapter 4, blood is healthy and life-enhancing provided that it is maintained as an integral part of the body. When it is spilt, whether by accident, intention or inevitability, then it is to be avoided, feared and ritualised. This was brought home to me most strongly when, shortly after my arrival in the field, my daughter tripped and cut herself on a sharp bush knife. The wound was deep and bled profusely over us both. My feeling was one of sheer helplessness when all the Temiars instantly vanished and did not appear again until later in the day when the wound was safely 'staunched' and all the blood had been cleared up. Some doctors conducting research in Malaysia informed me that when they arrived in a village to take some blood samples, the Temiars had just disappeared. The doctors had sent advance warning of their intention! We also discussed in Chapter 3 how the fear of blood is not only linked with coming into contact with it, but also the serious results of being too close to the smell of blood. If women and children venture too near to the smell of blood of certain slaughtered animals it results in *pocuk* illness, with symptoms of giddiness and loss of physical control.

Temiar men and women recognise that women menstruate every month and that it is the cessation of menstrual flow that indicates pregnancy. They are also clear that one cannot become pregnant unless one has started to menstruate. Women refer to their periods as *lɔɔt* (blood), and *ʔəd, na-jiʔ lɔɔt* (ill), or sometimes the Malay word *sakit* (ill) will be used. They also use words like *laʔəs* (bad, dirty). Men avoid mentioning it at all, but if they do, they use an avoidance term, *ʔɛsnɨs*. Benjamin suggests that this word is related to the noun for badness and filth, *ʔɛsnəs*. He also came across phrases which meant 'bad day' and 'cast-aside day' (1967b:172).

Any attempts at conversations with men about menstruation produce acute embarrassment and distaste and an insistence on avoidance of the topic. The little information that we could glean from men was that they must not have intercourse during menstrual bleeding and must not eat food prepared by a menstruating woman. Any man who has contact with menstrual blood even through food preparation will get severe wasting of the body, vomiting and convulsions. Healing seances may be held for an individual suffering in this way but it is considered to be frequently fatal.

However, for a shaman to have contact with menstrual blood is considered even more dangerous and he is likely not only to lose his spirit-guides (Benjamin 1967a:162) but also the menstrual blood that he touches will turn into a tiger and enter his *hup* and gnaw away at his feelings.

These powerful sanctions concerning menstruation mean that it is the one time when women must completely rely on each others' company. When on their own they will talk about their periods, symptoms and avoidances and there is a certain camaraderie in comparing notes. As I have said, women use their own language when talking to each other about periods and if they feel sufficiently ill due to either cramps or heavy bleeding they will consult the midwife. Women are not allowed to cook for their families, must sleep apart from their husbands, and are not allowed to bathe in the river while they are menstruating. They will usually wash themselves at the back of the house or at the edge of the forest, using water brought from the river. Bathing in the river is seen as making the river dirty or dangerous for other people, especially men. Old pieces of cloth are worn and then buried at the edge of the forest. Again, bloodstained clothing must not be allowed near or in the river. Not all of the younger women, particularly the unmarried ones, obeyed these river rules. Occasionally they would complain of being too hot and needing to bathe, and very occasionally they would wash a stained cloth in the river and let it dry. They would ensure that older women did not know they were doing this, and asked me not to give them away.

Women did not need to announce that they were inaccessible. The fact that they cooked for themselves, and that they were usually alone or with other menstruating women, and that another female relative would cook for their husbands and children, were non-verbal public statements. Although I did little cooking since I employed a family to cook for me, it was noticeable that men in the village always avoided coming to my house when I was menstruating. I was curious to know how they knew. Women who were menstruating have to avoid certain foods, in particular flesh, some vegetables, spices and salt, usually a milder set of prohibitions than those adhered to during the post-partum time, discussed on page 38. Contemporary research had demonstrated that women who live in close proximity with each other for more than six months usually synchronise their periods. I was given to speculation concerning the past, when most Temiars lived in communal long houses, as to whether there was any relationship between the lunar work cycle of the men and the menstrual cycle of the women.

The Temiars do make use of a lunar month when calculating their work routine of hunting and house building. The calculations vary by a few days and no one could give me the exact ordering of in-village and out-of-village activity. It must remain purely an etic speculation now that families as a rule live in separate houses whether the passage into the forest coincided with the inaccessibility of groups of women in the lunar and menstrual cycle.

Dentan (1968:99) has brief menstrual information about the Semai. He mentions food prohibition and avoidance of the river and intercourse, but not such extreme dangers as I and others found with the Temiars. One of his informants, however, said that menstrual fluid is like 'fish poison' and that if a menstruating woman joins in poisoning fish she will turn into a tiger. Thus the Semai link menstrual blood that is out of place with transformation into tigers.

In describing the prohibitions for the Mendriq, Batek Teh and some Batek De', Endicott (1979:90) says that women may not bathe in a stream during their periods. The reason given is that the thunder god and *naga'* do not like the smell of menstrual blood (and certain other blood from animals). The odour is supposed to rise like smoke and reach the thunder god. Endicott says that generally the Batek do not consider menstrual blood very polluting and are not concerned about the 'dirtiness'.

Apart from the avoidance of some foods, the river, and men generally, menstruating is not ritualised, as is a girl's first menstruation. At the first bleeding, the girl is taken by her mother and sometimes the village midwife to the edge of the forest. They take with them water that has been warmed on the fire in a large bamboo tube. The girl's sarong is removed and she stands naked under the tree. Her mother pours the warmed water through the leaves of the tree so that it goes over the girl's head and body and trickles down her pubic area. Her mother then dresses her in a new sarong and takes her back into the house, where she oils the girl's hair and then combs it. This only happens at first menstruation and is discreetly carried out at the back of the house at the forest edge with only women present. It is similar to post-partum ritual which I shall describe on page 145.

Menstruation, symbolically and in reality, belongs exclusively to the world of Temiar women. There is no male 'equivalent' in terms of blood, though we shall examine other male/female themes later, and it is a time when its own language, food and women's company are practised.

The letting of the blood of animals by human beings illustrates the relationship between men and ground-dwelling animals – as opposed to those animals which live off-the-ground. Other animals are too dangerous to bring near the village unless they have already been transformed in some way, as these animals have lower-body souls whose blood can seriously affect women and children. Conversely, lower-body blood from women can equally affect the safety of men and at its most serious cause transformation into a tiger, the most feared ground-dwelling animal. The persistent links between blood and tiger recur at all conceptual levels, alongside the reality of a real tiger's attraction to spilt blood. The essential human property of blood within the body can be seen to complement the permissible spilt blood of slaughtered animals of the forest. These categories are kept discrete in relation to gender, space and prepared food.

Although I will be discussing childbirth and pregnancy in further detail in Chapter 8, I want to address the actual birth and its accompanying beliefs as part of the management of dangerous blood belonging to the domain of women.

In many cultures, post-partum blood is as powerful and polluting as menstrual blood. The cleansing rituals in the Judaeo/Christian tradition are apt examples of this. The very term 'confinement' implies the setting apart of women at childbirth. Temiar women are usually confined to the kitchen area next to the fire for the delivery. The delivery room/kitchen is always on the jungle side of the house. As noted earlier, paths in and out of the village and especially the communal path down to the river, are always routed so that they do not pass people's back doors. One family who built a new compartment for an imminent delivery had to get some help to re-route the path to the river. The girl's father was adamant that the path must not go past the delivery room and met with older men in the village to discuss it. They agreed that they should cut through the undergrowth to make a new path round the other side of the house. In the room where the delivery takes place, the husband constructs a backboard of bamboo slanted at an angle of 45 degrees on a sturdy frame, against which the mother will lean during the birth. He also makes sure there is a plentiful supply of water and logs for the fire.

The midwife ascertains that the ground underneath the delivery room is well hoed so that any fluid will drain away without gathering into puddles on the surface. She also makes sure that there is a quantity of newly-cut branches that will be piled beneath the house to help absorb the fluid. The underneath of the delivery room with the hoed ground and the piled branches contrasts with the normally flat earth and cleared undergrowth of dwelling places.

If there has been shamanic intervention during the pregnancy, then there may still be leaves hanging from the ceiling which have been used to attract the good influences. The midwife makes sure that she has access to charcoal and ash from the fire, and coconut oil. She also makes use of other substances including fish bones and the leaves of the jack fruit – it varies with the individual midwife. There will also be plenty of children and young people nearby willing to go and fetch certain ingredients if required, and the father is usually on hand to carry out any heavy tasks. The midwife, and sometimes the shaman, makes bark *jampii?* water, using the same bark that is often tied round foreheads for a fever or headaches.

When labour pains start with any regularity, the expectant mother goes into the delivery room with the midwife and other close or older females. Usually a midwife will have a helper, a young woman who herself intends to practice one day; sometimes her daughter may be interested in becoming a midwife (see Plate 13). From the onset of labour (and sometimes before) the midwife keeps examining the woman internally to determine how far the cervix has dilated. The woman leans against the backboard with her legs well drawn up in a squatting position. Her sarong is tied tightly round her waist and she is usually bare from the waist upwards.

During these early stages the atmosphere is fairly informal. Women wander in and out and compare notes about their deliveries. Small girls sit in the doorway curious about what is going on and

Plate 13 Temiar traditional midwife

watching very intently. Sometimes small 'brave' boys peep through the floor slats if no one is looking. Different women take it in turns to massage the woman's shoulders and arms if she experiences discomfort. Men and boys stay at a distance, but near enough to carry out any lifting work such as fetching more logs and water. Once regular contractions start, the atmosphere becomes far more serious. The midwife herself attempts to manually dilate the cervix with the insertion of one finger at a time. She showed me how she needs to insert three fingers before the baby can be born, and she uses oil to help the dilation.

Nothing causes more anxiety than for the labour to be protracted. Everything possible is done to speed up the delivery process once the contractions are regular. I was initially quite shocked when I realised that beliefs concerning 'natural childbirth' which many people in the West have about primitive peoples were certainly fantasy as far as the Temiars are concerned. The Temiars quite consciously intervene in what for them is a highly dangerous process – the journey from intra-uterine to extra-uterine. In fact it is considered so dangerous that if it lasts more than a few hours the shaman is called to intervene.

While the midwife is internally manipulating between the contractions, she asks one of the stronger women to also assist her. Often, since I am larger than most Temiar men and women, she would ask me! On each contraction the helper holds the woman firmly round the waist and shakes her vigorously backwards and forwards. The woman is still squatting on the floor, so the act of lifting only takes her weight away from the backboard. This shaking is supposed to help quicken the contractions and hurry up the birth.

By this time there are usually just a few women, young and old, sitting at a distance just outside the delivery room, and perhaps one or two small girls discreetly watching. Some women will pop in briefly to see how the birth is progressing. The midwife may well have one or more helpers, apart from her assistant who will be doing the shaking (taking it in turns if one gets tired) and also continue to massage the woman's shoulders and arms. The midwife or her assistant starts to massage the woman's stomach with oil, and also gives her drinks of the bark water 'to keep her cool'. The mother is free to shout, moan or call out for people such as her mother or grandfather.

The midwife is very firm with the mother, particularly concerning her breathing. When she starts to breathe more shallowly, or even to hyper-ventilate, the midwife tells her to breathe more slowly and demonstrates, sometimes with a hand on her own diaphragm, to illustrate what she means. The midwife also gives the woman oil to drink as this is supposed to help ease the delivery. The oil is thus being taken internally, being massaged externally and also being used to dilate internally.

The bark water will not only be drunk from time to time but the midwife will also hold it a foot or so above the woman's abdomen and pour it so that it can trickle down over the pubic area. A paste made from mixing ground fish bones and leaves from the jack fruit with oil is sometimes spread across the abdomen by the midwife. These two ingredients, which are prohibited during pregnancy, are now used externally to help birth. As the dilation is increased, the midwife attempts to hold the head and gently pulls it on contractions.

As the birth becomes imminent, most people slip away, or remove themselves to a much further distance. Just before the birth itself, there are usually the midwife and her assistant present, with two or three others sitting outside.

The following example illustrates a typical childbirth:

The contractions have been regular since the middle of the afternoon and I and Halimah have been doing the 'shaking' at each contraction. The birth seems quite imminent now; the midwife has stopped doing internal examinations which she appears to do over-frequently, and says she can now get three fingers in and will check that I can as well, which I can.

The midwife draws a line from the woman's navel to her vulva with a paste made from charcoal and oil and starts to chant and ask 'Dato' Lengri' [see Chapter 8] to help the baby be born quickly.

She and her assistant spit-blow on to the abdomen and keep stroking downwards with the different medicines. She pours the water over her abdomen again. 'Come out, come out', she says intensely, and continues chanting.

The atmosphere is building up with extraordinary tension and those watching nearby are hushed and expectant. The midwife signals with a shout for things to 'open', and those sitting nearby opened their legs as wide as they could; they removed the lids of saucepans, opened the suitcases and opened the fishing net and laid it flat, and put up two umbrellas. All of us were carefully orchestrated into the group 'opening' as the baby was ejected onto the floor. There was a pause as the assistant put a foot on the mother's abdomen and pressed while the midwife held the cord. The placenta followed very rapidly.

(fieldwork notes)

The midwife calls out the sex of the child loud enough for the husband to hear. Once the baby is born, some waiting people go home, not wanting to be too near the blood. The baby is left lying on the slatted floor, still attached to the placenta, while attention is paid to the mother. The midwife uses water that has been warmed in a bamboo tube on the fire to wash the mother and remove all traces of blood from the pubic area.

The midwife then helps the mother to her feet, removes her stained sarong and holds a bamboo containing warm water at a height and pours it so that it runs down over her head and body to her pubic area. The mother is then dressed in a clean, but not new, sarong, and the midwife sits her on a pile of warmed leaves taken from the tops of cassave stems. She then combs and oils the mother's hair. The midwife then turns her attention to the baby while the mother, although quite exhausted, may start to rinse some of the blood out of her stained clothing, which is soaking in water.

The midwife measures the cord to the baby's knee and then cuts it with a sliver of new bamboo. It is not tied but later sprinkled with turmeric. The midwife washes the baby very thoroughly with warm water and then massages it with her hands which she keeps warming at the fire, and pays particular attention to the head. She wraps the baby in an old piece of sarong and hands it to the mother so that she can hold it to the breast to get to 'know it'. One woman wanted to sleep after the delivery and the midwife said sharply, 'Give him the breast or he will forget'.

While the child is being held to the mother's breast and there is an expectation that there will be some attempt at suckling, the midwife bathes herself and all those who have been involved in the actual delivery, i.e. those who have handled the mother and baby at the birth (not those who have been joining in the 'opening' outside the room). She makes sure that there is no blood still on them, and washes their feet and the floor area before finally washing her own hands and feet.

Having washed away any excess blood from the placenta, she wraps it in a cloth or places it in a bag, and calls the father, who has been waiting nearby; he takes the placenta into the forest and ties it to a tree. Once all the washing is complete, the branches underneath the house are removed and thrown into the bushes at the edge of the forest and the ground is hoed again by the midwife or one of the women to make sure that all fluid has drained away. If the birth occurs during the night, everyone will prepare to sleep; the father comes in to see the baby and speak with his wife for a few moments, but he does not stay. The midwife sleeps with the mother who is made comfortable next to the fire, with the baby, well padded out with cloth, lying next to her.

I have considered in some detail the circumstances surrounding childbirth which shares many similar beliefs with menstruation generally and also ritual similarities with first menstruation.

The birth itself is a time predominantly for women, when older women will assist in the early stages and talk with the midwife; a younger woman may help and younger girls will be around both to help and to watch as much as they are allowed. Men stay very much at a distance, except for the husband who fetches and carries. Other men, if they are around, may call out across the village to enquire about the progress of the delivery. However, as the birth becomes imminent, only the most 'brave' of Temiar women stay for the actual birth. Great care is taken after the birth over the bathing of the mother who has been in a state of ritual danger, an 'in-between', liminal stage that the Temiars believe is so dangerous; hence the speeding up of the labour with voluntary shaking and cervical dilation. Post-partum blood is considered as polluting or dangerous as menstrual blood. All women who have attended the birth, although they do not stay in the house where the birth took place, nevertheless keep the same dietary taboos and do not go to the river during the post-partum time.

As with menstruation there is the fear of contamination from post-partum blood and the mother and midwife stay together in the house until the flow has stopped. Not only is there a fear of contagion but again, concern about the smell of blood. There is also the fear of unwelcome attention from malevolent spirits and predatory ground-dwelling animals who might be attracted by the smell of blood. The husband therefore lights fires just outside the delivery room to keep away any unwelcome attention. Often he will put chilli branches on the fire as a deterrent (cf. death and sickness rituals discussed in Chapter 8).

The dietary restrictions after childbirth both for the mother and the midwife are the most severe of all food avoidance. At the end of the post-partum period, mother and midwife are able to have additional foods, although they are still restricted. The father also maintains food restrictions but they are not as severe as for the mother and the midwife.

In both the post-partum time and the menstrual period, women are restricted in their social contact, their spatial freedom and their diet. Just as the girl at her first menstruation is taken to the forest edge, her clothes removed, and bathed with warm water poured from a height through a bamboo tube, similarly the newly-delivered mother is bathed inside the house while naked with warm water poured from a height through bamboo. The girl is dressed in a new sarong whereas the mother is dressed in a clean but old sarong. There was strong insistence on this when I questioned the midwife. She said that the new baby must also not have new clothing.

One could suggest that the first menstruation was the move into a new status, whereas with the mother it was the beginning of a return to an old status. Conceptually the relationship between first menstruation and childbirth could be represented by the following:

to become fertile			to give birth
	:	:	
ground			off-the-ground
	:	:	
new			old
	:	:	
outside			inside

Ground/off-the-ground categories apply to location of the ritual; during first menstruation the water is poured from a height through the leaves of the tree, and the leaves that are used for the mother to sit on during the post-partum bleeding are from the top of the ubiquitous cassava plant (though this association is not consciously articulated by the Temiar).

We have seen how in both menstruation and childbirth women manage blood that pours *involuntarily* from the body. They manage it by regulation of diet, clothing, spatial freedom, social contact and more specifically their relationship with men. A dominent theme is the avoidance of the river in case the water itself becomes dangerous. We have seen how the biggest fear is the contamination of men resulting in serious illness or death if they come into contact with this blood.

However, there is also a *voluntary* act where women manage blood and are seen to be very powerful, and this is the thunder ritual.

It has been described to me by many women and they have shown me the scars on their legs where they have cut themselves with bush knives. However, I did not witness an actual performance (Benjamin also reports a similar lack of firsthand evidence (1967a:215)). In Chapter 3 I mentioned various prohibitions which, if contravened, could result in major thunderstorms. *Karey*, the thunder deity, comes closer to look at what is going on and possibly sends down the large cords that can enter the house, catch people by the throat and pull them into the fire.

I have already described the usual discouragement of thunder through the burning of hair on a log and the blowing of smoke towards the storm. However, if the storm worsens there is a transition from the hair to the blood ritual, the former usually taking place in a doorway at the back of the house, the latter being performed on the ground in the centre of the village. The following graphic description from Slimming (1954) features the wife of *Pɛnghulu Dalam*, one of my informants and also an experienced midwife.

Dalam's wife bundled all her possessions in a piece of cloth and carried them to the doorway. She stood on the top step with several other women and they screamed and shouted at the storm, clenching their fists and shaking them at the sky. The men sat, silent, by the fire waiting for the storm to finish, but the women defied it and cried out in anger and fear.

'Go away, storm! Go away! Either you go or we shall go!'

'Either you leave or we shall leave!'

'Go! Go!'

And they clung on to their small bundles of possessions and shook them up at the sky. They had pulled out their hair-combs and now their hair was hanging forward, plastered over their faces. Dalam's wife ran back into the room towards the fire ... and several of the other women followed her. She searched for a *parang* – reached for it – and cut her leg, lightly, below the knee. I suddenly realised that this was the blood sacrifice that I heard about and had never seen. Blood from the wound trickled down her calf and she caught some of it in a bamboo cup – the other women were cutting themselves; one of them standing on the hot embers of the fire as she did so and not noticing it. Each carried a cup with blood in it and they slopped water in with the blood and ran out into the thundering darkness. The cleared space was lit up with flashes of blue-white light and the women ran about in the mud, scattering blood on the ground and calling out above the noise of the pounding rain.

(Slimming 1954:154–5)

Temiar women described to me how they cut their legs with bush knives and catch the blood in bamboo tubes, mix it with rain-water and then throw it towards the thunder while shouting at *Karey* to go away. They said that the only reason I had not seen it was that there was not a sufficiently bad storm to warrant it. I would add that, if there is the sound of thunder in the distance, men and women alike will shake a fist or a bush knife towards the sound and shout for it to stay away. Apart from ear piercing in which there seems to be no blood flow as it is done so gradually, this appears to be the only act of voluntary blood-letting by humans, and always by women, although we saw in Chapter 4 how tattooing had been performed in the past. Dentan (1968) and Endicott (1979) report similar thunder rituals in their ethnographies. Endicott reports several suggestions as to how it accomplishes its purpose. However, he says that they are fully formed alternative conceptions and not just confused variations of a single interpretation (see especially Chapter 5, p. 159).

I would suggest that the significance of the blood ritual lies in the response to cosmic 'disorder'. Thunder is seen as malevolent, punishing and bad, and likely to bring about disruption and danger if it comes too close. Therefore it 'makes sense' for the Temiars to respond to this 'disorder' in the human domain, i.e. the opposition of the normal integrity of the body where blood must be maintained. In this instance it is spilt in order to dissuade thunder from staying near. Why it is supposed to work the Temiars could not say, except that there appeared to be some idea that thunder would be pleased, unlike other preventive practices such as the burning of chilli branches and hair which are considered unpleasant for *Karey* – they said the chilli smoke would get in his eyes. Perhaps to ask *why* the Temiars participate in and initiate such rituals is not the most helpful of questions. One could as easily answer *why not*. As Lewis says in his Gnau study, if we focus our attention on the search for meaning in ritual and symbol, may we not in fact misunderstand the very nature of ritual? He suggests that what is clear in ritual is knowing 'how to do it' rather than 'knowing what it means'. He says:

The efficacy of substitutes or symbols lies in their ability to release a response and this depends on a combination of their intrinsic attributes, the context in which they are set, and the power of expectation (the mental set, arousal and readiness to respond) on the part of the animal or person who perceives them.

(1980:116)

Benjamin (1994) suggests that free blood – i.e. bleeding – is acceptable when used deliberately to achieve some balance in the world, as in the blood-offering rituals, since it is counterbalanced by the fact that free blood is not usually acceptable. However, he suggests that menstrual blood presents a problem because it does *not* have a counterbalance such as the shedding of hair.

I have discussed the central role of Temiar women in relation to female blood and in its management. The first two examples concern the involuntary blood of menstruation and post-partum blood. Women generally and midwives in particular are managing the blood of individuals and are ensuring the protection of other individuals through essential action witnessed only by select women. In the blood ritual for thunder, women are the managers of a voluntary blood flow to ensure the safety of the community as a whole, and it is conducted in the public domain.

In a society that maintains various age stages – play, fertility and wisdom – and maintains the integrity of the parents and small children, we can see that in the management of blood there is a separation of gender more than in any other activity. This is a domain in which all women participate by the very fact that they menstruate, while men cannot. In the domain of blood the separation is absolute, so powerful are the resultant illnesses if prohibitions are broken.

However, we must also be aware that cross-cutting the separation of gender is the connection of blood with the Temiars' most feared entities, tiger and blood. Women are not just responsible for the protection of their menfolk; they also have great responsibilities and power to act for the community as a whole by maintaining the distance of these most feared, larger-than-life, epic metaphors. Just as thunder and tiger are ways of being able to express and talk about the presence of evil, so blood, a polysemic metaphor *par excellence*, is powerful enough if appropriately managed to lessen the possibility of the proximity of evil. Nevertheless, the very rituals themselves alert Temiar men and women to the presence of the very things that they fear.

Chapter 8

Temiar healers
Shaman and midwives

Every physician must also be metaphysician.
(Meier quoted in Fordham 1978)

The Doctor:
Unnatural deeds
Do breed unnatural troubles; infected minds
To their deaf pillows will discharge their secrets,
More needs she the divine than the physician.
(*Macbeth*, Act 5.i)

In this chapter I want to concentrate in more detail on styles and practices of Temiar healing and on the healers themselves. I have already discussed the role of the midwife when I described the rituals surrounding childbirth and menstruation, and throughout I have had to refer to the activities of the shaman. Indeed the need to anticipate and cross-reference stems from the problem of isolating the subject, as it permeates every level of Temiar existence. It is impossible to talk about the Temiars without reference to their shamanistic practices. However, I shall argue that since shamanism takes place in what I term the more visible domain, it has led to an imbalance in writings on the Temiars. Midwifery takes place in the less visible and therefore less accessible sector of Temiar life. Hence my emphasis on the significance and essential complementarity of midwifery practices.

The Temiars say that most ordinary mortals can become shaman and midwives, and that it is a matter of personal choice whether or not individuals choose to develop their potential. The Temiar term for a shaman is *halaa?*, spelt variously in the literature as *halakk*, *halaag* and *halaa*. Occasionally they use the Malay words of *bomoh* or *pawang*. *Halaa?* also describes the potential for being a shaman and the meeting of an individual with a person's spirit-guide in dreams (see Chapter 6). Dentan (1968:181), when discussing the Semai, uses the word adept for shaman when he says, 'all Senoi believe that people may be more or less "adept" (*halaag*)', and the word is used extensively in subsequent literature by other researchers (see for example, Benjamin 1967b; Roseman 1984, 1993).

Almost without exception, the Temiar *halaaʔ* are male. In the sparse accounts of Temiar female *halaaʔ* they are described as being particularly powerful. Benjamin (1967b:285) refers to a female shaman by the name of *ʔalɔb* who lived in a more remote region in Perak and of whom the Kelantan Temiars were very frightened (ibid:284). She had a reputation of harming strangers, in particular 'fat children, handsome young men and shaman' (ibid:285). During my stay I heard of only one female shaman, *ʔamɔɔʔ Luŋ* by repute from the village of Lambok, who was said to be very clever, particularly in the *ciɲcɛm*. It would seem that midwifery, which itself uses similar practices, medicines and chants to those of the shaman, is the usual healing role for women. Midwifery too attracts apprentices. Roseman also mentions a female *halaaʔ* whom I suggest is the same woman mentioned above:

> Women more rarely become adept as *halaaʔ* though the precedent exists: for example there was one woman of renown in Lambok, Amok Jerwan Long, who was a *halaaʔ* of several types of spirit-guides and vocal genres, including *ciɲcɛm* (spirits of dead humans), *ʔɛŋkuu ʔ* (thunder) and *poɲey* (a type of flower).
>
> (1984:416)

This is the only instance I have come across of thunder as spirit-guide. I have already discussed the link between women and thunder in Chapter 7. Dentan, for the Semai, also mentions the skill of the female *halaaʔ*:

> There are varying degrees of *halaaʔ*. Women are very rarely more than just a little *halaaʔ*, but a really *halaaʔ* woman is more successful than most male *halaaʔ* in the diagnosis and cure of diseases.
>
> (1968:85)

The Temiar say that there are two ways of becoming a shaman, either through self-teaching and the gradual building up of a reputation, or else by being an apprentice to an established shaman and working as his assistant. I met shaman in both categories, including young hopeful aspirants as well as trainees, and also the older more established practitioners. Above all a shaman has to be mature; it is only by having lived long enough that the Temiars believe a shaman (or other specialist) really knows. They use the expression *na-lɛk* (she/he knows) to indicate not just factual knowledgeability but wisdom as a person. Becoming a shaman is considered to be a great responsibility and to require time and commitment to the occupation. Many Temiars choose not to develop their shamanistic potential but nevertheless practice healing in a small way from time to time, and certainly would not refuse to assist (*toloŋ*) if asked.

We saw in Chapter 6 how most people from adolescence onwards will dream of a *gonig* (spirit-guide) who meets with the person in their dreams. The *gonig* appears as both the dreamer's child and teacher in the form of a small person, yet it is recognisable as a fruit, flower or off-the-ground animal. The dreamer takes notice if the dream encounters are persistent, and in these encounters the dreamer may be taught something new that can be imparted to the community. We say earlier how the teaching can be of practical day-to-day use such as hunting and also essentially creative in terms of new songs, dances and cures. An aspiring shaman teaches the new song or dance to the community at a seance and it is this public acceptance of his personal dream revelation that is considered to be the start of his progress to shaman status. The villagers are usually excited and eager to learn, and a seance is held at which the new piece is taught. Ultimately however, a successful shaman depends specifically on successful healing, and more generally on the head-soul protection of the community. He has to be able to demonstrate regularly his competence in preventive medicine at the seances, as well as curative medicine in both non-seance as well as seance healing. Head-soul (*rəwaay*) management is at the root of the shaman's practice, whether collectively at the seance performances or individually in more private healing rituals.

The Temiar refer to several grades of shaman although these distinctions are not absolute and I found variations in different people's perceptions of particular shaman. Broadly speaking they use the categories of minor, middle and major shaman respectively (*ʔamɛs, gagid* and *rayaaʔ*), but they also use a fourth category, *halaaʔ mənuuʔ*, meaning great shaman. Great shaman are usually the highest grade of shaman, the tiger shaman of whom there are very few at any one time, the title passing down in each river valley. The tiger shaman's skills and practice are described in more detail in relation to the tiger seances. Most shaman begin as minor shaman following the guidance of dream revelation; spirit-guides of *off-the-ground* species. Higher grades of shaman have spirit-guides from *on-the-ground* species. It is the major and great shaman that are able to accept power not just from the head-souls of off-the-ground and ground species, but also from the heart/blood-soul, the lower body soul, of species on-the-ground.

Midwives are not graded in the same way as shaman though some are more popular than others. The government-appointed midwife for the Betis area (the same midwife mentioned in the Introduction who was angry that I 'stole' her voice, namely by capturing it on tape) was generally not liked by expectant mothers for delivering their babies. Although they were somewhat in awe of her training and techniques, together with her rudimentary equipment, they nevertheless referred to her as unlike the village midwives with their traditional knowledge.[1] She was considered new (*paay*) rather than traditional (*manah*). Most women are considered to have the knowledge to deliver children, especially if they have given birth themselves (see Chapter 1 for Kleiman's definition of 'popular health care', p. 19). When I first demurred at being a midwife, the village midwife who asked me said that I must know what to do since I had had children myself. Midwives are called *bidat* and are considered brave, clever and having knowledge and experience. Midwifery, like shamanism, is not an occupation that is undertaken lightly. Most women avoid being present at the actual birth, although they are willing to assist during labour.

I began to understand the reluctance to become a midwife when *Busuuʔ*, my Temiar assistant, discussed his children with me. He said he would like his children to be clever and to attend school and then perhaps to work. Perhaps his daughter could work in Kuala Lumpur, he thought. When I asked him if he meant at the aboriginal hospital as a nurse, he reacted very strongly: 'All that blood; it's very dirty and she would have to touch all those sick bodies. It's not nice. No, I don't want her to be a nurse' (fieldwork notes).

Busuuʔ kept using the Temiar word for filth (*ʔɛsnəs*) the word often used to refer to women's periods, and he expressed disgust at the thought of her having contact with blood. Temiar midwives are considered brave to be in constant contact with blood, they are also recognised for having to accept the burden of constant avoidance and restrictions. We saw in Chapter 7 how midwives have to observe the same food restrictions as their newly-delivered mothers. These restrictions can last for most of her life if she is regularly delivering children. The midwife as well as the new mother is thought to influence the head-soul of the new-born infant. Since most midwives are older women past child-bearing age, the avoidances they practice are a continuation of those they have already maintained during their own years of fertility. Dalam's wife, who is childless, told me she became a midwife when she was quite young, when she realised she could not have children of her own. She said that midwives had to be on a restricted diet all their lives, that it was part of their job and she did not see it as undue hardship.

Midwives without exception are female; I have heard of no instance (except for the following exception) of a man or shaman delivering a child. The one exception reported to me was in the case of ʔabiləm, a major shaman from the village of Bawik. He and others told me that a woman had been close to death because the baby was in the wrong position to be born (transverse presentation); according to all the reports, ʔabiləm manipulated the baby internally, delivered it, and both mother and child lived. However, shaman are sometimes summoned by the midwife to perform *jampii?* or *tɛnhool* on the woman's head if she is believed to be seriously ill. If that happens then a screen is hung behind the backboard and the shaman stands behind it, and only has contact with the woman's head (see case history 1, p. 148). Sometimes a shaman recites *jampii?* at a distance and does not even come into the house. He may send some water and medicinal bark that has been chanted over, and this is drunk by or poured over the woman during labour. Dentan (1968:97) report that in Semai childbirth, the husband helps the midwife during labour and will knead the woman's stomach or sprinkle her with water to keep her supernaturally cool. Whereas with the Batek, according to Endicott (1979:99), all men including the husband withdraw from the birth hut before birth takes place. However, as with the Temiars, a man may recite some *jampii?* at a discreet distance if there are complications.

Minonɔɔʔ, the daughter of Mentri Suleiman, the retired headman of the region, has a well-established reputation as a good midwife both in the village of Asam where we were based, as well as generally in the Betis area. She delivered her younger daughter's baby as well as her granddaughter's while I was there. It was from her that I learned most about midwifery practice following her request that I and my daughter act as her assistants. As with shamanism, an aspiring midwife will become an assistant to one who is practising and experienced. *Minonɔɔʔ*'s middle daughter, a woman with two children herself, assisted in several deliveries. Women in the same family often become midwives, though the Temiars did not see it as hereditary; rather they saw it as an opportunity to learn from a more experienced relative. Although there are some midwives who are the wives of shaman there did not appear to be an observable pattern to this. Dalam and his wife were the most strongly active partnership in shamanism and midwifery. However, although his wife assisted regularly at seances, he did not assist at childbirth unless at a distance, like other shaman.

Midwives are not referred to as *halaaʔ* in any systematic way and do not usually talk about spirit-guide appearances any more than do other ordinary non-shaman Temiars. Dentan (1968:96) says that the Semai consider midwives to be a 'little *halaaʔ*' because childbirth involves dealing with such mysterious dangers. However, we saw how older women and midwives call upon *Datoʔ Leŋgriʔ*, one of the most powerful and feared tiger-souls, said to be the heart-soul of the Mikong who was traditionally the intermediary between the Orang-Asli and the Malays. Bejamin (1976b:27) says that *Datoʔ Leŋgriʔ* is 'a vast tiger spirit guarding the debouchement of the Nenggiri river'. *Datoʔ Leŋgriʔ* is called upon by women both in childbirth and also in the hair-rituals practised to appease thunder.

Both midwives and shaman are called by their patients *tohaat* (healer); the term is used by patients during and after successful treatment; and children who have been delivered by the midwife as they grow up learn to call her *tohaat*. Conversely shaman and midwives refer to their patients as *cɔɔʔ*, the same term that the Temiars use towards their pets which underlies the dependent relationship. *Tohaat* is also the term used by the Temiars for the deity in charge of the flower garden of the afterlife where the head-souls of dead Temiars reside. They also refer to *Yaaʔ-Podɛɛw*, granny sunset (see Benjamin 1967b:147), as being in charge of the garden. We will also recall that *Cɛŋkey* was the founding shaman-midwife-ancestress of the Temiars. If questioned repeatedly on afterlife, the Temiars say that it is all to do with *tohaat*.

The Batek believe in a deity called *Tohan* 'who lived where the sun goes down' (Endicott 1979:83), who occurs in their original creation myth and is also considered to be a god, who is able to enforce sanction, and is believed to both give and retrieve life-souls. *Tohan* for the Batek is a shaman. However, Dentan suggests that the West Semai have been influenced by Malay beliefs when they say that the *halaa?* of midwives enable them to be in touch with the 'First Midwife'. He says that they seek aid from the first midwife who:

> dwells in the uppermost tier of the seven layered heavens and from the six other Midwives in the other tiers. Since six is the magic number of the Semai and seven of the Malays, there is some reason to think that the notion of the 'Seven Midwives' was originally Malay.
>
> (1979:96)

We can see that the term *tohaat* is used to describe both the role of healer for shaman and midwives as well as the deity responsible for both creation and the afterlife. Both in the supernatural sense as well as in the human setting of childbirth and shamanic healing, the term *tohaat* subsumes gender differentiation and incorporates the essential complementarity of male and female creation, healing and afterlife roles.

Midwives and shaman employ various techniques and substances for driving out illness and implanting soul-essence in the sick and/or pregnant woman. The most common are as follows:

Techniques	Substances
blowing	oil
sucking	water
tongue-clucking	smoke
spitting	saliva
massage	and specific medicines
spraying	(*?obad*)
chanting	
shouting	
muttering	

The most common is *tenhool*, the Temiar word for the technique of blowing through a clenched hand on to the person's head-soul, heart-soul or on to that area of the body where an offending substance or object is supposed to be. When the shaman uses *tenhool* it is usually preceded by the milking of his own heart-soul to obtain some of the spirit-guide essence. However, the breath is also linked with the *hup*, the seat of feelings and will and where the heart soul resides, so the breath itself is seen as having healing properties. The shaman usually commences with noisy sucking through the clenched hand to extract any offending substance, often accompanied by clucking of the tongue. He may extract either an actual object (see case history 6,

p. 150), or will say that he, as shaman, can see an object (although no one else can). Either way, the object is disposed of and then the *tɛnhool* is thought to impart some strength to the patient.

Both midwives and shaman spit with their own saliva during healing. Spitting usually intersperses chanting or muttering of incantations (*jampii ?*), and is like a spit-blow which allows a fine spray of saliva to reach the offending principle that is believed to be causing the illness, the head- or heart-soul or a wound or bite, scratch or burn. The midwife shouts to the baby to come out. The shouting can be also interspersed with spitting or spraying. Spraying is also used by the shaman at a healing seance. He collects fluid from the spirit-guides which are thought to be resting on the central decorations and uses it to transmit the healing substance to everyone in the room. Sometimes he will have a bowl of water underneath the decorations in which the essence is believed to collect and he dips the whisk in the water before spraying the assembled community. Midwives do not use a whisk but will sprinkle *jampii?* water with their fingers or pour the water from above the woman and let it trickle down her pubic area. We saw in Chapter 7 how the midwife or older woman blows the smoke from burned hair towards thunder, to try and persuade it to go away. Similarly they place branches of smouldering chilli in the paths leading to the village for people to stand over if they have visited a sick or dead person. The burning chilli is supposed to discourage any sickness or ghost that may have accompanied the person on their return. After a seance of the more serious kind, older women take a tray of burning charcoal that has been sprinkled with aromatic herbs to each person who has been heavily entranced and assists them in bathing their body, but especially their head, in the smoke. Similarly, specially prepared cigarettes are placed in the mouths of those sitting in a dazed condition after trancing. Smoke emanating from evil-smelling substances is used to keep undesired entities away from the village, whereas perfumed smoke is used inside the house to attract the person's head-soul back to them and to integrate them into the conscious life again.

Both shaman and midwives use massage in their healing. A shaman often massages a patient's head-soul or heart/blood-soul or another part of the body which is thought to contain the offending substance. He also applies pressure with the flat of his hand on the forehead, crown of the head, the chest and the stomach as a way of transmitting his curative power. He uses a similar technique *pərɛnluʰb* when passing on his spirit-guide essence to an apprentice shaman. He stands behind the trainee, places his hand on his chest and sways with him; usually the younger man starts to stagger and bounce round the room, entranced by the essence from the spirit-guide via the shaman medium. We saw in Chapter 7 how midwives massage newborn babies from birth for the first few months. They pay particular attention to the closure of the fontanelle gap, and the massage is said to strengthen the head-soul which is weak and unformed at birth. The midwife also massages the woman during labour, and other women will assist by massaging her neck and shoulders. She is often massaged after the birth too, to relieve aching muscles. Midwives and older women massage the husbands' backs which ache after long expeditions in the forest, and I noticed one shaman being massaged by his daughter walking on his back when he was in particular pain.

Water is used as a therapeutic medium by both shaman and midwives; however, I observed oil being used only by midwives. Principally she makes use of it for massaging a woman in labour, and for dilating the cervix; she also encourages the mother to drink it so that the baby will be born more easily. After the baby is born and all the clearing up is complete, she oils the hair of the newly-delivered mother before combing it in a similar ritual to that of first menstruation.

I have described the various physical techniques used by shaman and midwives together with the healing application of water, oil, saliva and smoke. There is also a range of medicines that are used by healers; my list is by no means complete and needs to be supplemented by further research. Medicines can be prescribed by all Temiar healers, although apart from the *jampii?* water described above, shaman prescribe fewer medicines than midwives. They both recommend various pastes made from mixing ash with oil, barks and roots, and these pastes are smeared on the forehead, cheeks, chest and stomach for a plethora of aches and pains. Shaman also give amulets made from wild garlic which are tied round the neck or wrist to ward off malevolent spirits or prevent colds and chills. If an infant is unwell, the baby and its mother will wear an amulet. Midwives usually brew medicines by boiling roots, leaves or bark in bamboo for menstruation and post partum difficulties. Midwives are also consulted by men for sexual problems concerning their virility. As I mentioned in Chapter 2, the Temiars recognise that the Negritos have stronger medicines than they possess and that their shaman are more powerful but also more dangerous. They do consult their Negrito neighbours about healing from time to time but this is always tinged with a sense of danger.

For minor ailments, whether a shaman or a midwife is involved, the treatment can either be done in the healer's or the patient's home. There is usually a small payment of two or three dollars, or a gift of a sarong or tobacco. Unlike the shaman's cures which are usually effected in the doorway or the main room of the house, the midwife generally performs her treatment at the back of the house, often in the kitchen by the fire. Even when not newly delivered, ill women sit by the fire and sometimes sleep there, clutching warm bunches of cassava leaves to their stomachs. Men lie next to the fire if they are seriously ill, otherwise they are in the main room or in their sleeping compartments.

If the illness is more serious, the shaman visits the patient's house. He is usually sent for by an anxious relative or the midwife. There may not be a local major shaman, so messages are sent to other villages. Minor shaman would already have tried their skills before a major shaman arrives or is summoned. Just as the midwife is committed to the infant and mother throughout the delivery and post-partum time, the shaman makes a similar commitment with serious illness. If he agrees to begin treatment then he is also obliged to stay in proximity to the patient until recovery. This places a heavy demand on the shaman, especially if he is not from the area, and shaman may refuse. The first requirement for the seriously ill person is to keep on a restricted diet and stay in the house and off-the-ground. The patient may be isolated behind a curtain or small partition with a separate fire. No visitors are allowed apart from close relatives who provide care. It is often an older man or woman, usually a relative, who cares for someone who is dangerously ill. The shaman performs *tɛnhool* and *jampii?* regularly during the day, and he will also return at night. The Temiars say that the sick person must be isolated for their own protection; they remain behind the curtain so that no shadow falls on them. This is also why visitors are not allowed. However, the concern expressed when I visited a very ill person lest I had brought back the illness or potential death on my person, suggests an additional fear of contagion.

I have described some of the techniques, media and medicines used in shamanistic and miwifery practice, but I also maintain that there are many dimensions which we are unable to understand. The following narrative from my fieldwork notes occurred after we had been staying with the Temiars for eight months or so. We had been staying in Lambok for two weeks as guests of Pɛnghulu Dalam when Hal, my 7-year-old son, developed a very high fever. I was extremely anxious, as Hal had a glazed look in his eyes and complained of severe pain in his throat.

We are staying at Trula with the Headman Dalam, who is also a shaman of big reputation. Hal has developed a high temperature, well over 100 degrees. We are due to leave for Betis tomorrow, but I am wondering whether to take Hal out by helicopter and get him to hospital. Dalam asked me if I would like him to try Temiar medicine, not to have a special seance but to treat him at his house. Hal and I went to Dalam's house and they sat in the doorway, Hal looked very poorly. Dalam started to massage him, first on his head and then his stomach. He performed *tɛnhool* (the sucking and blowing routine), blew on him and then continued the massage. He concentrated on Hal's stomach and then opened his hand and showed Hal a *pebble*. Hal was overwhelmed and said, 'Was that in my tummy?' Dalam said that it was and that was why he was very ill. Hal's temperature dropped noticeably and I privately thought that Dalam must have had the opportunity to conceal the stone in the cloth wound round his head. I said nothing and Hal looked definitely brighter.

Acknowledging Temiar custom I said to Dalam that I knew Hal should stay within his care until he was quite recovered. Dalam told me that it was all right, as he was going to ask one of his friends to look after us, and we can still travel to Betis. I assumed that he meant a fellow shaman living further down the river. We set off in Busu's log boat and had been poling for about twenty minutes when Busu said quietly to me, 'Look up there'.

I looked and there was a big bird that had flown out of the jungle and was circling over the boat. I looked at Busu cryptically and he said, very impressed, 'Dalam said he would ask a friend to look after Hal'.

I scorned the idea, and Busu shrugged his shoulders and said, 'Wait and see'.

The brown bird, (not often seen in travels up and down the rivers) followed us all the way to Betis – occasionally coming out of the jungle and circling over the boat. Once we had reached Betis it flew away and we did not see it again.

(fieldwork notes)

After I arrived in Betis I was still in two minds whether to take Hal to hospital. His temperature was now normal and although a little tired from the fever he seemed well enough. I decided to monitor his progress for a few days and, if there was any deterioration, to take him to hospital. There was no relapse, but a month later we all went for a check-up; the doctor remarked on Hal's speedy recovery from such a high fever, due he thought to an ear and throat infection.

The following are brief case histories from my fieldnotes which illustrate the variation in healing practices and also attitudes towards self-healing and western medicine.

CASE HISTORIES

1   I went to Mentri Suleiman's house and Mereja was crying; his eyes were hurting and he had been rubbing them. Mentri was quietly doing some *jampi* on his eyes and gently spitting on them with a fine spray. I sat and watched and asked if English medicine would be useful. It was obvious that Mereja had conjunctivitis and was in a lot of pain. Mentri welcomed the idea of other medicines, so I gave him aureomycin and lent him my dark glasses, which cheered him up immediately. The eyes began to improve in twenty-four hours, and Mentri and I both continued our treatment conjointly.

2   I went to visit Jemino in the house opposite mine and she was sitting in the doorway looking miserable. She said she had a bad headache but did not need the shaman (or my painkillers!). Her husband *Long* had got her some special bark strips which she had soaked in water and tied round her head like a bandanna. I remember on another occasion she had put a Chinese plaster on her forehead which is *hot* for the same ailment, as opposed to the bark which is very cool.

3   Today I am walking to Pos Lambok as the medical helicopter is coming and I want to meet the doctor and talk to him. *Along* has asked me to get some antibiotics for him, and Mentri Suleiman wants cough mixture and I have run out. (He coughs badly at night – previously he has had TB.) On my return to Asam, *Long* is delighted with the antibiotics, but to my surprise does not take them with water as prescribed, but opens up two spansules [capsules] and mixes the powder with some water and smears it on some bamboo cuts on his leg that look infected. He can't see the sense of *eating* them when his leg hurts!

4   Lima has not been out for a couple of days. She is pregnant and

has never looked particularly well. I went over to her house and her mother said she was in *pantang* (taboo). She is sitting in a secluded place at the back of the house with a sarong acting as a partition. I was told not to go too near her until she is better. We talked from a distance and she said she felt ill and hot. She had access to the platform at the back of the house, presumably to defecate and urinate, as she was not allowed to go out of the house, even to the river. Busu Selbon (a shaman) came from Kuala Betis and did some *jampi* and said she must stay in *pantang*. She is not allowed any non-Temiar medicine and is being kept on a bland diet, seclusion and *jampi* from the shaman.

I was interested in the difference between case history 1, where the shaman concerned was quite happy with the combined treatment, and case history 4, where there was an explicit ban on non-Temiar medicine. In all the cases of childbirth that I attended and also instances where small babies were ill, only the midwife and shaman prescribed the treatment and there is avoidance of anything *gɔb* (foreign). I was also not permitted to take photographs of sick people, and there is a total ban on taking pictures at or after childbirth or for some weeks after the birth. The following case histories develop further the theme of childbirth, and the involvement of both shaman and midwife.

5   The children have all been kept away from Lima's house tonight and there is a lot of noise. She is the woman who has been ill during her pregnancy and has been put in *pantang* by the *hala'*, usually Mereja her uncle. I went over to the house and quietly watched; it was too busy for me to ask questions. There was the midwife and Mbong, her daughter, pressing on Lima's abdomen. It had black smudges on it from some medicine, and she was calling to the baby to be born. Lima was leaning against a back platform and behind that hung a screen; behind the screen stood Mereja who was working himself into quite a state (entranced?), chanting and calling out, with his hand pressed on Lima's hand. The chanting and shouting orchestrated together and reached a climax when the baby was ejected onto the bamboo slats of the floor. At that point Mereja left and returned much later to do some *jampi*. Meanwhile the midwife and helper commenced the cleaning up while I and some others watched at a distance. First she ritually bathed the mother and then cut the cord with a piece

of bamboo. Ayeh, the baby's father, was in the background bringing more water and handing it up into the house. He lit two fires outside at the corners of the compartment where the baby was born. The midwife then gave him the placenta in a cloth, which she told me would tie to a tree in the forest.

6   Jelimo has now been in labour for six days. Her midwife (also her mother) keeps examining her and asks me to do the same. I am not sure that she is actually in labour, I think it may have been induced. However, there is more and more anxiety, and women have come from the surrounding villages to observe and then leave. All the shaman small and large have been to do their particular thing. Some have performed the full seance-style healing ritual on her stomach. Others have done their own '*jampi*', or made suggestions. One shaman said that no wonder it had not been born because her bed was facing *up-river* – if her bed was turned round, so it was down-river, then the baby would be born, and he demonstrated the flow of the river with his hands.

Another said that she had eaten too much sappy fruit during pregnancy and that was impeding the birth.

The next day the baby was born with the midwife and a helper, with no shaman there for the birth. The baby was born with the most elongated head I have ever seen, and by next morning the midwife had massaged it back into shape again.

7   I was returning from Trula and had only reached the edge of the village when Busu came running to fetch me: 'Come quickly and help. Adoi is having her baby'.

I went across and the midwife and her daughter were in full attendance and the older women from the village were sitting around. Adoi was suffering some discomfort, but not in full labour yet. I was asked to shake her during the contractions. She called out for various relatives to come and help her when the pains got severe. She was drinking coconut oil and said it would make the baby be born more easily. The midwife sent over to the shaman for some *jampi* water, which Adoi sipped intermittently. Once during the labour the shaman was called over to see how things were going, but he did not enter the delivery room.

From the above case histories one can see the degrees of involvement of one or more shaman depending on the seriousness of complications. The one that attracted most attention was case history 6. Extended labour for the Temiars causes extreme anxiety, and once labour has started, the belief is that the baby must be born as quickly as possible. The purpose of shaking the mother around the waist is the belief that this will encourage a speedier delivery. This confinement attracted advice and comment from many different shaman and midwives. They placed ritual decorations in her room and one shaman danced around in the style of a healing seance (see page 162), and shouted at the baby to come out. People commented on the baby's misshapen head and said that it proved that the mother had eaten the wrong fruit during pregnancy because the baby's head was shaped like a jack fruit and was covered in sticky fluid which resembled its sap.

So why do Temiars consult a shaman or midwife about their health? They have often attempted self-medication first and will have tried to puzzle out some explanation for their illness which might be put right. For example, we saw in Chapter 3 how *Busuu?*, my assistant, punctured holes in tins because his daughter had a persistent runny nose and he thought it was caused by *tɘracɔɔg*. Vomiting and weight loss are usually attributed to *sabat* and the illness is considered to have resulted from eating a prohibited food, or from a child experimenting with a new food too soon. A person may also dream of the cause of their illness and avoid the food in future. The more severe illness of *tɛnruu?* which manifests in involuntary shaking or noisy breathing (*na-sɘlood*) needs immediate shamanic intervention and the person is usually isolated immediately. Diarrhoea is generally believed to result from an individual's carelessness with *misik* avoidance. Severe *gɛnhaa?* illness and *pocuk*, which both have symptoms of convulsions, shaking, giddiness and nausea, need shamanic intervention. Although most of the avoidances described in Chapter 3 can result in illness of some kind (*sabat, misik, gɛnhaa?, pocuk, tɘracɔɔg, tɛnruu?*), the most common reason for serious shamanic intervention is soul-sickness: either head-soul sickness (*rɛywaay*) or blood/heart-soul sickness (*na-ji?hup*). It is very often in these circumstances, when other forms of treatment have failed, that the relatives ask for a healing seance for the patient. Healing seances are not held lightly; the shaman charges fees which the relatives worry they cannot pay. However, if a seance is felt to be necessary the resources are always found, even if payment is delayed.

In this chapter we have considered the two important Temiar healing roles, shaman and midwife, and looked at their complementarity. Both roles share similar practices, the noticeable difference being the public nature of shamanic healing and the very private practice of the midwife.

Chapter 9

Healing performances
Dance-dramas of prevention and cure

> But the paradox remains. Some representations arouse *actual* sorrow
> or terror – sorrow for actual people they remind us of, terror of horrors
> we think we might actually face – or an objectless mood of anxiety,
> and it would appear that we sometimes seek and enjoy these
> experiences.
>
> (Walton 1990:256)

> Like ritual, custom gives explicit guidance on what should or should
> not be done. I have not gone further than repeating that ritual is one
> kind of custom.
>
> (G. Lewis 1980:11)

Before I describe a specific healing seance in detail, I want to discuss
healing performances more generally. Although seance performances
are held for the specific purpose of healing an individual, there are
healing elements in all performances, from the more playful,
spontaneous play-dance to the most serious and planned tiger-seance.
The following constitute the range of seances but the categories are
not discrete as, in common with so much of Temiar life, there are
similarities between categories, and one such seance can lead to
another in the course of the same evening.

COMMUNAL SINGING (*GƏNABAG*) OR PLAY-DANCE (*SISƐ? JEHWAH*)

These light-hearted sessions often take place on the spur of the
moment; usually there are no decorations and there is not the
intention of calling down spirit-guides. Music and dancing can lead
into vigorous trancing with much flailing and collapsing. It is at these
performances that older people often curb the exuberance of the
young people if it gets out of control.

PLAY-SEANCE (*PƐHNƆƆH JEHWAH*)

There is at least minimal decoration for these performances and shaman call down the spirit-guides (see below). They are considered to have a preventive function, i.e. to maintain well-being. Shaman and any trainees may spontaneously perform *tɛnhool* on the heads of children or others feeling unwell. There is singing, dancing and vigorous and less vigorous trancing.

SEANCE (*PƐHNƆƆH*)

This is the typical trance-dance performance complete with decorations, ritual objects (described below) and healing elements. Dancing in the early part of the seance is brief, as trance is the main objective of the performance. However, dancing is often resumed after the main trance session is finished or as an interlude until another trance session takes place.

A variation of this seance is held in the house of a sick individual or in the main house if the person is well enough to attend. The most striking variation is the individual healing performance given by the shaman in trance, with the patient lying in the centre of the room and everyone else watching. It may be performed within the context of the customary *pɛhnɔɔh*.

BURSTING OF THE MOURNING (LITERAL TRANSLATION OF *TƏRƐNPHK TƐNMƆƆH*)

This seance is held at the end of the mourning period and lasts for three nights before the village resumes normal life again. It is characterised by the music being in a minor key, and absence of new clothes and face-paint on the first night. Trancing is usually limited to close relatives on the first night. The seance is preceded by a communal feast. Gifts are presented to visitors.

TIGER-SEANCE (*PƐHNƆƆH KƏBUT*)

This is the most infrequent seance of all and is considered the most powerful and the most dangerous. It is characterised by an absence of dance, the construction of a special shelter inside the house to contain the shaman/tiger, and the whole seance being held in darkness. It is usually held to heal sick individuals but also to improve an ailing community.

I have described a play-dance (*sisɛʔjɛhwah*) in some detail in Chapter 4. I want to discuss the more formal seance (*pɛhnɔɔh*) and the preparations that are involved. These sessions take place with more forethought and planning, which may be on the morning of the day itself, or a day or two before. However, the actual preparations start on the morning of the seance. Women and children fetch the leaves and foliage to make the decorations. The men assist in hanging them under the roof but the shaman arranges the central decoration for his own use. Women weave head-dresses from *kəwaar* palm fronds, making intricate patterns by cutting them with a small blade (Plate 14), or they plait together circlets of marigold flowers. These are only worn by the men, with the addition of a bunch of *kəwaar* stuck into the back of their sarongs like a tail. Women wear a single flower in their hair and often paint their faces (Plate 15). The palm fronds and leaves are usually hung at intervals so that the entire room is decorated. The centrepiece is rattan tied in the shape of a hoop, from which are hung leaves and sweet-smelling herbs to attract the positive spirit-guides. Home-grown tobacco is rolled very carefully into cigarettes and arranged in a pattern on a tray near the fire, where there may also be a dish of charcoal containing incense or fragrant herbs. A banana log for the musicians to stomp their rhythm on is placed at the side and the pairs of bamboo stompers, one longer than the other, are checked for any cracks or holes. If they are damaged then new ones are cut. The musicians are almost always women who echo the shaman in his singing (for a musical analysis of the Temiars see Roseman 1986 and 1993).

In a typical *pɛhnɔɔh* which I describe below there is a drawing together of the many elements of Temiar shamanism and seances. Although the main business of the evening is serious trancing (*lɛslããs*) when people are said to have forgotten their feeling (*wəl hup*), there will also be spontaneous trancing, dancing, playing-at-seance by children, healing, flirting, joking, and maybe some firm admonishment from the shaman as well. Trancing must not be confused with Temiar shamanism *per se*; as we have seen, shaman perform in several domains, and it is in the seance domain that their prime task is to call down the spirit-guides so that their good essence is available to everyone. Shaman do not necessarily trance at seances, unless they are engaged in healing a specific person. It is noticeable that they are in a lighter state of dissociation than the participants. Young people when talking about trance say, 'When I'm trancing I'm free. It's like flying', whereas older people disavow the erotic aspect,

Plate 14 Making the decorations

Plate 15 Face paint and hair flowers (photo ʔaluŋ Andy)

Plate 16 Seance about to trance

saying that trance is 'forgetting' and they cannot recall the sensation. Following Benjamin's (1967b:273) distinction, there is a shift away from the ecstatic experience in youth towards an ascetic experience in the more serious trance among older people. I.M. Lewis makes a similar general point:

> The state of mental dissociation (which may vary considerably in degree) and which for convenience we call trance, is, in the circumstances in which it occurs, open to different cultural controls and to various cultural interpretations.
>
> (1971:44)

The following is a description of a seance (*pɛhnɔɔh*) which also involves healing. It was a performance held at Asam (Plate 16) which the entire village attended. There was a sense of anxiety following several official visits, and the proximity of *gɔb* (foreigners) to the seasonal fruit trees. It contains most of the elements of this kind of performance.

> A sense of anticipation builds up throughout the day as the preparation and decorations are nearing completion. Once darkness falls there is a feeling of urgency to get started. Most of the village will be present and any visitors from other villages who have heard about it, or are passing through. They all assemble in the main dancing area and the women, often with babies slung across their backs, take up a position sitting or squatting behind the banana log. There is a settling down period while they get in sequence beating out a steady rhythm.
>
> The shaman who is going to lead the proceedings squats by the women on the stompers. The fire is dampened down, the children are hushed, the chatter dies away, and as everyone watches, the only illumination is from the kerosene wick. The shaman sings to make contact with his spirit-guide who will assist him in the seance, and to coax the small shy spirits on to the roof of the house, or even to come down to the central leaf decoration. As the singing builds up, the shaman stands and holds on to this centrepiece, through which the power from the spirits can enter him. He is thought to catch it in his palm in the form of a fluid, which he can use to transmit their good influence. At this point he enters a light trance but is in complete control of the proceedings.
>
> Men of all ages get up and make a big circle round the shaman,

and with the walking step described above [see Chapter 4, p. 72], accent the rhythm in their movements. The women play the stompers and increase the intensity of their singing. Those not involved in the music watch and discuss the dancers, sometimes giggling, though not too loudly. Boys dance with the men, and girls either help with the stompers, or sit with their friends. In the shadows younger people may use the opportunity to flirt as in a play-dance until the trancing becomes serious.

The shaman tries to control the development of the session, restraining those who fall into trance too soon so that there can be a slow build up to a climax by the group as a whole. The rhythm and singing become louder and the dancing starts to get faster; soon some people start to trance spontaneously, those who are not going to trance stand aside as do the young boys.

The circle breaks up and those already in trance start bouncing round the floor in their own circle. The shaman gives attention to those who are not in trance, and either flicks water with his fan, presses their chest, or puts his forehead against theirs, and soon everyone left in the centre is bouncing, twirling and spinning; their arms flail, they may overbalance and fall over.

The onlookers are intrigued, elated, scared and even amused. They step to one side to avoid being hit by a flailing limb while assisting anyone who may be overbalancing. If the trancing is very chaotic, the musicians break up and move away until the proceedings have calmed down. By contrast, the older men are unobtrusively fanning themselves and gently moving backwards and forwards into a trance state, which they achieve with minimum movement as compared with the vigorous efforts required by younger people. Whether trancing or dancing, or just watching, the entire house is involved in this highly charged and energetic experience.

Some of the entranced sink unconscious to the floor, others spontaneously recover. The shaman watches those in trance very intently and gives attention to those who are unconscious by massaging their heads, or blowing into their head-soul through a clenched fist, *tɛnhool*. As they slowly emerge from the trance looking dazed and disorientated, cigarettes are placed in their mouths and often they are bathed in smoke by the shaman or by one of the elderly women from a dish containing charcoal and aromatic herbs [Plate 17]. During the evening, the shaman may see to any illnesses, other shaman may take a session and also

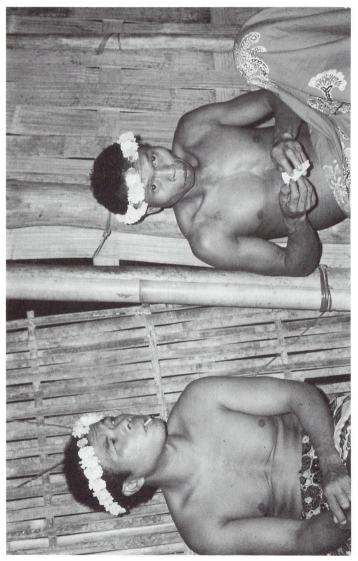

Plate 17 Still dazed from trance (photo ʔaluŋ Andy)

heal. Sometimes there is a break in the proceedings while everyone smokes cigarettes before starting again.

The observer feels that the entire Temiar group had been involved in the experience that is essentially Temiar, whether in trance or not, binding them together into a whole, composed of many contrasting elements.

(fieldwork notes)

It would appear that on some occasions a seance is arranged in response to a level of anxiety or tension in the village. For example, there would be anxiety after visits from outside officials, especially from government departments, or an army patrol looking for communist guerillas. I could also observe a general level of irritability and, in my perception, body movements suggested greater social distance between people. It is as if the Temiars embody these feelings without being able to articulate them verbally. Gestures are more angular than rounded, movement and speech are more staccato, and generally people appear more in control of than at ease with their bodies. On these occasions, one of the older men or women suggests a trance-dance for the same evening.

However, I am not proposing a general theory of tension release for Temiar seances. I have discussed elsewhere that a tension release theory is contradicted by the fact that those with most to be anxious about are precisely those who must observe avoidance of trance, such as parents of young children and sick people.

The trance-dance builds up through a spirit of elation that is infectious, and the spectators play almost as important a part in engendering it as the dancers themselves. Thus those who are prohibited by their condition from full social existence are at least permitted to enter the dance vicariously, and the joint occasion that brings the village together as a group has the effect of drawing in the more marginal members, dispelling their anxieties.

(Jennings 1985a:62)

The Temiars long for the trance experience; they say they cannot exist without it for long, which is why they often get very impatient with the taboo on seances during the mourning period. Roseman also suggests that a tension release model is inappropriate in understanding the Temiar trance-dance:

Singing and trance-dancing ceremonies do not, however merely function as a 'stress release' when they relieve accumulated longing and discomfort. A stress release model would not explain the aesthetic elaboration, the poetics of this particular release. The Temiar in fact are longing for the activity which is the release of longing; the ceremony *intensifies* the sentiment of longing in order to effect its 'release'. A Temiar spirit seance gets rid of longing by *playing* on it – a modulation rather than a simple evacuation.

(1986:213)

I will return to the theme of 'aesthetic elaboration' and the 'poetics' in Chapter 10.

When a shaman holds a healing seance for an individual patient, he performs a stylised dance round the patient while everyone else watches intently. An important seance of this kind usually leads on to a dance session, and while people are dancing the shaman takes advantage of the presence in strength of the spirit-guides and treats other minor illnesses. The following describes a seance (*pɛhnɔɔh*) for healing held in Bawik for a middle-aged woman complaining of chest pains:

> People gathered in the main dancing room with all the decorations: some had travelled from other villages. The shaman opened the seance by the usual singing and then invited the patient to lie in the centre of the room under the cluster of leaves. Still singing he held on to the leaves in the centrepiece, and rocking backwards and forwards he went into trance. He started to dance slowly round the patient, using elongated walks and angular arm gestures, touching all the periphery of the ill body with the *kəwaar* whisk. Then he massaged the patient's stomach, while muttering incantations. He noisily sucked through a clenched fist to bring out whatever was causing the trouble; he opened his hand and we all strained to see, but there was nothing actually there. He still disposed of the offending 'substance' outside the door of the hut. Then he milked his heart with his right hand and blew through a clenched fist into the same area, before repeating his preliminary dance.

(fieldwork notes)

I described in Chapter 6 how the soul essence manifests itself in the form of liquid which the shaman transmits to the sick person (and also to others) directly from his whisk and clenched or flat hand and also indirectly from his own *hup* where the substance has accumulated. The following is an account of a more spectacular seance conducted by *?abiləm*, who is very creative.

Abilum has asked me to go to a very special seance *pɛhnɔɔh* tonight at Bawik. A young boy is ill and he is holding a special seance for him. I was asked not to take my tape recorder or camera. The cameras have been referred to before as I have not been allowed to take pictures of anyone in trance, but tonight there is also a taboo on recording any of the songs. I remember the midwife from Blau blaming me for her sore throat, saying that I had trapped her voice on the tape. Tonight this is also connected with building up the atmosphere and attention for this big performance.

When we arrived the decorations were all up in the main house which has a huge central area for performances and sleeping quarters for the shaman's two wives at either end. It is not a typical long house of the communal variety. We were given flower head-dresses and very fine *kəwaar* crowns were made for the menfolk, as well as bunches to put in the backs of their sarongs. Abilum was not there and we were told he was in *pantang* (seclusion) getting things ready for the healing. He was outside somewhere near the edge of the jungle. I could discern a pale light but not what he was doing. About fifteen minutes later he came into the house and placed an egg on a rice tray with the whisk, and cigarettes near the damped-down fire. He started singing in the usual way, calling down the spirits, the atmosphere was quite electric. 'Last time he used the egg, he got a frog out of a man's stomach', said a Temiar sitting next to me. The intensity of the music built up with staccato singing from Abilum after a gentle swaying beginning. The boy was lying in the centre, wide-eyed, looking as if he wondered what was going to happen to him. He is about 9 years old and is suffering from severe stomach pains. Abilum starts to sway and appears disorientated. He lets go of the circlet that he has been holding, picks up the whisk and moves towards the patient. He dances round him with grandiose movements, a stylised form of dance and using the whisk makes large sweeping movements down the boy's trunk and arms. Abilum talks to us while he is doing it – like a running commentary – the singing has stopped for the time being. He seems such a showman, slowly building us up to the suspense of the climax. Putting down the whisk, he takes the egg and holds it as he passes it all over the boy's body and eventually lays it on his stomach. He does all the sucking and clucking very noisily and with a flourish removes the egg and places it on the floor. He asked the audience what they think is in it, and they call things such as a frog (as before), leaves. . . . He cuts it open with a bush knife and feels around in the yolk and produces what looks like a black seed-pod with a thorn in it, hard and shiny, no bigger than my finger-nail. 'Of course he was in pain', said Abilum.

The audience all look impressed, and the boy is amazed at what is going on. Abilum gets rid of the pod at the door and then starts the milking of his heart and the blowing. The audience relax as the main performance is over. The specific healing complete, Abilum leads an ordinary trance and dance and most people join in. The boy sits at the side and watches.

(I tried to get hold of the eggshell to see if in fact it had been opened before by Abilum in his preparations, but it had gone. I could not decide whether it was sleight of hand after opening, or whether it was inserted before.)

(fieldwork notes)

This performance was in marked contrast to another healing seance that I attended, which was being held for a woman in her late thirties/early forties who, it was said, had a weak head-soul. It was far more of a communal seance than one person's stylised perform-ance and included several shaman, performing one after the other. Although described as *pɛhnɔɔh* it was certainly nearer to *pɛhnɔɔh jɛhwah* than the previous example.

We arrived just after dusk and were told that there was a seance and that we could go. But there would not be much dancing for us as it was to heal someone. We attended as usual and the singing had already started with one of the old men taking the lead. The woman was lying in the centre with her head on a cushion. Several of the older men took over the singing, urging the chorus of girls to sing better. The shaman sang, squatting in the middle and then stood up under the central bunch of leaves (not a circlet this time); they smelt like herbs of various sorts. He did not appear particularly disassociated but in extreme concentration. He went over to the woman and started to blow on her head-soul, then the usual sucking noises. Then he did the same on her chest – *hup* – sucking and clucking – driving out the substance. Then milked his heart and blew it into her chest and head. He went back into the centre and went on singing and some of the older men repeated the

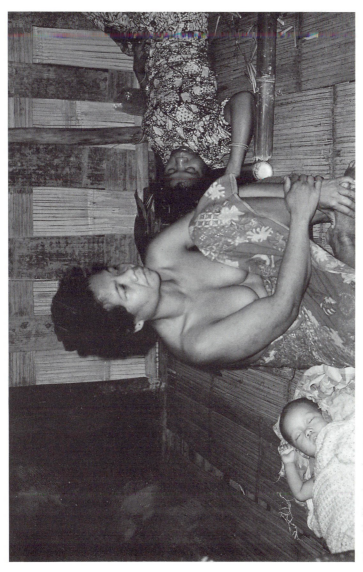

Plate 18 Sleeping after the seance

procedure on her head – i.e. the sucking and blowing. The woman seemed quite inert and listless all the way through. She was helped to the side afterwards and the evening developed into singing and trancing, several men taking it in turns to be in charge of the proceedings. It went on very late and slowly we all curled up to sleep where we were [Plate 18]. The singing went on most of the night.

(fieldwork notes)

Although there are regional variations, and differences between the practices of individual performers, there are some constant elements in the healing seance. If the seance is for healing then *particular* care is taken with the decorations and the ritual objects. The shaman himself goes into trance, whether lighter or heavier. However, in the healing seance the patient never goes into trance. A sick person already has a weak head-soul so it would be foolish to weaken it further (cf. Chapter 3, p. 38). It is the shaman himself, drawing on the power of his spirit-guides and being able to free his own head-soul, who will strengthen the head-soul of the sick patient.

Following death, as we saw in Chapter 6, there is a period of mourning which can last for some weeks and up to three months. This depends on the status of the person (e.g. a shaman's relative), the wishes of the close family and the recommendations of the shaman and older members of the community.

During this time (*tɛnmɔɔh*) there is a total ban on dancing, singing, trancing and listening to the radio. There is only essential passage in and out of the village, and others do not visit socially. All the villagers wear their old clothes. I realised that one of the delays in my moving into Asam was because they were still in mourning, and the seance that we had been invited to was the last stages of the breaking of that mourning. The following is the description of a seance to mark the end of the mourning period for a headman's wife who had died a month previously:

We arrived in the afternoon and the village was a hive of industry. Each house is busy cooking and some people are also busy making decorations in the large house that the headman had moved into. There is a piece of rattan strung from one side of the room to the other with a row of new sarongs and muslin cloths hanging from it. The evening started with a communal meal and I was invited to join the big circle with the men, although the women are at the side. The shaman started to sing and the musicians followed him, very slowly and gently. The songs are all in a minor key and there is not the build-up and urgency of the usual seances. The close relatives began to cry as the shaman said what a good woman she had been, but now she must rest and not come to the village to bother people. In the middle of the singing her husband, the headman, got to his feet and gave an enormous shriek, and stumbled, obviously entranced, to the centre of the room. The shaman kept on singing and then performed the blowing sucking routine on his head. The singing continued in chorus for about an hour.

Then the headman's son reached up, and one at a time gave out the new sarongs and cloths. They were given to all the visitors to the village but not to the mourners, and we had to wrap them round ourselves straight away. The singing then continued until people went to sleep, but there was no more dancing or trancing.

The second day everything had changed, people were much more lively, some of the people went out foraging. They told me that tonight there is dancing and trancing. Everyone is dressed up in new clothes and there was a usual trance *pɛhnɔɔh* with plenty of dancing and vigorous trancing, which of course everyone had been deprived of for several weeks. The seance went on until dawn and everyone fell asleep exhausted with only one or two individuals returning to their own homes. The seance continued for a third night by which time everyone seemed tranquil though exhausted.

(fieldwork notes)

This is the only seance which is always preceded by a communal meal. The seance can continue for many nights, but the first two nights are the most important. The first night is the final ending of the mourning with placatory songs to the deceased, the wearing of old clothes and the gifts of new clothes to the visitors. The second night marks the return to normal activity, with previously tabooed singing, dancing and trancing. In the above account, people had begun to move in and out of the village after the first day, and then dressed up in their newest clothes in the evening.

The tiger-seance is thought to be the most powerful, the most awesome and also the most dangerous for shaman and others alike. It is not often performed and I was fortunate enough to witness two such seances during my stay. The specific principle behind the tiger-seance is that the shaman concerned is powerful enough to have the tiger as his spirit helper, and also has many other spirit-guides who belong to off-the-ground and ground categories.

An ordinary seance usually follows a tiger-seance (*pɛhnɔɔh mənuuʔ*), so the house is already decorated in the usual way with flowers, herbs and ritual objects. However, there are particular preparations for the tiger-seance. A shelter of palm branches is built inside the house, i.e. a house within a house, similar to the temporary shelters built by the Temiars when travelling in the forest. Unlike the preparations for the other seances which are made by women and children, the building of the shelter is done exclusively by men; often the shaman himself supervises its size, balance and so on.

Before the seance begins, fresh flowers are placed on a mat outside the shelter. The atmosphere is tense and anxious; the fires are damped right down and there is no illumination. No one is allowed to leave or enter the house once the seance has started and everyone is perfectly quiet. It is very much in contrast with the ordinary banter and joking in the everyday seances and the flirting between the young people. The shaman enters the shelter through a small gap in the palms and sits down. He starts to sing, accompanied by the women on stompers, and he sings *as the tiger* roaming over the countryside, interspersing his singing with growls. Once the singing has started there is absolute silence; everyone is straining to see in the dark, and not even cigarettes are allowed. The singing continues and the growling increases, and the shaman's helper – usually a trainee shaman – is standing nearby. He does not look into or touch the hut as the power of the tiger is too great. He helps the patient to move near the hut, though not to come in contact with it. The tiger-shaman is considered to be in a trance as the growling increases and he starts scratching – one can hear the leaves rustle inside the shelter (and audience members jump). The Temiars believe that the shaman then actually changes into a tiger. Even the sceptical individuals who consider themselves 'modern' in other ways (for example, more relaxed with food taboos) assured me on this point. They insisted that they had seen the tiger's claws disappear from the ends of the shaman's fingers as the seance ended and the lights went up.

The moment of transformation, when the growling and scratching become more pronounced, is believed to be the moment of the greatest power and the watchers express not just interest but also concern and fear. The Temiars say that the tiger does not actually come into the house, but stays nearby and sends threads (again a recurring theme as with the thunder and the good spirits) under the house that only the entranced shaman can see. These come up into the hut and enable the metamorphosis to take place.

When the shaman emerges dazed from the hut, the fire is rekindled and everyone lights cigarettes and breathes a big sigh. After a break the evening can become an ordinary seance, with dance, trance, calling down the spirits and more general healing. The tiger is supposed to disappear with the first light from the embers and not stay around. The flowers either disappear or wilt and die.

The tiger-seance is usually performed to cure a sick individual but it is also thought to benefit the community as a whole. It is sometimes done after recurring bad fortune, crop failure, deaths and illnesses. Only for serious matters does the tiger-shaman call upon his most powerful *gonig*.

The following is an account of the first tiger-seance that I attended:

We had been staying for a few days at Trula with Penghulu Dalam and had many talks with him about shamanism and healing. His wife is the important midwife, and they have no children of their own. She has been showing me the dances in the old style. Dalam says there will be a seance tonight and the usual preparations are being made. However he does not tell me in advance that it will be a tiger-seance. We do not know until just before it starts, when we see the men are carrying in the palms to make the shelter. Dalam says that a young woman is ill, but also implies that it is going to be a good thing – that it is good for the village. His wife is very good at organising everyone, shushing the children and reminding people about the darkness and no cigarettes. She puts flowers in front of the hut.

The fires are damped right down, the doors are shut and Dalam very modestly squeezes inside the shelter. The bamboo rhythm starts – Dalam's wife sits near the girls (she is almost like a stage manager) who are making the music; there are some very powerful singers here. Dalam starts to sing, quite unlike any of the other singing we had heard. Much shorter and staccato, and what I realise are the growls in between. I can catch just a few of the words which seem to be describing a journey through the jungle and the mountains, from a long way.... It's pitch dark, so I cannot write anything down. As I look round, everyone is concentrating very hard, Dalam's male helper is hovering near the shelter and watching and listening and the young woman is lying on a cushion. She is much less the centre of attention than in the ordinary healing seances, the focus of all is on the hut, with Dalam's wife keeping an eye on the proceedings. The patient does not appear to be chronically ill, but it was said that she had a sick *hup*, pains in her chest, and didn't breathe easily. She looks listless and very frightened.

The singing gets more intense and the growls more frequent. Then there is a rustling noise from inside the house and there are more growls and scratchy sounds. Dalam stops singing and one of the older men takes over and keeps up the chorus. The scratching and growls get very intense, not a muscle twitches in the house as all eyes are straining to see something. The singing reaches a peak of tension and then relaxes. The noises stop quite abruptly and Dalam emerges from the hut, rubbing his eyes. Someone stirs up the fire to a glow and lights a couple of kerosene lamps. Everyone starts lighting up cigarettes, the tiger-seance is over.

After a short pause on this occasion the ordinary-style seance started and continued well into the night. Dalam and other shaman danced and called down spirits and danced and tranced. The hut was dismantled before we went on. The tiger had really gone away.

(fieldwork notes)

There is a marked contrast between the tensions, darkness, silence and lack of active engagement in the tiger-seance, and the release, increased light, noise and participation at many levels of the ordinary seances. The evening as a whole could be seen as continuum from tiger to conventional seance in terms of a balanced performance; on the one hand the tiger-seance calls up the most feared character and draws upon his power and, on the other hand, the ordinary seance complements this with the lesser, yet nevertheless potent good influences that are within the direct reach of everyone through their private dream encounters.

The second tiger-seance that I was invited to at Bawik was to be led by the very charismatic shaman called *ʔabiləm* whose seances I have described before. There had been several deaths in the village and a lot of illness. Mentri Suleiman had been called in on more than one occasion to help heal someone who was very ill. This seance was set up without any of the sick people actually being there, and *ʔabiləm* said that it was not specifically for the ill people but also to make 'the head-soul of the village strong'. There had been some problems in *ʔabiləm*'s village, with division between sections and break-away groups. *ʔabiləm* was trying to unite everyone to live and work together as a whole; the village had several family units coming together and was one of the sites for a government project for larger-scale crop growing. He was worried about the illnesses and about people from other villages staying away. People from our village asked us not to go on more than one occasion, in case we should bring the illness back with us. We were also aware that the people in our village, and some people in Bawik, say that *ʔabiləm* is not *really* a tiger-shaman anyway. However, those who work closely with him say that he is a great shaman with many powers.

The following is a description of *ʔabiləm*'s tiger-seance:

Abilum has invited us to go for a meal before the seance. The older of his two wives is not well, but the other with the young baby cooks for us. His older wife appears to be fed up with the new pretty wife, and tells me that she gets more presents. The room is fully decorated as it always is at Bawik, and the decorations hang from the whole ceiling, with the centrepiece in the middle. The men are still making a hut from the palm branches (like the ones the roofs are thatched with); Abilum is not around.

People drift in and chat as the final touches are put to the decorations. Abilum's helper asks me to be sure not to take any pictures or recordings. He seems to be Abilum's constant companion and assistant, and is always helping with the healing though does not refer to himself as a healer. Everyone gathers round and I get the impression amongst some of sheer disbelief as to whether Abilum can actually do it. Others are talking of seances they have been to in the past, and what happened, and inevitably the discussion of seeing tiger's claws comes up again. Abilum comes in and everyone falls silent. He nods to the girls to start singing, and they start beating out a rhythm and singing snatches of phrases. They find it more difficult to sustain in chorus than some of the other groups I have heard. Abilum gets inside the shelter and starts to sing somewhat falteringly to begin with, and the girls have difficulty in picking up the sequence. He then seems to get into his stride and appears confident. There are lots of growls and grunts, very loud, and people look at each other as if saying, 'told you so'; the proceedings are under way. His assistant stays near during the whole proceedings and looks around, checking that there is no light; darkness is essential.

The noises are becoming more and more realistic and the tension increases. Very loud scratching noises start – Abilum has changed and his audience wait expectantly. Another man sings for a while and his assistant stays near, looking very anxious. Abilum stumbles out a few moments later, after the 'tiger' noises have subsided. He looks around him and someone lights the lamps and throws something on the fire. The house is suddenly illuminated very brightly and we all jump. Abilum seems to recover very quickly, and before the tension and formality have gone, picks up the fresh flowers that were in front of the hut and holds them up for all to see. 'Look', is all he says. The flowers are all drooping and withered. We are all suitably impressed.

Everyone starts to chat and compare the seance with others they have witnessed. Since there are very few of these seances they have not many to compare with, and they go way back in their memories. Some of the young people, and many of the children, have never witnessed one. Abilum comes over to me and asks me what I thought of it.

(fieldwork notes)

In this chapter on healers, taken in conjunction with Chapters 6 and 7, we have elaborated the concepts that are central to the Temiar way of life. Linking them with the themes concerning bodies and space, we can now see how prevention and healing through the practices of midwives and shaman, through the management of souls and blood, enable the Temiars to maintain their essentially Temiar identity in relationship with, but separate from, the non-human and supernatural world.

There is a parallel in the seances between the integrity of the human body and that of the domestic house and the need in both cases to maintain strict boundaries. Horizontal and vertical spatial divisions provide a physical as well as a conceptual framework that is mirrored in the beliefs and practices concerning the human frame. The construction and maintenance of these boundaries prevent the entry of unwelcome harmful substances and permit the entry of desirable good influences. All these substances have the potential for transformation either for good or evil. Whereas tiger can bring death as transformed menstrual blood, it can also be a source of powerful good when harnessed and transformed through the tiger-shaman.

Men and women have clearly defined roles in relation to thunder and tiger and the management of their potentially evil influences. Tiger and thunder both send down strong cords of evil which are contrasted with the delicate threads of the spirit-guide substance used by shaman in healing. In addition, the positive fluid which flows from the head-souls of the spirit-guides has healing powers, in contrast with the dangerous, illness-causing fluid which flows from the lower body of women, which has to be ritualised and controlled by midwives (see also Benjamin 1994).

The seance represents the Temiar world as a whole by integrating the dominant conceptual dichotomies: public/private, off-the-ground/ground, order/disorder, male/female, individual/group, illness/health, life/death. In the seances the essential human-ness of Temiars in general as well as their Temiar-ness specifically, is affirmed in relation to the outside world. All acceptable things coming in from the outside are transformed in order to be integrated within Temiar life, whether they are words borrowed from Malay, hunted animals brought back from the forest or stories from other Aslian groups. The Temiars have a strong sense of the transformational possibility of desired phenomena and their own ability to effect those transformations and to keep the undesired at bay.

This account may suggest a constant awareness by the Temiars of the presence of evil (cf. Benjamin 1967:243) and indicate that the restrictions and avoidance impose a permanent seriousness on the lives of these people. To a certain extent these are valid impressions. The larger-than-life projections, these epic metaphors of tiger and thunder, contrast sharply with the shy, small, elusive qualities of the positive spirit-guides that the Temiars themselves appear to emulate. Given a society in which the accusation of stinginess is the greatest insult, it is not surprising that many features of Temiar life are seen as desirable by outsiders, including myself and my children. By projecting punishment and retribution on to outside forces, the Temiars are able to be indulgent towards their children, to respect their bodies and their autonomy. As the Temiars say, you cannot *make* a human being do anything. So in conclusion, I want to stress the essential playfulness of the Temiars. Playing, dreaming, singing, flirting and trancing are all highly enjoyable activities. Soul freedom in dreams and trance enable creativity and imaginary release with feelings of flying and waterborne journeying 'from source to estuary'. The controlled abandon in dance and trance is almost addictive as seances continue for nights in a row. The sense of well-being for both individuals as well as the community is noticeable for days after a seance: 'We cannot live for long without trance.'[1]

Chapter 10

The epic metaphor
The paradox of healing

'I can't explain *myself*, I'm afraid sir', said Alice, 'because I'm not myself, you see.'

(Lewis Carroll, *Alice in Wonderland*)

The instruments of darkness tell us truths;
Win us with honest trifles, to betray's
In deepest consequence.

(*Macbeth*, Act 1.iii)

This final chapter draws together dominant themes from the Temiar world view in relation to their healing seances and the specialist roles of midwife and shaman. In earlier chapters I have explored the play of children; bodily and spatial concepts; beliefs concerning dreams, souls and trance; the significance of women and blood, and healers and healing performances. I now wish to return this data to the framework of ideas about drama, theatre and ritual outlined in Chapter 1. I develop the argument that these three dramatic forms are variations on a central theme, based on the fundamental human nature of the dramatic act and its revelatory quality. Its transformation and healing potential is manifested in the epic metaphor. Crucial to this understanding is the embodiment of both introjected and projected 'self and other'.

In Chapter 1, I stated the fundamental importance of play activity in the development of social and cultural human beings. I emphasised that pre-play experience through embodiment, projection and role enable the emergence of dramatic play. We have seen how the play of Temiar children within boundaries imposed by adults and sanctioned by thunder anticipates and reinforces roles, relationships and beliefs that constitute Temiar individual and collective identity. For example, there is little emphasis on gender differences in infants and young children. In family games girls *and* boys play the parents and mirror the roles and behaviour of parents (who *jointly* 'parent' their small children). The main separation is in relation to the play-space of jungle and village, and play-tasks of hunting and cooking. Gender separation gradually develops at puberty with girls' first menstruation rituals and the increased tendency for same-gender peer groups to sleep, play or work together. Boys often accompany older men on less dangerous hunting expeditions and girls join older women on foraging. The playing-at-seance becomes the play-seance which takes place inside the house rather than outside (Plates 19 and 20). In the play-trance and dance sessions, dance movement is similar for men and women and there is equal excitement about participation in ecstatic trance. However, there is a tendency for more girls to trance if the proceedings are being held by an attractive aspiring shaman (Jennings 1985a), with the ensuing possibility of erotic physical touch. These sessions provide an opportunity for both playful and serious courtship, as well as rehearsals for role competence and separation between shaman and musicians.

From an early age, children learn the importance attached to dream experiences. Individual dreams, which for example warn a child about food avoidance, encourage the emergence of individual autonomy, a quality valued by the Temiars. Children are encouraged to dream and to report their dreams to their parents. Similar excitement is aroused if someone reports that they have dreamed, as when they have a story to tell. The Temiars always listen to other people's dreams, as they always listen to stories. Although sleep and dreaming are associated, like trance, with temporary absence of *rǝwaay*, Benjamin suggests that it is in fact a *controlled* activity:

> [D]reaming is a very highly valued activity, and it *is* an *activity* in the sense that there is real agency involved. Temiars do discuss each other's dreams with each other in the morning or on any other appropriate occasion, particularly after waking up in the morning, so much so that I think it could truly be said that Temiar dreaming is very largely a controlled activity. It is not something about which the subject is passive – but is actually active.
>
> (1979a:3)

What interests me is the dramatic structure of dreams, a kind of private internal theatre that often enables some resolution to take place, and for the Temiars, in this internal theatre as in their everyday life, autonomy is encouraged and valued. Temiar dreams are essentially problem solving, prophetic or innovative. Decisions can

Plate 19 Playing at seance (ii)

Plate 20 An elaborate seance (photo ʔaluŋ Andy)

be made when outcomes are presented in dreams; successful hunting can ensue from directions given in a dream; adversaries can be struggled with and overcome in dreams; and new technology and art can begin in a dream. People dream of new dances, songs or cures, and the fact that they are dreamed about gives them an initial authenticity. However, it is through the process of teaching it to others and its acceptance by the community that the dances or songs are validated; individual revelation on its own is not enough.

Perhaps most important for the Temiars is the relationship between the private world of dreaming and the meeting of one's personal spirit-guide who is both child and teacher to the dreamer. Anyone is considered to have the capacity to meet a spirit-guide in their dreams, but it is the public declaration of this and its integration into the seance practice that places an individual on the path to shamanism. I will not repeat the nature and type of spirit-guides which I discussed earlier; in this context I want to emphasise the links between dreaming, trancing and the creative process.

For the Temiars it is the absence of head-soul that enables the dreaming and trancing and thus the creativity to emerge through dreams and trance in music and dance. I have compared this (Jennings 1992b) with current thinking in relation to right and left brain hemispheres (see p. 4). The left brain, the dominant sphere, controls logic, scientific thought, ordering and speech; the non-dominant, right hemisphere is intuitive, creative, artistic and innovative; it responds through metaphor and symbol. Dreaming and trance, a 'letting go' of conscious controls, allow spontaneous creativity to emerge, but it is controlled and instructed by the left brain. It is the emergence of the head-soul in the infant that produces a human being of culture. Furthermore, just as the dream involves the dramatic interaction between dreamer and spirit-guide, the seance also involves dramatic interaction whereby the shaman allows the 'healing essence' inside him, and acts and reacts with his audience and patient *in a different role*.

Throughout the socialisation of children and into adult life, we have seen how the maintenance of avoidances and limits concerns what enters the body and what emanates from it: the separation of, ground/off-the-ground and jungle/village; and the regularisation of familial and social relationships (i.e. the bodily, spatial and social) maintains well-being not only in all these domains but also preserves a cosmological balance and order. Any disruption in one domain will bring about a reaction in another. For example, incest (*gɛɛs*) will result in an illness of swollen groin and legs involving the people in question, as well as a major thunderstorm; noisy playing by children brings about intervention by thunder; the spilling of blood on the ground, other than menstrual or post-partum, means the transformation of the blood into tiger. These wide-ranging prohibitions together with institutionalised generosity (the obligation to give if someone asks for something) place a great responsibility on the individual in relation to society. Most of one's actions do not just carry implications for the individual but also for the group and thus society as a whole. We must also remember the emphasis placed on Temiar individual self-autonomy, the individuated self; and the idea that you cannot impose your will on another, you cannot *make* anybody do anything. This is well borne out in the rearing of children where they are free to say 'no' to parental requests, and physical punishment of children is virtually unknown. However, we need to understand parental indulgence in the context of Temiar child-rearing, otherwise it could present a rather idealised picture. Children are taught from birth to *fear* thunder and later tiger. Thunder's presence is more obvious in sounds and lightning flashes (whereas tiger could be described as the silent enemy), and both are described as malevolent, angry and so dangerous that their real names cannot be used. Anger, violence and enmity are projected outwards on to tiger and thunder, which I call *epic metaphors* (Jennings 1986c).

Both thunder and tiger are experienced as being able to take control: to invade the world of people (their bodies and their space) if sufficient care has not been taken in the maintenance of boundaries. The non-imposition of the self on other, and the obligation to give on request to another, regulate and maintain social relationships that otherwise would result in violent intervention from outside forces, whether tiger, thunder or illness.

As public group feelings of anger and violence are projected on to forces outside the Temiar social world, what about individual feelings that are not acceptable to the Temiars? Stewart (1947) suggests that they are repressed and directed into the dream life of the Temiars. Many dream theorists suggest that they allow us to experience thoughts and feelings that cannot be expressed in other ways. For the Temiars, the active encounter in dreams with the idealised 'other' enables transformation of raw emotion into resolution and creativity. In dreams we join our spirit-guide on journeys from 'source to estuary'; in playing in the fields and on the fruit trees; and we are also taught creative innovations.

However, the individual and group experiences are brought into juxtaposition at all forms of seances. Seance performances encapsulate and transform the epic metaphor of tiger and thunder which enable these themes to resonate at deep levels both for individuals and the Temiar as a society. Thus the seances provide, through enacted and embodied ritual dramas, socialisation and cultural learning of dominant symbols. The seances alert the Temiars to the qualities they most fear on the one hand and those they seek to emulate on the other, as well as providing the means of innovation and change. As G. Lewis says when he suggests that ritual is primarily action:

> [a] way of doing, making, creating, showing, expressing, arousing
> – a complex form of stimulus to which people respond. Things done in ritual have the power to arouse or to release, to serve as substitutes, as focuses for fantasy: they meet needs and stem from motivations.

(1980:118)

I will return to the theme of seance performance later in this chapter; first I want to look further at the roles of shaman and midwives.

The midwife establishes individual relationships with people who are ill, pregnant, and newly-delivered women and newborn babies. Although her 'patients' tend to be women, men also consult her for sexual problems. A lifelong named relationship *tohaat-cɔɔʔ* is established with individual people to whom she is midwife. Although the shaman will carry out individual healing on request, he also takes the responsibility for the public seances for the community as a whole. Although individuals receive healing rites within these seances, particular attention is paid to the community and the beneficence bestowed collectively from the benign spirits. The midwife's healing practice takes place more privately and is usually carried out at the back of the house, away from public paths and social intercourse. The shaman, unless he is attending a secluded sick individual, will conduct his healing at the front of the house, often in the doorway, with people dropping by for chats or to watch the proceedings. The shaman, as we have seen in Chapter 8, is mainly responsible for the management of head-souls and their freedom or loss. The midwife is, by contrast, concerned with the lower body, particularly in relation to menstrual and post-partum blood. Only in exceptional circumstances does a male shaman intervene in childbirth and, when he does, it is usually through 'head-soul' methods.

The complementarity between upper body and lower body, between blood and hair exemplified in these roles, has already been discussed in detail. However, there is an essential paradox in relation to shaman and midwives. Although midwives can be identified with the lower body and with blood, it is essentially shaman who deal with soul sickness – whether of *rəwaay* (head-soul) and its relationship with dreams and trance, or *hup* (blood/heart-soul) and its relationship with feelings, and breathing. It is only in its infancy that the midwife is responsible for the emergent 'whole child', from the cutting of the cord to the massaging of the fontanelle, and the general protection of the infant whose head-soul is yet unformed. A shaman only intervenes if an infant is seriously ill. However, the midwife manipulates both hair and blood in the thunder rituals. Thus apart from seances the shaman manages blood/heart- and head-soul sickness for individuals, and the midwife manages the redressive potential of hair and blood to appease thunder for the community (but see also Benjamin 1994).

Thus the relationship between the blood/heart-soul and tiger reinforces connections with the ground and the jungle. As we have seen earlier, the ground and the forest are particularly the domains of men, and the tiger-seance exemplifies the ultimate power of the great shaman to have the guidance of the most feared 'ground' animal, tiger. There is an obvious association of women with blood in childbirth and menstruation, and the midwives with the management of these domains. But if we consider more closely beliefs about menstrual blood I think we may discern a relationship between shaman and midwife that is more than one of separation, opposition or subordination. Men and women alike will refer to it as dirty and polluting and both will make sure that men have no contact with menstrual blood, the belief being that they will be ill as a result. It is also believed that *if a shaman comes into contact with menstrual blood it will actually turn into a tiger inside his body*. Benjamin also describes this: 'A shaman furthermore suffers not only from the loss of his spirit-guides, but any menstrual blood that he touches is believed to enter his *hup* and change into a tiger – a straight case of lycanthropy' (1967b:162).

Whereas Benjamin discusses this in relation to soul beliefs and blood, I am struck by its relationship to male and female power. Recent writings on women (e.g. Shuttle and Redgrove 1978; Knight 1983; Laws *et al.* 1985) have suggested that many beliefs are concerned with the *power* of women because they menstruate, particularly when they live close together and synchronise their monthly cycles. The great religions are all concerned with avoidance of the *pollutant* qualities of menstruating women. An etic (*vis-à-vis* emic) observation is that the Temiar expressions of disgust and the use of words like dirty came from later Malay Muslim influence; whereas within the Temiar beliefs it is the loss of power of the shaman by losing his spirit-guides that is important.[1,2] The additional danger is the possible introjection of tiger, the most powerful of animals, in a context where the shaman is not able to control it, as in the tiger-seance.

Thus I would argue an interpretation closest to the Temiar position that shaman and midwives have complementary roles of comparable power in relation to the healing of bodies of individuals and the community, demarcated by particular spaces. At particular times one or the other has a total responsibility for the upper and lower body. However, although the midwife takes responsibility for appeasing thunder, the most fearful cosmological symbol above ground, ultimate power rests with the great shaman who alone can transform tiger into a positive spirit-guide. The transformative power of the great shaman in relation to tiger is echoed in the following reflection on Greek tragedy:

> Through the Oresteia we may recognise the god within ourselves, transform Dionysus into a spirit of morality and say 'Thou are indeed just Lord, if I contend with thee.'
>
> For only if we contend with Dionysus, will he stimulate our hopes for human victory; and Aeschylus his celebrant translates these hopes into clear dramatic forms.
>
> (Eagles and Stanford 1977)

The relationship between tiger and the blood/heart-soul of human beings is polarised in ordinary life: tiger is kept outside human bodies and space, and provides a dominant symbol for negative projections of darkness and destruction. Within the ritual life of the tiger-seance, the shaman's blood/heart-soul is able to make room for the powerful essence from his tiger spirit-guide, and transform its destructiveness into positive healing power. Providing the great shaman contends with tiger then there is hope and healing for the Temiars both individually and collectively.

We can see from the healing and preventive seances of the Temiars that the fundamental nature of the dramatic act is expressed in all their rituals.

Whereas in Chapter 1, I was concerned with dramatic play and the importance of drama and theatre experience in society generally, I want now to discuss further the intrinsic healing properties in drama, theatre and ritual.

Apart from physical forms of treatment, most therapy in twentieth-century society has been dominated by verbal psychotherapy and psychoanalysis. Bodies and space are held constant while words are used to explore the inner regions of the conscious and unconscious mind. It is only comparatively recently that creative arts therapies have become recognised as alternative modes of treatment. Drama-therapy makes use of play and the dramatic act to explore the 'world' of the patient through myth and metaphor: 'Dramatherapy is a healing process in which dramatic engagement is interactively explored through multiple levels of metaphor' (Jennings 1985b:1).

However, traditional verbal psychotherapy contains many dra-matic elements such as the role of therapist and clients; the 'as if' quality of transference and counter-transference; and the evolving of many layers of metaphor. It also has the ritual qualities of time and space 'set apart' and the special 'language' within which the therapeutic encounter is expressed, and explores internal dramas of dreams and fantasies. Although some psychotherapists make use of literature, art and images to facilitate therapeutic disclosure and to expand understanding, the total experience is nevertheless 'held' in the bodily and spatial parameters. Moving into the therapeutic alliance (the dynamic between therapist and client) is a metaphorical movement which may allow psychic movement. The psychotherapist makes use of and is informed by certain aspects of the dramatic and play process. The dramatic process is central to neither the psycho-therapists' personal experience nor to their methodology and practice.

However, for the dramatherapist, the drama is *central* to the *modus operandi* of dramatic encounter with clients. Dramatherapists use their own dramatic experience which has been informed by the range and depth of their theatrical roles in plays and improvisations; for example, taking part in a Shakespearean production will bring another dimension to that gained by merely reading it to oneself or in a group or seeing it performed in a theatre. The very roles that have been played are informed and expanded by movements, mime and voice development, the exploration of the senses, the play of objects, shapes, forms, colours, environments – the whole panoply of the theatre. The dramatherapist views as a piece of 'personal theatre' the disclosures, themes and scenarios that are brought into the thera-peutic present. This 'personal theatre' of the patient is not one-dimensional; it resonates and interacts with the therapist's 'personal theatre', that of the group, society and the theatre as a whole. Just as theatre is an encapsulated 'world' of the world, so the patient's 'personal theatre' encapsulates life as a whole, his or her own 'world': The dramatherapy, as a theatre of healing, uses the theatre structures and themes to enable a transformation of personal experience into the metaphysical resolution (Artaud 1958).

Let me illustrate this further with dramatherapeutic examples. In my work with women who have abused their children (and who have usually been abused themselves), I reach some understanding by examining my violent feelings towards my own children. I am further moved by reading *Macbeth* and seeing it performed, in particular where Lady Macbeth says:

> I have given suck, and know
> How tender 'tis to love the babe that milks me;
> I would while it was smiling in my face
> Have plucked my nipple from its boneless gums
> And dash'd the brains out, had I so sworn
> As you have done to this.
>
> (*Macbeth*, Act 1.vii)

However, this understanding reached very different levels when I played the part of Queen Margaret in *Henry VI Part 3*, where she flings the blood-stained napkin in the face of York – a napkin soaked in the blood of York's young son, whom Margaret had had murdered.

> Look York, I stained this napkin with the blood
> That valiant Clifford with his rapier's point
> Made issue from the bosom of thy boy.
> And if thine eyes can water for his death,
> I give thee this to dry thy cheeks with.
>
> (*Henry VI Part 3*, Act 1.iv)

In the dramatherapeutic situation, expressions such as 'I want to take a hammer and beat his brains out', or 'I'll wrap his entrails round his throat', have all the force of epic metaphors that express the most profound feelings of frustration linked with the despair which characterises these particular women, who are victims and perpe-trators of child abuse. The expression of these feelings within the dramatherapeutic situation, without fear of reprisal or admonition, facilitates exploration through visual and role media, a whole range of violent feelings. This process is facilitated by the conscious and unconscious processes of both dramatherapist and patient in resonance, dissonance and consonance.

It is the internal 'patient' role of the therapist, that aspect that has 'suffered into truth' (Aeschylus, The *Eumenides*), that is available to the patient as well as the therapeutic role. One of the goals of all psychotherapeutic and dramatherapeutic healing is surely for the patient to discover his or her internal 'therapist' during the journey from unwell to well-being. The therapist is facilitator and guide on this journey, a frontiers person or liminal specialist.

It is in the *meeting* 'betwixt and between' of the conscious/ unconscious individuals and groups that there can be illumination in the chaos. Murray Cox emphasises how the therapist is *involved* in the treatment process:

> Therefore, when the therapist also experiences ontological insecurity it can ease the burden for his patient who does not have to 'go it alone'. The therapist can never be a merely neutral, impassive facilitator of cognitive–affective self-awareness for his patient, because he also shares the predicament of humanness. Paradoxically, it is precisely because of the ontological insecurity in the therapist that the patient dares to trust him enough to risk the 'abandonment to therapeutic space'.
>
> (1978:107)

The theme of 'abandonment' is crucial – it happens in theatre as well as therapy and participants need to trust the structure as well as the specialists that it will be safe. Abandonment occurs frequently in considerations of shamanic practice, drama and theatre – in fact all activities that involve catharsis. It is often equated with a loss of control and total freedom. However, as we saw in Temiar seances, the degree of control is socially conditioned and supernaturally sanctioned. Young people who flail and fall in erotic and ecstatic trance experience are controlled by the shaman and other adults present. With maturity, older people maintain an *internal* control and are able to achieve dissociation with minimal physical movement. The degree of abandonment or loss of control is culturally determined within ritual drama, seances and theatre. We saw earlier that some men choose not to become shaman because of the overwhelming demands of their dream life and spirit-guides. Similarly there is a belief that the power that is present in the tiger-seance can overwhelm people and be dangerous if they are too close. The tiger-shaman gives up part of himself (the *hup*) in order to introject the power from the tiger, but in turn he must keep an appropriate distance from people in order not to overwhelm them. This contrasts interestingly with Wilshire's description of enactment in the theatre when he says that the actor and audience are engaged in a dramatic encounter which is brought about by giving up, or holding constant, the conscious self. He describes it as artistically controlled engulfment:

> To articulate fusion and engulfment, the actor allows artistically controlled engulfment with his audience to occur. As they feed off his characterisation, he feeds off their passivity, their fusing and their objectivity in regard to the character before them. His artistry consists in maintaining a precarious balance between abandonment to archaic fusion authorised by the audience, and artistic control of what enactment is allowed.
>
> (1982:100)

We can see from the Temiar examples given that several people, including the shaman, retain an executive controlling role. It is noticeable that the deeper the trance of the participants the more shallow is that of the shaman. Ritual and theatre share degrees of controlled freedom, a paradoxical statement surely, to facilitate the encounter between performers and audience. Both have a designated time and space set apart, with ritual rules to contain the encounter. It is within the limits set by these rules that theatrical or ritual *abandonment* can take place. The degree of abandonment will vary according to structure, expectation and external control.

There has recently been growing interest, shared increasingly by anthropologists' in universal aspects of healing processes. There were attempts initially to disprove Freudian claims of universalism; more recently there have been innovations to explore possible universals in what has been termed 'symbolic healing' (Moerman 1979). In my own research in dramatherapy, in which anthropological theory contributes an important frame of reference, I have been concerned by attempts to transplant symbolic healing forms from one culture to another without consideration of context. My initial foray into anthropology was as a result of frustration with western psychoanalytic and psychotherapeutic models, and with their frequent one-dimensional interpretations of symbols.

Transcultural psychiatry and psychotherapy is a burgeoning field (e.g. Littlewood and Lipsedge 1982; Cox 1986; Kareem 1991) against which in the future I intend to further consider my Temiar data. Two writers have recently defined the psychotherapeutic process in traditional and contemporary psychotherapy. Pottier says:

> Scanning the available but sparse literature on 'traditional' mental treatments in Central Africa, I have developed the argument that authentic psychotherapy is essentially a 'bargaining exercise' between, on the one hand, the insecure individual, and on the other the anxiety producing social environment from which the patient had fled.
>
> (1985:82)

This implies that there is a two-way process engaged in the therapeutic endeavour. Pottier also brings together the individual and collective self into the therapeutic process:

> At the level of the individual Self it is 'suggested' that 'yes, you are strong enough to take up the challenge of identity synthesis'; at the level of the collective Self (or the 'generalised Other' Kapferer 1979:118), which equally undergoes treatment, it is 'suggested' that the socio-cultural changes that emanate from the impact of encroaching alternative value systems are 'not something to be afraid of'.
>
> (ibid:83)

However, Dow (1986) appears to place all the power in the hands of the shaman/therapist. He proposes an outline of the structure of all symbolic healing, both what he terms magical healing and psychotherapy. He summarises thus:

1   A generalised cultural mythic world is established by universalizing the experiences of healers, initiates or prophets, or by otherwise generalizing emotional experiences.
2   A healer persuades the patient that it is possible to define the patient's relationship to a particularized part of the mythic world, and makes the definition.
    The healer attaches the patient's emotions to transactional symbols in this particularized mythic world.
4   The healer manipulates the transactional symbols to assist the transaction of emotion.

> (1986:56)

Dow's paper provides a big step forward in consideration of therapy practice but this is not the place for a full critique of his ideas. Although broadly in sympathy with his schema I want to challenge certain uses of language such as 'persuade', 'manipulate', as if *all* the power rests with the therapist or shaman. Both bring an executive control to the situation which helps to contain experience and maintain boundaries. Some therapists and some shaman present directives and concrete interpretation, and 'persuade', as Dow suggests. Other shaman and therapists are like the oracle at Delphi: 'The lord whose oracle is at Delphi neither speaks nor conceals but gives signs' (Heraclitus). H. Stack Sullivan, quoted in Littlewood, says: 'Any problem in psychopathology becomes a problem of symbol functioning, a matter of seeking to understand and interpret eccentric symbol performance' (1986:37).

Recent developments in western psychotherapy have moved from the hierarchy of the blank screen and the ritual couch to a more interactionist model which acknowledges the active engagement of both the therapist and the patient in the process. This applies to work with individuals as well as groups. It is my contention that both traditional and contemporary healers enter a therapeutic 'frame' or 'stage' within which the therapeutic procedures are related to the cultural values, but which allows some flexibility within this liminal time. Turner (1969, 1982) suggests that liminality is the realm of primitive hypothesis.

To recapitulate, it is the capacity of the therapist/shaman/actor to allow 'controlled abandon' that enables healing potential within the therapeutic space. The healer allows the patient to explore the disjunction between what appears to be real in an empirical sense, and what is experientially real, i.e. what is felt somatically by the patient. The therapist may use transference to enable the exploration of past and present 'others'; to re-experience unsatisfactory introjected others. The therapy may be heightened by the use of myth or literature and the creation of the therapeutic theatre. The outcome is intended to be a tolerable equilibrium for the patient between inner experience and outer reality. In dramatherapy this is facilitated by the re-experiencing of the pre-play processes of embodiment, projection and role, dramatic play and exploration within the 'personal theatre' of the individual and the creation of the healing theatre of the group as a whole.

The following is an example of dramatherapeutic practice which in retrospect I realise was influenced by the Temiar spatial concepts of under, on and off the ground. The work was with a very 'stuck' client group, unable to initiate and in complete contrast to the vociferous group of women described earlier. They needed some help to 'move' in every sense of the word. I used as a stimulus the poem by Eleanor Wylie called *The Eagle and the Mole*. In this poem Wylie evokes underground images by describing a subterranean river and an isolated mole; on the ground, flocks of sheep huddle for warmth while a remote and isolated eagle flies above the earth and then poises on a crag.

The dramatherapeutic process was first activated by some embodiment exercises of being in the dark and flowing and burrowing, emerging into the light and crawling with others; and of being separate and then flying and looking down on the world. After a reading of the poem, members of the group then enacted non-verbally the image that had stayed with them most strongly (the river, the mole, the sheep or the eagle). Further exploration in small groups resulted in a wealth of personal experience in relation to dark and light – 'I'm in the dark', 'going with the flow', or 'beavering away'. The isolation and remoteness of the eagle contrasted with the huddled warmth and danger of loss of identity with the sheep – the struggle between individual autonomy and group identity.

After personal and group exploration of dominant themes, we then moved to an epic representation, whereby we created masks for the different creatures. Through improvisation, a dramatic enactment was played through of the oppositions between these metaphors and the essential need for a reconciliation between them. Through the epic enactment, people were able to explore or re-explore their own internal 'self and other', e.g. by staying with the safety of my sheep-likeness I am not allowing the strength and discernment of my eagle-likeness; and, my sheep and eagle-likeness help me to avoid exploration of my subterranean, dark side. These metaphors resonated a whole series of cross-cutting selves and others that had relevance for individuals and the group as a whole. It was the dramatic movement between self and the group and between personal and epic levels that allowed resolution and integration to take place.

Does the dramatherapist always develop 'epic scale' work? The epic metaphor, as with the abusing women (Jennings 1986d), can be expressed within a fast-moving discourse about the price of baked beans and disposable nappies, and explored within the relatively 'small-scale' theatre of the group sitting round the table with finger paints and crayons. Paradoxically, the 'epic drama' quality of many of these women's lives, a recounting of life histories, takes on the quality of a Greek or Shakespearean tragedy, suggesting that form has to be flexible in relation to the needs of the particular client group. With the 'stuck' group the epic drama facilitated the metaphor and enabled more profound understanding to be achieved. With the abused women the metaphors were already available and needed form and context in which they could be safely expressed, understood and made manageable – transformed and integrated (see also Jennings and Minde 1994).

In dramatherapy, i.e. drama and theatre in the curative sense and also in designated healing rituals, the exploration is intended to bring about balance, insight and understanding in the experience of disorder and 'unwellness'. As Turner says:

> But the ritual and its progeny, notably the performance arts, derive from the subjunctive, liminal, reflexive, exploratory heart of social dramas, where the structure of group experiences are replicated, dismembered, remembered, re-fashioned, and mutely or vocally made meaningful – even when, as is so often the case in declining cultures, 'the meaning is that there is no meaning'.
>
> (Turner and Bruner 1986:43)

I have always been somewhat reluctant to look for similarities between the contemporary dramatherapist and the indigenous shaman and have for some time remained in a polarised position myself. I have particularly wanted to guard against assumptions based on ethnocentric universalism. I tentatively suggested in an earlier paper (Jennings 1983a, 1983b) that dramatherapists and shaman are specialists in liminality. I now feel more confident, having worked through this study, to make that claim. Nevertheless, I do not want to suggest a mode of 'shamanic dramatherapy'; I think 'metaphysical' is more appropriate to describe this healing theatre. Both dramatherapists and shaman make use of dramatic ritual and multiple media to enable unwell people to embark on a therapeutic journey. They provide ritual boundaries in time and space set apart to contain undifferentiated experience that is expressed through multiple layers of metaphor. The core of this experience is the *embodied and enacted 'world'* through which the polysemic qualities of drama enable profound inner experience and epic metaphors to resonate, reveal and achieve resolution. The drama-therapist and shaman are mediators through and managers of this liminal experience. Turner poetically describes liminality and liminal personae:

> The attributes of liminality or of liminal personae (threshold people) are necessarily ambiguous, since this condition and these people elude or slip through the network of classification that normally locate places and positions in cultural space. Liminal entities are neither here nor there; they are betwixt and between the positions assigned and arrayed by law, custom, convention and ceremonial. As such their ambiguous and indeterminate attributes are expressed by a rich variety of symbols in the many societies that ritualise social and cultural transitions. This liminality is likened frequently to – death, to being in the womb, to invisibility, to darkness, to bisexuality, to the wilderness and to an eclipse of the sun or moon.
>
> (1969:95)

However, we can also recognise that within the suggested chaos there is potential for creativity. Out of the disorientation there are illuminations of clarity and perception. For example, Nathan Scott says that the liminal period is also 'an enormously fruitful seedbed of spiritual creativity' (1985:5).

Halifax, when discussing the role of the shaman as wounded healer, says:

> The shaman as artist and performer utilizes the imagination to give form to a cosmos that is unpredictable. Even in the course of wild initiatory trances, the mythological renderings of a chaotic psyche is essential. Order is imposed on chaos; form is given to psychic confusion; the journey finds its direction.
>
> (1982:18)

This experience, the journey that finds a direction only once it has been embarked upon, is essentially revelatory. I stated in Chapter 1 that the original meaning of the Greek word for theatre, *theatron*, means a place of seeing, where things are made visible. Wilshire quotes from Kerenyi who points out the links between *theatron*, *theoria* and *theos* (the Greek word for God). Kerenyi said that *theoria* means 'to look God in the face', an essentially revelatory experience. Wilshire asks how can God/*theos* be looked in the face and at the same time be linked with theory/*theoria*? 'It can only be because god was considered to be a living body and that awareness of body was considered fundamentally revealing' (1982:33).

The very stuff that great drama is about – blood, destruction, relationships, life and death, good and evil – are the selfsame themes which preoccupy our clients. They are themes that preoccupy us all in the struggle of the human dilemma. The understanding of the power of the mimetic and poetic encounter illustrated in ritual and epic theatre has in turn helped me to understand more fully the scope and effectiveness of preventive and curative healing rituals of the Senoi Temiars. Healing theatre is one which ultimately allows for the journey from everyday reality to dramatic reality and back again.

My journey has taken me from my own culture and experience to that of the Temiars and back again. My encounter with the Temiars, both mimetic and mundane, has enabled some light to be cast on the unilluminated areas both of my own personal development and that of my children, and also that of my practice with my clients. It has also firmly brought me back to my own culture and especially to appreciate the epic qualities of Shakespearean and other theatre understanding and metaphor. It has enabled me not only to be clearer about my own identity as a woman, but also, I hope, to redress some balance of the perceptions and experience of women in anthropology and therapy.

Although this is *my* closing statement, albeit so much informed by others, I must at this stage of the journey allow the Temiars to have the closing story:

THE TIGER-SEANCE: EPIC METAPHOR *PAR EXCELLENCE*

The rarely performed tiger-seance is an apt example of the healing power of the epic metaphor and its integrative function of bringing the dominant symbols of a culture into juxtaposition with one another. As powerful as any piece of Greek theatre, the tiger-seance has the good shaman, and the metaphorical evil other (which in other contexts would be in opposition) in a dialectical relationship which results in a final transformation and embodiment of the evil by the good.

The shaman's wife, the midwife, stage manages this performance and quietens everybody down. She makes sure that cigarettes and fires are extinguished. Darkness is provided for the forces of darkness. The 'forest style' shelter is created within the domestic house in this pardoxical theatre. It is completely closed in total contrast with the usual seance decorations; the open circlet of herbs and flowers where the shy small spirits come to rest. Small flowers are placed near the tiger shaman's shelter in which he will experience his metamorphosis. Individuals in need of healing are brought near the shelter. No touch is involved, such is the power emanating from this fusion; in fact too much proximity is considered dangerous. The musicians start playing and the shaman as tiger starts to tell of his journey 'from source to estuary'; scratching and growls start to get louder. The fusion has taken place. Some minutes later the shaman stumbles from the shelter, and the midwife lights the fire and places a cigarette in his mouth. She draws attention to the drooping flowers. The tiger-seance is over.

The souls of shaman and tiger have allowed a fusion of human and non-human; the shaman has embodied the power of the tiger in an epic poetic and mimetic encounter. Poiesis (bringing forth) and mimesis achieve and celebrate a triumph of good over evil.

Every physician must also be a metaphysician.

Notes

INTRODUCTION

1   Dramatherapeutic change comes about through 'understanding' being allowed to emerge rather than 'explanations' being given; hence the reluctance of dramatherapists – this one in particular – to interpret the client's symbolism.

2   'Acting out' is a term used in therapy to mean that clients and patients break acceptable boundaries and express themselves 'inappropriately'. My contention is that the nature of the communication has been misunderstood and needs to be contextualised within the 'epic-micro' paradigm.

3   I had dismissed the persistent rustling and squeaking in the roof of our first house in Kuala Betis as birds; it turned out to be a large black cobra chasing mice!

4   I am preparing a book which explores the resources of a family engaged in fieldwork and the particular dynamic it creates for the family itself.

2 INTRODUCING THE TEMIAR

1   For a beautiful description of Temiar courtship see Benjamin 1967b:1.

2   A detailed study of children's games with comparative data between areas should prove most useful. I only have information from the Kuala Betis area (see Map 2, page xv).

3   Constant breast-feeding inhibits the production of the hormone prolactin which is essential for ovulation.

4   A middle-aged, childless couple in the village of Asam 'borrowed' two children from a larger family in another village; they said they were lonely without children.

5   See, e.g., Stacey (1953), *The Hostile Sun*.

4 TEMIAR BODY: CONTROL AND INVASION

1   Doctors at Gombak Hospital reported that Temiar women were not concerned about 'waist upward' examinations but most discomforted

by examinations of the genital and pubic area.

2   Temiar decorative arts consist of weaving: mats, pouches and baskets, both plain and dyed; carving: hair combs, blowpipes and quivers, and nose flutes from bamboo and sheaths and handles for bush knives.

3   Burning hair on logs, chilli on fires and other noxious substances are supposed to discourage *Karey* – to keep him outside.

4   Doctors told me of comparative research being carried out between Temiar home-grown tobacco and shop-bought cigarettes; those Temiars who only smoked the former had no lung traces.

5 TEMIAR SPACE: ORDER AND DISORDER

1   My children's pet puppy was savaged by a dog; although it was suffering and obviously dying, the Temiars would not kill it.

2   Covering up mirrors during thunderstorms is a widespread custom; in Lancashire mirrors and knives are covered during storms.

3   The umbilicus may be worn round the child's neck to ward off evil.

4   Some Temiars reported that the 'special shelter' is built at the edge of the forest.

5   *Hun-tɛ?*, although disorderly, is also powerful; cf. Negrito shamanic practices.

6 DREAMS, SOULS AND TRANCE

1   See *Orang Asli Studies Newsletter* No. 2, September 1983, and No. 3, August 1984; both contain an extensive bibliography on Senoi dream therapy including Stewart's own publications and many others where his work is discussed.

2   Skeat (1900) says that the Malay conception of the human soul (*semangat*) is that of a species of 'thumbling': a thin insubstantial human image, or mannikin, which is temporarily absent from the body in sleep, trance and disease and permanently absent after death.

3   Benjamin (1967a:36) describes a definitive version of a Temiar creation myth which he recorded at a 'seminar' during fieldwork.

7 WOMEN AND BLOOD

1   See Knight (1991) for the most detailed menstrual study by an anthropologist.

8 TEMIAR HEALERS: SHAMAN AND MIDWIVES

1   Nevertheless, certain midwives are called upon over an area of several villages because of their experience, whereas others only deliver in their own village.

9 HEALING PERFORMANCES: DANCE-DRAMAS OF PREVENTION AND CURE

1   Temiars say that they cannot imagine life without tobacco, trancing and dreaming: a relationship to be discussed elsewhere.

10 THE EPIC METAPHOR: THE PARADOX OF HEALING

1   Benjamin (1994) suggests psychological thematisation of physiological processes. By making the blood and *hup* of the mother stand out, it further enhances concern for the infant who is dependent on her souls.
2   My current focus is on the biological basis of drama and that we are *born* dramatic; absence of 'drama' seems to bring about dramatically destructive behaviours (1995, in press).

Bibliography

Ardener, E. (1975) 'Belief of the Problem of Women', and 'The Problem Revisited', in S. Ardener (ed.) *Perceiving Women*, London: Malaby.

Artaud, A. (1958) *The Theatre and Its Double*, New York: Grove Press.

Beattie, J. (1977) 'Spirit Mediumship as Theatre', *RAI News*, No. 2.

Bell, D., Caplan, P. and Karim, W.J. (1993) *Gendered Fields: Women, Men and Ethnography*, London: Routledge.

Benjamin, G. (1966) 'Temiar Social Groupings', *Federation Museums Journal*, 11:1–25.

—— (1967a) 'Temiar Religion', PhD dissertation, University of Cambridge.

—— (1967b) 'Temiar Kinship', *Federation Museums Journal*, 12:1–25.

—— (1968a) 'Temiar Personal Names', *Bijdragen tot de Taal-, Land- en Volkenkunde*, 124:99–134.

—— (1968b) 'Headmanship and Leadership in Temiar Society', *Federation Museums Journal*, 13:1–43.

—— (1976a) 'Austroasiatic Subgroupings and Prehistory in the Malay Peninsula', in Philip N. Jenner, Laurence C. Thompson and Stanley Starosta (eds) *Austroasiatic Studies, Part I*, Honolulu: University Press of Hawaii.

—— (1976b) 'An Outline of Temiar Grammar', in Philip N. Jenner, Laurence C. Thompson and Stanley Starosta (eds) *Austroasiatic Studies, Part I*, Honolulu: University Press of Hawaii.

—— (1979a) 'The Place of Trance in Temiar Culture', paper presented at International Conference on Traditional Asian Medicine, Canberra, Australia.

—— (1979b) 'Indigenous Religious Systems of the Malay Peninsula', in Aram Yengoyan and Alton L. Becker (eds) *The Imagination of Reality: Essays in Southeast Asian Coherence Systems*, Norwood, NJ: Ablex Publishing Corporation.

—— (1983a) 'The Anthropology of Grammar: Self and Other in Temiar', unpublished manuscript, 147pp, University of Singapore.

—— (1983b) 'Peninsular Malaysia' and part of 'Southern Mainland Southeast Asia' (with notes), in Stephen A. Wurm and Shiro Hattôri (eds) *Language Atlas of the Pacific Area, Volume 2*, Canberra: Australian

Academy of the Humanities and Tokyo: The Japan Academy, maps 37 and 38. (Distributed by Geocenter, Stuttgart.)

—— (1985) 'In the Long Term: Three Themes in Malayan Cultural Ecology', in Karl L. Hutterer, A. Terry Rambo and George Lovelace (eds) *Cultural Values and Human Ecology in Southeast Asia*, Ann Arbor, MI: Centre for South and Southeast Asian Studies, University of Michigan.

—— (1987) 'Ethnohistorical Perspectives on Kelantan's Prehistory', in Nik Hassan Shuhaimi bin Nik Abdul Rahman (ed.) *Kelantan Zaman Awal: Kajian Arkeologi dan Sejarah di Malaysia*, Kota Bharu: Perpaduan Muzium Negeri Kelantan.

—— (1991) 'Achievements and Gaps in Orang Asli Studies', in Hood Mohamed Salleh (ed.) *Orang Asli Studies: Issues and Orientations* [=*Akademika: Journal of Social Science and Humanities Volume 35*], Bangi: Penerbit Universiti Kebangsaan Malaysia.

—— (1993a) 'Process and Structure in Temiar Social Organisation', in Hood Mohamed Salleh, Kamaruddin M. Said and Awang Hasmadi Mois (eds) *Mereka Yang Terpinggir: Masyarakat Terasing di Indonesia dan Orang Asli di Malaysia*, Department of Anthropology and Sociology, Universiti Kebangsaan Malaysia, Bangi, Selangor.

—— (1993b) 'Temiar', in Paul Hockings (ed.) *Encyclopedia of World Cultures, Volume V: East and Southeast Asia*, Boston, MA: G.K. Hall.

—— (1994) 'Danger and Dialectic in Temiar Childhood', to appear Autumn 1994 (in French translation) in Josianne Massard and Jeannie Koubi (eds) *Enfants et Sociétés d'Asie du Sud-Est*, Paris: Harmattan.

Blacking, J. (ed.) (1977) *The Anthropology of the Body*, London: Academic Press.

Bloch, M. and Bloch, J. (1980) 'Women and the Dialectics of Nature in 18th Century Thought', in C. MacCormack and M. Strathern (eds) *Nature, Culture and Gender*, Cambridge: Cambridge University Press.

Brook, P. (1972) *The Empty Space*, Harmondsworth: Pelican.

Callow, S. (1985) *Being An Actor*, Harmondsworth: Penguin.

Carey, I. (1961) 'Tengleq Kui Serok', Kuala Lumpur: Government Press.

Carruthers, M. (1992) *Why Humans Have Cultures*, Oxford: Oxford University Press.

Casement, P. (1985) *On Learning from the Patient*, London: Tavistock Press.

Courtney, R. (1980) *The Dramatic Curriculum*, London: Heinemann.

Cox, J.L. (ed.) (1986) *Transcultural Psychiatry*, London: Croom Helm.

Cox, M. (1978) *Structuring the Therapeutic Process, Compromise with Chaos*, Oxford: Pergamon. (Reprinted 1988, Jessica Kingsley.)

Dentan, R.K. (1968) *The Semai. A Non-Violent People of Malaya*, New York: Holt, Reinhart & Winston.

—— (1983a) 'Senoi Dream Praxis', *Dream Network Bulletin*, 2(5).

—— (1983b) 'A Dream of Senoi', Special Studies Series, Council of International Studies, Buffalo: State University of New York.

Domhoff, G.W. (1985) *The Mystique of Dreams: A Search for Utopia Through Senoi Dream Theory*, Berkeley, CA: University of California Press.

Douglas, M. (1970) *Natural Symbols. Explorations in Cosmology*, London: Barrie & Rockliffe.

Dow, J. (1986) 'Universal Aspects of Symbolic Healing', *American Anthropologist*, 88.

Duvignaud, J. (1972) *The Sociology of Art*, London: Paladin.

Eagles and Stanford (1977) Translation of Aeschylus's *The Oresteia*, Harmondsworth: Penguin.

Endicott, K. (1979) *Batek Negrito Religion*, Oxford: Oxford University Press.

—— (1983) 'The Effects of Slave Raiding on the Aborigines of the Malay Peninsular' in A. Reid and J. Brewster (eds) *Slavery, Bondage and Dependency in South East Asia*, Brisbane: University of Queensland Press.

Evans, I.H.N. (1937) *The Negritos of Malaya*, London: Frank Cass.

Faraday, A. and Wren-Lewis, J. (1984) 'Temiar Dreaming', *Dream Network Bulletin*, 2(3), August.

Fiddes, N. (1991) *Meat: A Natural Symbol*, London: Routledge.

Fordham, M. (1978/1986) *Jungian Psychotherapy*, London: Maresfield Library.

Gillison, G. (1980) 'Images of Nature in Gimi Thought', in C. MacCormack and M. Strathern (eds) *Nature, Culture and Gender*, Cambridge: Cambridge University Press.

Goffman, E. (1969) *The Presentation of Self in Everyday Life*, Harmondsworth: Pelican.

Grotowski, J. (1969) *Towards a Poor Theatre*, London: Eyre Methuen.

Halifax, J. (1982) *Shaman The Wounded Healer*, London: Thames & Hudson.

Harré, R. (1981) 'Psychological Variety' in H. Locke and P. Helas (eds) *Indigenous Psychologies, The Anthropology of the Self*, London: Academic Press.

Harris, O. (1980) 'The Power of Signs: Gender, Culture and the Wild in the Bolivian Andes', in C. MacCormack and M. Strathern (eds) *Nature, Culture and Gender*, Cambridge: Cambridge University Press.

Harwood, R. (1984) *All the World's A Stage*, London: Methuen.

Heathcote, D. (1971) 'Drama and Education: Subject or System?', in N.Dodd and W. Hickson (eds) *Drama and Theatre in Education*, London: Heinemann.

Helman, C. (1984) *Culture, Health and Illness*, London: Wright PSG.

—— (1994) *Body Myths*, London: Chatto.

Hogbin, I. (1970) *The Island of Menstruating Men*, London: Chandler.

Holman, D. (1958/1984) *Noone of the Ulu*, Oxford: Oxford University Press.

Howell, S. and Willis, R. (1989) *Societies at Peace*, London: Routledge.

Hudson, J. and O'Connor, C. (1981) 'Peace Process: A Modified Technique for Children's Nightmares', *The School Counsellor*, 28(5).

Huizinga, J. (1949) *Homo Ludens: A Study of the Play-Element in Culture*, London: Routledge & Kegan Paul.

Jennings, S. (1975) 'The Importance of the Body in Non-Verbal Methods of Therapy', in S. Jennings (ed.) *Creative Therapy*, Banbury: Kemble Press.

———— (1977) 'Dramatherapy: The Anomalous Profession', *Journal of Dramatherapy*, 4.

———— (1979) 'Ritual and the Learning Process', *Journal of Dramatherapy*, 13(4).

———— (1983a) 'Rites of Healing', paper presented to Dramatherapy Conference, London.

———— (1983b) 'The Importance of Social Anthropology for Therapists', talk given to Royal Anthropological Institute, London.

———— (1985a) 'Temiar Dance and the Maintenance of Order', in P. Spencer (ed.) *Society and the Dance*, Cambridge: Cambridge University Press.

———— (1985b) 'The Drama and the Ritual, with Reference to Group Analysis', paper presented to Spring Seminar Group Analytic Society.

———— (1986a) *Creative Drama and Groupwork*, Vicester: Winslow Press.

———— (1986b) 'Playing with Ideas of Play', paper presented to Art Therapy and Dramatherapy Summer School, St Albans.

———— (1986c) 'The Loneliness of the Long Distance Therapist', paper presented to Jungian Summer Seminar, *British Journal of Psychotherapy*, 3.

———— (1986d) 'Metaphors of Violence', paper presented to International Congress of Group Psychotherapy, Zagreb.

———— (ed.) (1987) *Dramatherapy, Theory and Practice 1*, London: Routledge.

———— (1990) *Dramatherapy with Families, Groups and Individuals*, London: Jessica Kingsley.

———— (ed.) (1992a) *Dramatherapy Theory and Practice 2*, London: Routledge.

———— (1992b) 'The Nature and Scope of Dramatherapy: Theatre of Healing', in M. Cox (ed.) *Shakespeare Comes to Broadmoor*, London: Jessica Kingsley.

———— (1993) *Play Therapy with Children: A Practitioner's Guide*, Oxford: Blackwell Scientific.

———— (1994) 'Unravelling Dramatherapy: Ariadne's Ball of Thread', *Family Context* (in press).

———— (1995) *Introduction to Dramatherapy*, London: Jessica Kingsley (in press).

Jennings, S. and Minde, A. (1994) *Art Therapy and Dramatherapy: Masks of The Soul*, London: Jessica Kingsley.

Johnstone, K. (1981) *Impro, Improvisation and the Theatre*, London: Methuen.

Kaplan-Williams, S. (1980) *Jungian-Senoi Dreamwork Manual*, Berkeley, CA: University of California Press.

Kareem, J. (ed.) (1991) *Intercultural Therapy*, Oxford: Oxford University Press.

Kleinman, A. (1980) *Patients and Healers in the Context of Culture*, Berkeley, CA: University of California Press.

Knight, C. (1983) 'Menstruation as Medicine', paper presented at BMAS Conference on Women as Healers: Women as Polluters.

———— (1991) *Blood Relations: Menstruation and The Origins of Culture*, London and New Haven: Yale University Press.

La Fontaine, J.S. (1985) *Initiation Ritual Dramas and Secret Knowledge Around the World*, Harmondsworth: Penguin.

Latner, J. and Sabini, M. (1972) 'Working the Dream Factory: Social Dreamwork', in *Voices* (fall).

Laws, S., Hey, V. and Eagon, A. (1985) *Seeing Red*, London: Hutchinson.

Lewis, G. (1980) *Day of Shining Red*, Cambridge: Cambridge University Press.

Lewis, I.M. (1971) *Ecstatic Religion*, Harmondsworth: Pelican.

Littlewood, R. (1986) 'Russian Dolls and Chinese Boxes: An Anthropological Approach to Implicit Models of Comparative Psychiatry', in J.L. Cox (ed.) *Transcultural Psychiatry*, London: Croom Helm.

Littlewood, R. and Lipsedge, M. (1982) *Aliens and Alienists*, Harmondsworth: Penguin.

MacCormack, C. (1980) *Ethnography of Fertility and Birth*, London: Academic Press.

MacCormack, C. and Strathern, M. (eds) (1982) *Nature, Culture and Gender*, Cambridge: Cambridge University Press.

Mead, G.H. (1934) *Mind, Self and Society*, C.W. Morris (ed.), Chicago: University of Chicago Press.

Moerman, D.E. (1979) 'Anthropology of Symbolic Healing', *Current Anthropology*, 20 (1).

Newman, G. (1865/1986) *Dream of Gerontius*, London: Mowbray.

Nietzsche, F. (1967) *The Birth of Tragedy*, London: Random House.

Noone, H.D. (1936) 'Report on the Settlements and Welfare of the Pre-Temiar School of the Perak-Kelantan Watershed', *Journal of Federation of Malay States Museums*, 9 (Part 1).

Orr, N. (1981) 'Are Masks Necessary in an Operating Theatre?', *Journal of the British Medical Association*.

Parkin, D. (1992) 'Ritual as Spatial and Bodily Division', in D. De Coppet (ed.) *Understanding Ritual*, London: Routledge.

Piaget, J. (1962) *Play, Dreams and Imitation in Childhood*, London: Routledge & Kegan Paul.

Pottier, J. (1985) 'Identity on Trial: Self and Other in Central African Psychotherapy', *Ethnos*, 1 (2).

Randall, A. (1953) 'The Terrible Truth of the Temiar Senoi', *Dream Network Bulletin*, February.

Reiter, R. (ed.) (1975) 'Towards an Anthropology of Women', New York and London: *Monthly Review Press*.

Roose Evans, J. (1984) *Experimental Theatre from Stanislavski to Peter Brook*, London: Routledge & Kegan Paul.

Roseman, R. (1988) 'Pragmatic of Aesthetics. The Performance of Healing Among Senoi Temiar', *Journal of Social Science and Medicine*, 27(7).

—— (1986) 'Sound in Ceremony: Power and Performance in Temiar Curing Rituals', PhD dissertation, University of Cornell.

—— (1993) *Healing Sounds from the Malaysian Rainforest*, Berkeley: University of California Press.

Schebesta, P. (1927) *Among the Forest Dwarfs of Malaya*, London: Hutchinson.

Scott, N.A. (1985) *The Poetics of Belief*, Chapel Hill and London: North Carolina University Press.

Shuttle, P. and Redgrove, P. (1978) *The Wise Wound*, London: Gollancz.

Skeat, W.W. (1900/1967) *Malay Magic*, New York: Dover Publications.

Skeat, W.W. and Blagden, C.O. (1906/1966) *Pagan Races of the Malay Peninsular*, London: Frank Cass.

Skultans, V. (1974) *Intimacy and Ritual*, London: Routledge & Kegan Paul.

——— (1979) *English Madness: Ideas on Insanity*, London: Routledge & Kegan Paul.

Slade, P. (1954) *Child Drama*, London: Routledge & Kegan Paul.

Slimming, J. (1954) *Temiar Jungle: A Malayan Journey*, London: John Murray.

Stacey, (1953) *The Hostile Sun*, London: Duckworth.

Stanislavski, C. (1950/1981) *Building a Character*, London: Methuen.

Stewart, K. (1947) 'Magico-Religious Beliefs and Practices in Primitive Societies: A Sociological Interpretation of Their Therapeutic Aspects', PhD dissertation, University of London.

——— (1953) 'Culture and Personality in Two Primitive Groups', *Complex*.

——— (1954) 'Mental Hygiene and World Peace', *Mental Hygiene*, 38(3).

——— (1975) *Pygmies and Dream Giants*, London: Harper & Row.

——— (1983) 'Bibliography and Discussion of Stewart's Work', *Orang Asli Studies Newsletter*, 2.

Storr, A. (1976) *The Dynamics of Creation*, Harmondsworth: Penguin.

Tambiah, S.J. (1985) *Culture, Thought and Social Action*, Cambridge, MA: Harvard University Press.

Turner, B.S. (1992) *Regulating Bodies: Essays in Medical Anthropology*, London: Routledge.

Turner, V.W. (1969) *The Ritual Process*, London: Routledge & Kegan Paul.

——— (1982) *From Ritual to Theatre, The Seriousness of Human Play*, Performing Arts Journal, Pubs NY.

Turner, V.W. and Bruner, E. (1986) *The Anthropology of Experience*, Illinois: Illinois University Press.

Turton, A. (1978) 'Architectural and Political Space in Thailand', in G.B. Milner (ed.) *Natural Symbols in S.E. Asia*, SOAS, University of London.

Walton, K. (1990) *Mimesis as Make-Believe*, Cambridge, MA: Harvard University Press.

Wilkinson, R.J. (1971) *Papers on Malay Subjects*, Oxford: Oxford University Press.

Williams-Hunt, F.D.R. (1952) *An Introduction to Malayan Aborigines*, Kuala Lumpur: Government Press.

Wilshire, B. (1982) *Role Playing and Identity*, Bloomington: Indiana University Press.

Winnicott, D.W. (1974) *Playing and Reality*, Harmondsworth: Pelican.

Wolheim, R. (1980) *Art and Its Objects* (2nd edn), Cambridge: Cambridge University Press.

Index